*Useful reading for policymakers managing the intersection of national security and a thriving commercial space ecosystem.*

**- DR. DIANE HOWARD,**

Principal, sur l'espace PLLC; Former Director of Commercial Space Policy at the National Space Council; *Making do with what we have: Creating Certainty in Private Space Law* (2009)

*This urgent critique is a wake-up call for policymakers to act decisively to improve America's space strategy—or risk surrendering the future of space to China.*

**- DR. MIR SADAT,**

Former National Security Council Policy Director (2019-2020)

# PRAISE FOR *SPACE SHOCK*

*A well-reasoned and chilling glimpse into the potential futures we must prepare for. Every national security leader needs to read this—now.*

**- LT GEN JOHN SHAW,**
U.S Space Force (Ret), Former Deputy Commander,
U.S. Space Command and Author of *Whither Space Power?*

*These scenarios don't just make you think—they make you uneasy. And that's exactly what good foresight should do. Read it, then ask yourself: what would we do if this happened tomorrow?*

**- JOEL B. MOZER, PHD,**
U.S. Space Force Chief Science Officer (retired)

*If America wants to survive and protect its values and world leadership, it must think strategically about the ultimate high ground of Space. Space Shock is a must read for all segments of society, from citizens to politicians. It asks the right questions, and uses compelling scenarios to help America think and compete in the brave new world that Space represents. The timing of this book is critical, and its recommendations are key to our success as a civilization. Bold action is required now!*

**- STEVE KWAST,**
Lieutenant General (Ret) and
Co-Founder of SpaceBilt Inc., a Space logistics company

*Simulations and wargaming can unlock insights that analysis alone cannot. We ignore these insights at our peril.*

**- JP PARKER,**
CEO, Escape Velocity and
Former Special Advisor to the Vice President for Space

*In* Space Shock, *Garretson and Harrison issue a no-nonsense alert to U.S. decision-makers: when crises arrive, soaring rhetoric undermined by deep cuts to budgets and misplaced priorities will leave us underprepared. The scenarios they highlight contrast China's all-in strategy, powered by sustained, coherent investments in security, science, and exploration, against America's splintered, underfunded commitments. The authors don't just diagnose the problem, they prescribe bold action to cement U.S. leadership of the future of humanity. My takeaway from the book is: enough with the rhetoric, it is time to be strategic and invest.*

**- DR. BHAVYA LAL,**
Former Acting Chief Technologist and
Associate Administrator for Technology, Policy, and
Strategy, NASA

*This plain-language assertion of urgency regarding space policy and investment puts readers squarely in the crosshairs of what could result from failure to act. Incremental advancements in space policy have become so much a part of the current US space posture that even highly qualified teams failed to respond with bold action when faced with scenarios simulated as part of the book's research. Harrison and Garretson boldly recommend specific actions to advance US national security through space capability.*

**- LEE STEINKE,**
Chief Operating Officer, CisLunar Industries

# SPACE SHOCK

**AMERICAN FOREIGN
POLICY COUNCIL**

ISBN (paperback): 978-1-968919-00-9
ISBN (ebook): 978-1-968919-01-6

Armin Lear Press, Inc.
215 W Riverside Drive, #4362
Estes Park, CO 80517

# SPACE SHOCK

## 18 THREATS THAT WILL
## DEFINE SPACE POWER

**PETER A. GARRETSON**
**RICHARD M. HARRISON**

AFPC

# CONTENTS

# ACKNOWLEDGMENTS

In 2023, Richard Harrison and Peter Garretson co-authored *The Next Space Race: A Blueprint for American Primacy*, which outlined the threats in space, China's plan for dominance, and the vast economic benefits—that book advocated for a proactive approach for U.S. space policy. As its successor, this book explores what a reactive approach might entail. We pitched the idea to AFPC president Herman Pirchner, Jr., who once again believed in our vision and helped identify funding for the project, for which we are greatly thankful. We are deeply grateful to our anonymous donor, whose generous financial support made this research possible and who shared our commitment to enhancing policymakers' and the public's understanding of critical space policy issues.

Several members of the AFPC team deserve recognition for their contributions. AFPC Senior Vice President Ilan Berman merits great thanks for his guidance throughout the publication process. We also extend our appreciation to Chloe Smith for her space program support and Lilly Harvey for her programmatic efforts on the project. Special thanks go to Chris Griffin, Christopher Stone, and Brent Ziarnick for their invaluable guidance during critical phases of the project. We also thank Laura Winter for her expert input and suggestion to include a crisis communications plan, along with her willingness to supply the majority of its' content and insight.

We are grateful to Amy Marks for editing the three after action reports that served as the foundation of this book. Special thanks to Calla O'Neil, whose diligent editorial assistance greatly improved the manuscript. Our full gratitude goes to Maryann Karinch for her expert editing and publication of the manuscript.

This project would not have been possible without the support and insights gained from the three wargaming workshops upon which this book is built. We would like to extend our sincere thanks to the researchers who supported these workshops: Avery Borens, Elizabeth Oakes, Walker Robinson, Shivani Sharma, Sophia Chang, and Aedan Yohannan. Their diligent preparation, excellent notetaking, and contributions to our reports were instrumental to the success of our mock National Space Council simulation and subsequent workshops. A complete list of workshop participants is provided in Appendix A. Additionally, a special thanks goes to Abigail Koch for her meticulous fact-checking of the book manuscript. All Images in the report were generated with the assistance of OpenAI's DALL·E.

## A PERSONAL WORD OF THANKS

Completing a co-authored book brings with it a deeper appreciation for those who make such work possible. Peter would like to thank his spouse Namrata for her patience and support and the many hours required to complete this book and for the continuing support of Peter W., Jerri, Madeleine, Aly, and Marcus.

Richard extends his heartfelt gratitude to his wife, Allyson, whose patience and encouragement never wavered, and to his sons, Nathan and James, whose boundless energy and curiosity continue to inspire his work. He is forever grateful to his parents, Monty and Sonia, and in-laws Ron and JoAnn, for their unwavering belief in this endeavor. Special appreciation goes to his sister Danielle Harrison, her husband Michael DeHart, and their children Riley and Everly, as well as to his brother-in-law Logan DiPaolo, his wife Wendy, and their children Parker, Kayla, and Morgan, for their enduring support throughout this journey.

# INTRODUCTION

## *Motivation for this Project*

On October 4, 1957, the Soviet Union (USSR) shocked the world when it successfully launched the world's first satellite, Sputnik 1. The event was deeply symbolic. The technological prowess required to engineer and execute the Sputnik launch confirmed that the USSR was a supremely powerful nation. It was also an event with clear implications for national—and indeed, international—security. As Lyndon B. Johnson famously observed at the time, "control of space means control of the world."[1] Sputnik's launch touched off the U.S.-Soviet space race. Fortunately, due to action the U.S. took years earlier, the U.S. was able to respond rapidly[2] and became the second nation to get to space with its launch of Explorer 1 on January 31, 1958. Policymakers framed the importance of space as a techno-ideological race against the USSR, and space development was pursued with a strong sense of national purpose.

As we enter a new era of intense space competition, the Sputnik episode is instructive. The psychological impact and strategic potential of Sputnik generated a significant public reaction and thereafter resulted in a substantial redistribution of the national budget per Gross Domestic Product (GDP) as the United States raced to catch up. Three major organizations were created as a result (National Aeronautics and Space Administration (NASA), Defense Advanced Research Projects Agency (DARPA), and the National Reconnaissance Office (NRO). A major human space-flight project was also started, advancing through the Mercury and Gemini efforts, culminating in a multi-phased Apollo Project (to land a man on the Moon by 1970)—which, at its peak commanded a significant fraction of the national budget.

More recently, the impact of China's successful bid to become the first nation to land on the far side of the Moon and its rapid build-up of anti-satellite (ASAT) weapons systems and doctrine, has played a major role in generating NASA's Artemis program, and served as an impetus for the creation of the U.S. Space Force (USSF). All of these historical events have one thing in common: the U.S. was responding to a threat, rather than being pro-active and anticipatory.

This history begs the following questions: what potential strategic and psychological space surprises lie ahead, and how can U.S. policymakers to anticipate them and adapt responses?

U.S. policymakers are currently still working to grasp the profound differences between the first space race (which was based on prestige before a global audience of newly independent and unaligned states), and the new space race (which is fundamentally about national security, sovereignty, and sustained economic development), and to craft the necessary policy, strategy, and legislation to enable the U.S. to be successful in the space domain. The confluence of existing trends and the announced plans of both state and non-state actors suggest significant surprises may lie ahead—surprises that could suddenly become significant for policymakers. However, there have as yet been few, if any, unclassified studies detailing how or what major space events might impact U.S. economic or national security in the near to mid-term future. Examining such scenarios provides policymakers with critical foresights that would assist future strategy, planning, concept development, and force design. Such unclassified studies can likewise help to engender winning competitive strategies and could illuminate key areas of operational competition and interagency tension that exist during the work needed to protect and defend U.S. interests.

## METHODOLOGY AND BOOK STRUCTURE

As the American Foreign Policy Council (AFPC) Space Policy Initiative co-directors, we designed a series of workshops to examine near-term scenarios that could have a significant strategic/*psychological impact on public perceptions* of space, and thus on resourcing and policy decision-making. For these workshops, we assembled teams of players who represent surrogates of the National Space Council (NSpC) and presented them with a set of scenarios that might simultaneously appear in the media, forcing players to shape a U.S. government response. This process allowed us to anticipate concerns, tensions, and cross-sector impacts of future developments in space. During the workshops, each space scenario was discussed, with a focus on addressing two primary questions:

- How do we anticipate the situation being framed in the public media, and what sort of action is likely to be demanded from public officials?

- What options exist for the United States, and which option should be selected and why?

Our aim was for these discussions to help policymakers make better decisions. By *anticipating what political pressures will be felt by U.S. government policymakers*—including how the public, the press, Congress, allies, and adversaries may respond—and *examining potential responses* for the U.S. (in new policies, executive orders, dedicated strategies, national-level guidance), we believe that U.S. policymakers can prepare for what might lie ahead—before those events occur—and arm them with the foresight and policy options needed to steer the wisest course.

Building on the success of previous off-the record exercises, we conducted three new simulation workshops to develop strategies for how policymakers can manage future space eventualities. Given the timeline of the scenarios that the workshops encompassed and the nature of the objectives, a seminar-style wargame was chosen. Each workshop contained six scenarios—most of which had the People's Republic of China as the first mover—and content was provided to the players in advance of each workshop (three workshops, with six scenarios each, totaling 18 potential space surprises). The players, collectively forming the National Space Council (NSpC), were given an hour to formulate and brainstorm different ideas and appropriate reactions to the scenario. No barriers to communication were implemented, though the wargame's inherent speed challenged the players to remain as concise as possible. Additionally, injections with headlines and various new incidents were interspersed throughout discussion time. At the end of the hour, participants were asked to present and reason out their chosen course of action.

To mitigate groupthink among the participants, one "External Press Agitator" serving as the White House Press Secretary was placed into the group and directed to challenge or question the group's decision-making. Without a red team to react to the players' actions, the press agitator was the next best option to encourage discussion of the possible consequences of their actions. To adjust for political bias during the recommendations in each workshop, the administration for the NSpC assumed a Democratic administration for three scenarios and a Republican administration for three scenarios, each with a divided U.S. House of Representatives.

Participants for the workshop were selected for their deep substantive knowledge on U.S. space activities or policy along with their likelihood to provide counsel or have the opportunity to serve at a senior level in future administrations. The participant list includes senior space leaders across the military, civilian, private, and academic sectors (see participant list for names and affiliations in Appendix A). The workshops followed Chatham House rules, so as to encourage brainstorming and experimentation.

The following positions formed the simulated NSpC for the workshops:

1. Vice President
2. Secretary of Defense
3. Director of National Intelligence
4. Secretary of Commerce
5. Secretary of State
6. NASA Administrator
7. Secretary of Energy / Subject Matter Expert
8. Assistant to the President for Domestic Policy
9. Director of the Office of Science and Technology Policy
10. Chinese Communist Party Subject Matter Expert
11. White House Press Secretary/External Press Agitator
12. Presidential Policy Advisor

The first workshop assessed how China, which has outlined a grand vision for space, over the next two decades has plans to—among other milestones—unveil incrementally improved space-based solar power satellites, a space nuclear reactor, a squadron of spaceplanes, develop a mature operational co-orbital anti-satellite constellation and continue to pursue and advance anti-satellite technology. Meanwhile, corporations will be vying for key orbital slots and commercial conflict between multi-national corporations may arise, with increased congestion and competition.

The second workshop evaluated how celestial bodies, particularly the Moon, is a major area of future strategic competition. As technology advances in coming decades, there will be several Moon-related scenarios worth investigating, including civil/commercial occupation of a key strategic sites, the PRC conducting a human landing mission, the risk of a nation state claiming territory, infrastructure building and 3-D printing on the Moon, commencement of Lunar regolith mining and solar cell deployment, and the need to contemplate a Lunar civil/commercial space rescue mission. These scenarios have both economic and strategic impacts that are worth considering.

The third workshop considered how to plan for and expect "inevitable surprises." As the push for access to space increases, there will inevitably be misunderstandings, accidents, and confrontations among stakeholders and nations. We should expect, *inter alia*, a major spacecraft collision and loss of human life and asteroids closely approaching and possibly impacting the Earth. Mining projects will also occur on asteroids, and nations have already signaled plans to develop the capability to capture asteroids and return them to Earth. Furthermore, middle powers could use kinetic anti-satellite interceptors, and engage in counterspace warfare, while great powers compete with reusable super heavy lift rockets. Policymakers will need to have plans in place to address these scenarios should they arise.

While it was certainly possible to commission an individual to research the implications of such space eventualities, the rich interaction of multiple individuals with deep experience in the space sector provided a more complete and holistic understanding of how competing interests and stakeholders are likely to respond. There is, additionally, great merit to exposing relevant thought leaders to such scenarios before they take place—and thereby build a more interconnected and prepared network of decisionmakers. Moreover, the workshop framework more closely mimics the environment in which such scenarios will be discussed and debated in the real world when they do eventually occur. Information and insights gleaned from the workshops were captured in three post-simulation reports summarizing the reactions, pitfalls, potential responses and escalation risks encapsulated in each scenario modeled. This book takes the analysis a step further by allowing us to provide a more thorough analysis with the benefit of having additional time and consideration to review each scenario in a more detailed manner and present a set of peer reviewed specific and macro space recommendations.

In the pages that follow, our first chapter begins by setting the stage for the book walking the reader through the promise of a burgeoning space economy, discussing how the United States can leverage the Moon, the benefits of space mining, outline China's impressive space ambitions, and the need to mitigate Sputnik like moments. After framing the issue, each subsequent chapter has the same structure. Our chapters are thematic groupings of the scenarios presented in the workshops and chapters include Crisis and Escalation, China's Bid for Space Energy Dominance, Conflicts on the Moon, and Space Safety and Rescue. We present a thematic introduction for the chapter, then present numerous scenarios that fit the theme. For each scenario, we begin with the selection rationale citing why the specific scenario is likely to occur, then the detailed scenario that was presented to the NSpC participants, followed by an AI generated discussion from each workshop, and our analysis and set of recommendations. Each chapter will include a chapter summary and a macro set of recommendations. The book closes with a chapter, Securing America's Space Future, on concluding remarks and recommendations for policymakers.

## PLANNING FOR AN UNCERTAIN SPACE FUTURE

We previously authored a book that identified the need for the U.S. to establish a comprehensive and enduring vision for space and advocated for proactive policies that enable the U.S. to be a leader in space and to guarantee U.S. economic and national security. While a proactive space policy can keep the United States ahead, it cannot completely avoid "inevitable surprises," nor can it control the actions of other spacefaring nations such as China. Thus, this project is meant to serve as a "Plan B" in case the U.S. follows a path that requires more reactive (as opposed to proactive) space policy dictated by China, among other spacefaring nations. By using simulations to preview potential reactions, ramifications, and responses, this project empowers policy by: (1) fostering relations between individuals who may ultimately help craft future space policy, (2) bringing neglected policy-challenging scenarios to wider attention, (3) exploring how the public and key stakeholders may react to these scenarios, and (4) suggesting the most useful policy responses. Ultimately, the study intends to prepare U.S. policymakers for a number of foreseeable scenarios they may encounter before those events occur and arm them with the foresight and policy options that enable them to steer the wisest course.

While we suspected that proactive planning would be superior to reactive policy responses, the results of these 18 wargames made *it clear that after-the-fact solutions were never truly adequate to the challenges presented. A failure to plan proactively for these potential futures was borderline catastrophic.* The players of our wargames were under immense time pressure to create solutions and often resulted in less than optimal, yet largely realistic outcomes. Almost universally, independent reviewers considered these policy frameworks wholly inadequate to the challenges. Hopefully this book is instructive in demonstrating there is a vital need for proactive space planning and suggesting the form it should take.

# CHAPTER 1

## *Celestial Competition on the Horizon*

### A NEW ERA OF GREAT POWER COMPETITION

"Now, make no mistake about it: We're in a space race today, just as we were in the 1960s, and the stakes are even higher. Last December, China became the first nation to land on the far side of the Moon and revealed their ambition to seize the lunar strategic high ground and become the world's preeminent spacefaring nation"[3]

—Mike Pence, former U.S. Vice President, March 26, 2019

"It is a fact: we're in a space race... And it is true that we better watch out that they [China] don't get to a place on the moon under the guise of scientific research. And it is not beyond the realm of possibility that they say, 'Keep out, we're here, this is our territory.'"[4]

—Bill Nelson, NASA Administrator, January 1, 2023

"The United States will once again consider itself a growing nation, one that increases our wealth, expands our territory, builds our cities, raises our expectations and carries our flag into new and beautiful horizons. And we will pursue our manifest destiny into the stars, launching American astronauts to plant the stars and stripes on the planet Mars."[5]

—President Donald J. Trump, January 20, 2025

Once America won the first space race—by landing on the Moon first in 1969—the reason to pursue space objectives for purely prestige purposes faded. However, the unipolar moment has long since passed, and great power competition among the United States, China, Russia, and others has refocused attention on outer space as a key domain. The stakes in this 21st-century space race are arguably higher than they were during the Cold War, because space activities today are tied to our economic vitality, national security, and control of critical infrastructure and resources. There is growing acknowledgment of the existence of a new space race for industrial development, with even higher stakes than the original.

## A BURGEONING SPACE ECONOMY

Movement toward the stars is inevitable, for both strategic and economic opportunities can be realized there. Previously, investment in space was not appealing or profitable due to high launch costs and commercially ambiguous legal frameworks, which kept the barriers for entry into the space market exceedingly high. However, the advent of reusable rockets has substantially decreased the cost of launches over the last decade. Launch costs are poised to drop even more substantially if ambitious next-generation rockets like the

SpaceX Starship super-heavy reusable rocket launches successfully and repeatedly. As recently outlined in a *Space Policy Review* paper, "the ability to launch 100 metric tons for $100 million provides an incredible gain in efficiency for U.S. spacefaring, as it means cutting the cost to orbit by nearly 40 percent from today's lowest-cost option ($1,520/kg on Falcon Heavy) to an unprecedented $970/kg."[6]

Nor is the U.S. the only nation working toward launch cost reduction through reusable launch systems, and as prices decrease and launch providers increase there will be a direct correlation with amplified space interest and activity.

As a result, in 2023 the space economy was valued at over $570 billion.[7] Enabled by low-cost launch and a host of new applications, the space economy is poised to expand dramatically (and increase value into the trillions of dollars) over the next two decades.[8] The implications of reusable space launch are only now becoming apparent. As heavy lift rockets improve, they will enable space tourism, facilitate space development on the Moon, provide easier access to space stations for medical research, and facilitate the development of space hotels. Those breakthroughs, in turn, hold the power to alter the astrostrategic and geostrategic landscape, changing both what nations might compete over and the tools with which we might do so.

## *In-space Service, Assembly, and Manufacturing (ISAM)*

One of the principal methods to effectively explore, extract resources, and develop an off-Earth supply chain is through the construction of large-scale projects by in-space service, assembly, and manufacturing (ISAM, previously known as on-orbit servicing, assembly, and manufacturing, or OSAM).[9] In-space service refers to the ability for satellites to be refueled on-orbit, thereby extending their useful life. Space assembly is necessary because future space infrastructure and space systems will be incredibly large and unable to fit inside current launch systems. Thus, for giant structures, assembly through artificial intelligence (AI) and robotic systems will likely become more common. Space manufacturing will involve the processes to manufacture the components and assemble the structures using technologies such as 3-D printers built for the Lunar environment or microgravity.[10]

Given these benefits and many others, the White House has recognized the importance of ISAM and advocated for it with an ISAM national strategy.[11] The development of ISAM will lead to further development of the extractive industries including Lunar and asteroid mining along with development and settlement on the Moon.

## THE MOON AS A STRATEGIC FOCAL POINT

It is almost unfathomable that despite all human accomplishments since Apollo, no human has walked on the Lunar surface in a half century.[12] Part of the rationale is due to the difficulties in accessibility, but equally important is the lack of a well-articulated and justifiable reason to visit the Lunar surface. Though not everyone subscribes to the argument that the Moon carries immense strategic value, both the Trump and Biden administrations believe exploring and expanding human presence there is a wise pursuit.[13] The White House Office of Science and Technology Policy stated, "the Moon is a driver of scientific advances and potential economic growth," in its November 2022 "National Cislunar Science and Technology Strategy."[14]

Human scientific experiments, exploration, and eventually settlement of the Moon certainly serve as a means for national prestige, but there are many reasons beyond mere spectacle to pursue Lunar initiatives.[15] As famed Lunar scientist Paul Spudis said, the Moon is close, interesting, and useful. The reduced gravitational pull (about 1/6th that of Earth) makes the Moon a desirable launch point for deep space exploration (if propellant is sourced there). Furthermore, the Moon is resource rich and is one of the closest celestial bodies to target for space mining and space-based manufacturing. The Lunar regolith on the surface of the Moon contains numerous useful minerals (including aluminum, oxygen, iron, silicon, magnesium, titanium, potassium, and phosphorus) and the incredibly rare and valuable helium-3, which may be vital for future fusion reactors.[16] Most importantly, millions of tons of water ice has been detected at the poles of the Moon, which can be used to provide drinkable water to the astronauts, be converted to breathable oxygen, and used to create propellant.[17] Moreover, the Moon has the ability to serve as the starting point for new space industrialization and a stepping-stone to mine asteroids, and bolster ISAM.

Therefore, it is no surprise that NASA has focused on the Moon through its Artemis program.[18] According to NASA (under the Biden Administration): "With Artemis missions, NASA will land the first woman and first person of color on the Moon, using innovative technologies to explore more of the Lunar surface than ever before. We will collaborate with commercial and international partners and establish the first long-term presence on the Moon."[19] The stated objectives of the Moon program are scientific discovery, to develop a Lunar economy, and to inspire a new generation through the construction of a Lunar base camp and an orbiting station around the Moon.[20]

While the specific date for the next human-led Moon landing has slipped, it is tentatively scheduled for 2027.[21] The renewed push for the Moon is further evidenced in the new White House *National Low Earth Orbit Research and Development Strategy*, which for the first time announces settlement as a goal of U.S. policy.[22] While the U.S. appears to be moving toward some bipartisan coherence in Lunar policy, there is no guarantee that this train will remain on the track without constant monitoring and maintenance. Meanwhile, U.S. adversaries, notably China, are moving forward with their own Lunar plans. As recently as late March 2023, senior Chinese space officials have called for Chinese development of the Earth-Moon industrial market, describing it as a "critical time."

## CHINA'S AMBITIONS AND THE BROADER GREAT POWER CONTEXT

Over the last several decades, China has steadily been improving its space prowess[23]—constructing its own space station, landing on the far side of the Moon (a feat not even the U.S. has accomplished), and successfully sending a rover to Mars and communicating with it (which Russia has not achieved), among many others. In a 2016 BBC interview, Wu Weiren, the chief designer of China's Lunar exploration program, laid out the plans for China's Lunar program: "Our short-term goal is to orbit the Moon, land on the Moon, and take samples back from the Moon. Our long-term goal is to explore, land and settle. We want a manned Lunar landing to stay for longer periods and establish a research base."[24] Yang Mengfei, chief commander of the PRC Chang'e-5 Lunar sample return mission and a member of the Chinese People's Political Consultative Conference (CPPCC) National Committee, similarly stated, "for our country, it is now a key opportunity to seize the opportunity and lead the Earth-moon space industrial market. It will have a great impact and far-reaching significance... Now is the critical time for space infrastructure to expand to the Earth-moon system."[25]

Beijing and Moscow are teaming to establish a Lunar base, having released an International Lunar Research Station Guide for Partnership in June 2021[26] and as of the time of this writing have signed up 13 participating states[27] and 40 non-governmental organizations and universities.[28] China has also articulated a broader plan for Cislunar infrastructure[29] as part of a solar system-wide resource utilization plan.[30] The PRC hopes to create a Moon-Earth economic zone with a continent's worth of economic output—$10 trillion annually by 2050.[31]

First mover advantages matter on the Moon, particularly in the limited number of vital locations near the poles. The Lunar poles, where ice is available, are quite likely the most valuable real estate in the solar system, which is why both China and the U.S. are eyeing the same landing areas for operation.[32] It remains unclear what norms and protocols are in place if Beijing arrives first and claims a location before other nations do. As Dr. Larry Wortzel, the former Chairman of the U.S.-China Economic and Security Review Commission, notes, China's predatory behavior on Earth (e.g., in the South and East China Seas) may hint at future behavior on the Moon. Notably, while some observers have proposed pathways for U.S.-China space cooperation on planetary exploration, Chinese officials have articulated a substantially different view. According to China's chief Moon scientist, Ouyang Ziyuan, "[T]he Moon could serve as a new and tremendous supplier of energy and resources for human beings . . . This is crucial to sustainable development of human beings on Earth . . . Whoever first conquers the Moon will benefit first . . . As for China, it needs to adopt a strategy based on its concrete economic power and technology level . . . We are also looking further out into the Solar System—to Mars."

Chinese officials tend to see space in territorial terms, likening it to islands in the South and East China seas. "The universe is an ocean, the moon is the Diaoyu Islands, Mars is Huangyan Island," says Ye Peijan, the former chief designer of the Chinese Lunar Exploration Program. "If we don't go there now even though we're capable of doing so, then we will be blamed by our descendants. If others go there, then they will take over, and you won't be able to go even if you want to. This is reason enough."[33]

Strategic competition on the Moon is happening, whether the U.S. is fully engaged or not, and the likelihood of challenges arising over location preferences and access to resources between nations are high. Here is how this fits into the bigger conversation about the new space race.

### China's Roadmap Through 2045

The U.S. cannot assume that competition for space resources will proceed in an orderly fashion. Time will tell whether the U.S. will pursue an ambitious vision for space. However, China does appear to be on just such a course. Whether or not the United States moves forward with a grand space vision, China has mapped out a plan for the next few decades.

The argument for the importance of space and the dangers of U.S. inaction has been clearly articulated in the last three annual *State of Space Industrial Base* reports, a project coordinated in partnership between the Air Force Research Laboratory, Defense Innovation Unit, and the U.S. Space Force with consultation from 120+ senior defense and space private sector, military, and government leaders.[34] To articulate this message to policymakers, *The*

*Next Space Race: A Blueprint for American Primacy* discuss the "pacing threat" posed by China's space ambitions, and its strategic implications for the United States. *The Next Space Race* outlines the enormous potential benefits of the space economy, provides an overview of the competitive security environment in that domain, and offers prioritized areas for space investments and high-level policy recommendations for the U.S. government.

China seeks to become the leading space power, eclipsing the U.S., by 2045. China has articulated a comprehensive and extremely ambitious space agenda, which includes the demonstration of numerous novel space technologies.[35] These technologies are likely to draw the interest of the public, be perceived as symbolic of a step-change in national power and suggest military capabilities they may enable—much like Sputnik back in its day.[36]

- **Space-Based Solar Power (SBSP).** China plans a scalable, 24-hr, baseload, green energy system, which would revolutionize in-space logistical capabilities, open entirely new markets, and provide very high levels of power (100s of kilowatts to gigawatts).[37] The industrial and logistical capabilities required to construct solar power satellites have broad implications for military mobilization, systems and logistics. They may create fears of the use of directed energy—the ability of solar power satellites to gather and direct megawatts of power might be repurposed.[38] Strategically, if one power corners the market in space-based energy, it could impact global energy security and have broad strategic implications in the Western and developing world.

- **In-Space Nuclear Power and Nuclear-Powered Spaceships.** China's ambitions include plans for in-space nuclear power and nuclear-powered spaceships, specifically to mine asteroids. Nuclear-powered rockets can have roughly twice the performance of today's best chemical rockets. The U.S. has historically avoided large-scale development of nuclear reactor-powered spacecraft over public safety and proliferation concerns. However, both DARPA and NASA are now pursuing nuclear power for Lunar surface operations and faster transit to Mars, reflecting an emerging race.[39] If China develops a nuclear-powered spacecraft—particularly one that outpaces the U.S. or operates at significantly higher power levels—it would likely draw substantial public attention and signal China's serious intent to secure asteroid mining resources. Returning even a small asteroid to Earth would likewise garner dramatic notice.

- **Heavy-Lift and Reusable Launch.** If the PRC demonstrates a successful heavy-lift reusable rocket, it will mean the U.S. may lose its lead in space access technology. All the potential advantages identified for U.S. heavy-lift reusable systems (like SpaceX Starship) would be available to China as well. Given the military applications of such large-scale boosters—and the PRC's track record of dropping rocket bodies in uncontrolled reentries—this could raise alarm.[40] A suborbital carrier rocket landing in Cuba, Venezuela, or Brazil, for example, would likely spur considerable public concern.

The sheer scale and scope of China's roadmap highlight that resource extraction—both on the Moon and beyond—is central to its strategy. All of China's off-world pursuits of achieving space-based solar power, nuclear propulsion, and heavy-lift reusability converge toward a space strategy that culminates in off-planet mining and manufacturing. These technologies are critical to sustaining large-scale operations in space and necessary for achieving the transformative space economy.

## SPACE MINING

While the Moon serves as a major point of focus for economic and strategic competition, it is far from the only one. The size and scale of what will be possible in space in the years ahead difficult to fathom. It has been estimated that the mineral wealth contained in the belt of asteroids between the orbits of Mars and Jupiter would be equivalent to $700 quintillion dollars—about $100 billion for every person on Earth today—and nation states are already mobilizing to compete for these resources.[41]

The concept of space mining refers to the extraction of raw materials/minerals from astronomical objects including asteroids, comets, the Moon, and other planets. Sourcing material in space supercharges ISAM, because it will obviate the need to bring materials up from Earth with costly rockets—and that has the additional benefit of reducing mining demand on Earth, which translates to a healthier climate. Major banks have already forecast that space mining has potential to be a profitable endeavor, and mining the Moon alone may account for 12 billion in sales by 2040.[42]

Asteroid mining, once technologically mature, would enable large-scale resource extraction for building space-based solar power satellites, settlements, and other major space structures. It could also reduce reliance on rare earth elements (REE), most of which are currently supplied by China. An extraterrestrial source could help the U.S. break the emerging Chinese monopoly over these strategic elements, which are included in most of our advanced military technology.[43] Furthermore, the extracted material could be used to construct many items in the defense technology sector (fiber optic cables, aircraft parts, and so on).

## Legal Ambiguities and National Approaches

Though some disagree, it is the consensus position, as expressed by the International Institute of Space Law (IISL) that, "both national legislation and the subsequent state practice to Articles I and II of the Outer Space Treaty ... do not lead to a different result: the legal framework governing activities in space does not prohibit the exploitation of resources as an activity open to States." However, it also notes,

> "Under the existing international legal framework, mining of
> space resources raises a range of legal issues that need to be
> addressed adequately. Such use of outer space is not explicitly
> mentioned in the Treaties and there is no specific legal order
> for such activities. However, any prudent interpretation of
> the *corpus iuris spatialis* leads to the conclusion that space
> resource mining is not prohibited per se and that it is an
> activity falling under the freedom of the use of outer space
> as laid down in Article I para. 2 Outer Space Treaty, limited
> however by the fact that according to Article I para. 1 such
> use must be for the benefit of all mankind and according to
> Articles IV and IX must be in conformity with the provisions
> concerning military uses and environmental considerations."[44]

Thus, from an international perspective, the Outer Space Treaty does not prohibit the exploitation of space resources per se, but it remains vague—especially on the line between "non-appropriation" of celestial bodies and the right to extract resources.[45]

In the United States, the *Commercial Space Launch Competitiveness Act* that American companies and citizens are "entitled to any asteroid resource or space resource obtained, including to possess, own, transport, use, and sell it according to applicable law, including U.S. international obligations."[46] The first Trump administration further advocated for the use of space resources with an executive order on *Encouraging International Support for the Recovery and Use of Space Resources*, which provided additional cover for private companies interested in space mining.[47] The U.S.-led Artemis Accords—joined by 50+ countries—reinforces the U.S. position on space resource collection.[48] Several other states (Luxembourg, Japan, the UAE, and now India) have taken similar stances.[49]

China, meanwhile, is planning its own space mining initiatives, including capturing an asteroid and returning it to Earth.[50] As Dr. Larry Wortzel writes in *The Next Space Race*, "over the past two decades, numerous papers and government studies have emphasized the importance and strategic value of space mining both in economic terms and as a way 'to address China's oil and energy shortages.' Nor is the PRC limiting its vision of space mining to asteroids. Rather, it is also considering mining the Moon, Mercury, and Mars." the PRC's studies have repeatedly emphasized the importance and strategic value of space mining, not only for economic gain but to address China's energy shortages. Beijing does not limit its mining vision to asteroids alone—the Moon, Mercury, and Mars are also in play.[51]

## INEVITABLE STRATEGIC SURPRISES AND RISKS

It is imperative that U.S. policymakers and defense officials are aware of the future planned scenarios that are likely to occur based on adversarial nations' space ambitions and roadmaps as outlined above. However, it is equally important to widen our adversary aperture to include civilian-based challenges, natural space occurrences, and second tier powers, all of which may intentionally or unintentionally have an impact on U.S. space policy.

North Korea and Iran, specifically, have long been known for their development of offensive missile programs. Long-range missile testing by these two middle powers has consistently rattled the international system, and particularly their neighbors.[52] As advanced nations increasingly rely on space-based assets for modern life (GPS, weather, telecommunications and so on) and also for intelligence collection and force planning, attacking satellites can be viewed as a great equalizer. The North Koreans, Iran, or even Pakistan—as a signal to India—may be tempted to conduct a kinetic anti-satellite (ASAT) test to demonstrate or evaluate the ability to attack satellites.[53] Moreover, in a conflict, these second tier powers may immediately conduct a kinetic counterspace war during a conflict with each other, and due to the nature of any resulting space debris from satellite destruction, the U.S.—and all other spacefaring nations—will be affected. This will not be too much of a surprise, given that satellites are not off-limits during war. During the Ukraine conflict, the Russians conducted non-kinetic attacks on U.S. private sector company SpaceX's Starlink satellites, since they were being used to help the Ukrainians in the fight.[54]

National security and war constitute one aspect of space, but there will also be unplanned civilian incidents that elicit a response as well. The U.S. space shuttle program was eventually shuttered due to extremely high costs, long turnaround time between flights, and too much risk for safety—as it had experienced casualties during launch and reentry missions.[55] As rockets increase their payload reliability, human presence in space will naturally increase.

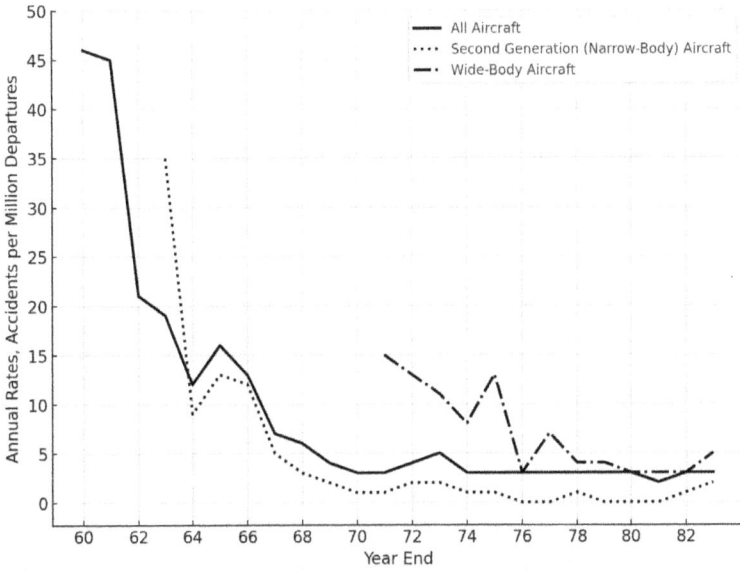

Figure 1. Annual Rates of Airline Accidents[56]

## Airline Safety Record
## Before and After Deregulation

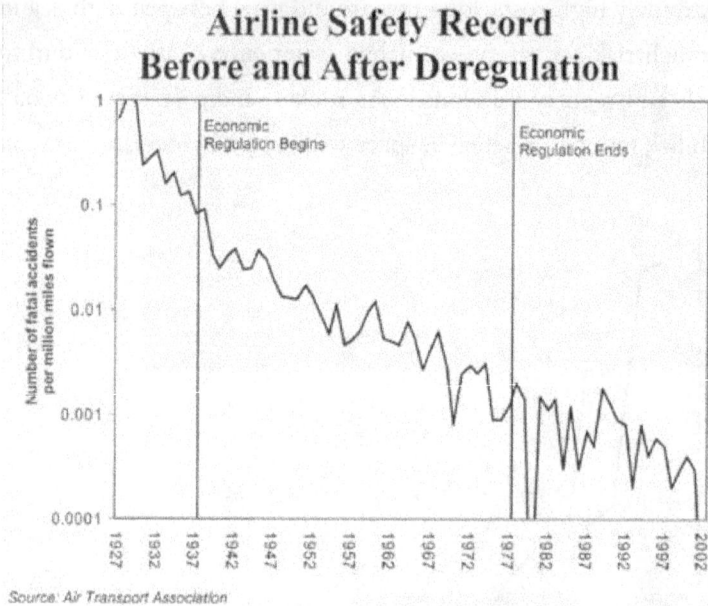

Figure 2. Airline Safety Record[57]

Rocket transportation is likely to mirror the experience in air transportation. Air transport is now a very safe form of transport, but in its infancy it experienced a number of fatal accidents, and experienced rapid and significant increases in safety, primarily from experience.

Unfortunately, civil/commercial launch failure and loss of human life is likely ineludible. The ever-expanding number of objects in space will translate to increased risk of major spacecraft collisions. Furthermore, as space hotels and space settlements become populated, there will be issues with handling problems with space tourist misbehavior. As problems arise in civil and commercial environments in space, who will conduct space rescue operations? There are also naturally occurring space phenomena that could pose challenges, such as the issue of defense against incoming asteroids.

The U.S. has conducted tests to deflect an asteroid, and China is also in the process of doing so. But should such an event occur, who will take the lead and ensure the safety of Earth?[58]

## MITIGATING "SPUTNIK MOMENTS": ESCALATION TRIGGERS AND POLICY RESPONSES

There are several Sputnik-like scenarios that could unfold. These may trigger a sudden national or international reaction—either by the U.S. or by adversaries to spirals of counteraction, acceleration, or efforts to check one another's advantage. How might this scramble of potential space scenarios manifest itself in the near-term? There are a number of objectives that have been announced by our adversaries that could have significant Sputnik-like effects on the part of the United States. Conversely, there are several goals laid out by the U.S. government and by private entities that could trigger Sputnik-like effects among our adversaries, creating spirals of reaction, acceleration, and attempts to check American advantage.

As adversarial nations, particularly China, continue to develop new technologies and pursue cutting-edge initiatives in space, the U.S. will need to adapt. While it may be impossible to predict space-related "black swan" events, there are numerous expected breakthroughs that can be addressed with the right planning. As outlined in *The Next Space Race*, China has a clear and coherent vision for space, complete with milestones for the next three decades. How should U.S. policymakers and the military respond when the PRC reaches these milestones? In turn, a few expected U.S. events and milestones could cause reactions from, or escalations by, other actors. And numerous "inevitable surprises" could likewise occur in the coming two decades.

These potential scenarios take place against an altered strategic landscape, both at home and abroad. While technology is evolving in the U.S. space sector, it is doing so faster than policymakers can adapt or understand. Assisting the U.S. government to properly assess and respond to developments in the space sector is consequently a high priority.

## CHAPTER 1 SUMMARY

- **Renewed Space Race & Great Power Stakes.** U.S. and China are engaged in intense strategic and economic competition in the space domain.

- **A Burgeoning Space Economy.** Today's $570+ billion space economy is poised to expand dramatically (and increase value into the trillions of dollars) over the next two decades. The implications of reusable space launch are only now becoming apparent. As heavy lift rockets improve, they will enable greater space tourism, facilitate space settlement on the Moon, provide easier access to space stations for medical research, and facilitate the development of space hotels. Those breakthroughs, in turn, hold the power to alter the astrostrategic and geostrategic landscape, changing both what nations might compete over and the tools with which we might do so.

- **The Moon is the Strategic Focal Point.** The Moon has approximately 1/6th the gravity of Earth, and this reduced gravitational pull makes the Moon significantly more desirable than Earth to serve as a launch point for deep space exploration. The Moon also can serve as the starting point for new space industrialization and a steppingstone to mine asteroids, and bolster in-space service, assembly, and manufacturing (ISAM). Both the U.S. (Artemis program) and China see the Moon as vital for science and resource extraction (helium-3, water ice). Lunar poles, rich in water ice, are especially contested; first arrivals may claim critical sites.

- **China's has Vast Space Ambitions.** China seeks to become the leading space power, eclipsing the U.S., by 2045. China has articulated a comprehensive and extremely ambitious space agenda, which includes developing a $10 trillion Moon-Earth economic zone the demonstration of numerous novel space technologies.

- **The Contest is for Space Resources.** Estimates show the mineral wealth contained in the belt of asteroids between Mars and Jupiter equivalent to ~$700 quintillion dollars. Extracted material could be used to construct many items in the defense technology sector and provide a new source of rare earth elements (REE)—all of which could help the U.S. overcome reliance on China for REEs. A major benefit will be the advancement of AI, robotics, and 3-D printing.

- **Risks, Surprises, & Potential "Sputnik Moments."** Middle-tier powers (Iran, North Korea) could test anti-satellite weapons, threatening orbital stability and sparking conflict. Increased human presence raises the risk of accidents, collisions, and the need for rescue or planetary defense. Significant Chinese milestones—like nuclear-powered spacecraft—could trigger major U.S. policy shifts, spurring a faster race for dominance.

- **Mitigating Sputnik Moments.** The U.S. must anticipate rapid technology changes, invest in key space infrastructure, and collaborate across public and private sectors. Clear legal guidelines and international cooperation will be critical to managing competition, preventing conflict, and harnessing space's vast economic potential.

# CHAPTER 2

## *Crisis and Escalation*

### INTRODUCTION

As American dependence upon our critical space infrastructure has become more apparent, U.S. policymakers must prepare for a range of crises that threatens America's quest for space supremacy and the preservation of its national security. This chapter examines six scenarios across three strategic dimensions: direct military confrontation, proliferation of asymmetric threats, and technological competition. Beginning with the immediate challenge of satellite attacks, we explore how China's development of co-orbital anti-satellite capabilities could systematically threaten U.S. critical space infrastructure. We then examine how emerging powers like North Korea and Iran, along with non-state actors, might further destabilize the space domain through both kinetic and non-kinetic means. Finally, we assess how China's technological breakthroughs in spaceplanes and heavy launch capabilities could fundamentally alter the balance of power in space, affecting both military capabilities and commercial competition. Each fictional scenario tests current response frameworks and highlights areas where enhanced capabilities or policy evolution is needed, particularly in situations requiring clear attribution and immediate crisis management.

## SCENARIO 1: INCIDENT IN THE COSMOS— THE DOWNING OF A U.S. SATELLITE

### SCENARIO RATIONALE

Recently the public has been made aware of close passes or inspections by adversary satellites,[59] but, as yet, they have not been made aware of a physical attack on a U.S. satellite. Were such an event to become public, it would likewise trigger attention and outrage like the violation of U.S. airspace by the Chinese spy balloon in early 2023. An article from March 3, 2023, in *Space.com* demonstrates the context for this scenario. According to the article, "the Chinese satellite TJS-3 has been inspecting other countries' assets in geostationary orbit . . . [The satellite] was sent up into geostationary orbit in late 2018. It then released a small subsatellite, possibly to help test TJS-3's capabilities."[60] The *Space.com* article continues, stating that "orbital data reveals that TJS-3 has been making close approaches to American satellites in recent months."[61] The Chinese are already capable of inflicting damage to U.S. space assets, but to date no Chinese physical attack using an inspector satellite has been publicly disclosed.

## *The Scenario*

### The Daily Astronomer | Front Page
*March 8, 2027*

A sudden and catastrophic failure of Satellite USA-2X7Y, a key U.S. space domain awareness asset in geosynchronous orbit, has ignited global alarm and intensified geopolitical tensions. The U.S. Space Surveillance Network detected the anomaly at 0600 EST, with preliminary telemetry strongly suggesting that the event was not accidental.

Within minutes of the incident, amateur satellite trackers took to social media, reporting a bright flash near the satellite's last known position, followed by a rapidly expanding debris cloud. Open-source analysis points to the presence of a foreign "inspector satellite" maneuvering near USA-2X7Y just hours before the failure, raising serious concerns over a possible deliberate act of aggression.

This incident unfolds against the backdrop of already fraught geopolitical negotiations. While the adversary nation has not explicitly claimed responsibility, state-controlled media issued stern warnings against the militarization of space and cautioned the U.S. against encroaching on what it called its "strategic orbital territory." The message, though ambiguous, has been widely interpreted as an implicit admission of involvement.

The destruction of USA-2X7Y has immediate and far-reaching consequences. The satellite played a crucial role in space domain awareness, and its loss exposes vulnerabilities in U.S. space assets. Global communications and surveillance capabilities face ripple effects, leaving allies increasingly concerned about their own orbital security. Many have called for a unified response, warning that failure to act decisively could set a dangerous precedent for unchecked aggression in space.

As news outlets break the story, a wave of public outcry erupts. The incident has drawn comparisons to the 2023 Chinese balloon controversy, fueling fears about national security vulnerabilities in the space domain. Social media platforms are flooded with trending hashtags such as #SpaceAggression and #SatelliteGate, amplifying demands for accountability and a clear U.S. response.

*NOTE: The President saw this article and is concerned. He has asked the Vice President to convene a National Space Council to provide the President with options and recommendations for immediate response and long-term programmatic response options.*

## SIMULATED NATIONAL SPACE COUNCIL DISCUSSION

Faced with the prospect of a Chinese inspector satellite suspected of destroying a critical American space domain asset, the council members grappled with how to respond effectively, with key points of conflict emerging.

One major tension was between projecting strength and preventing escalation. The Vice President and some advisors believed a strong response was necessary to deter China from further aggression. However, the Department of Defense and others *cautioned against escalation without definitive proof.* While it would be possible to eliminate Chinese inspector satellites, with no concrete intelligence it would be a massive escalation. They highlighted America's greater dependence on space capabilities compared to China, the U.S. reliance on China for a robust industrial supply chain, and the potential for a devastating space arms race.

Another point of contention was the choice between a military or diplomatic response. If necessary, the Department of Defense could put forward a range of options: maneuvering our assets in low Earth orbit, conducting retaliatory anti-satellite attacks, or employing a jamming and non-kinetic response.[62] The Department of Defense pushed for options involving the U.S. Space Force, while the Department of State and the Office of Science and Technology Policy advocated for a more diplomatic approach. They proposed building an international coalition to pressure China and emphasized the importance of upholding space norms—the thought was to use lack of adherence to norms to penalize China with sanctions.

Transparency versus strategy also presented a challenge. Some advisors stressed the need for public transparency, but the White House Press Secretary prioritized keeping the President out of the spotlight until facts are clear. The consensus was for a swift political reaction and for sending officials to brief Congress in the interim. Additionally, participants thought public briefings should not discuss the need to deescalate and should not mention jamming any communications to Chinese inspector satellites, stating instead that defensive actions are being taken.

There was a level of paralysis from the NSpC in responding

without having full intelligence or clear attribution and contingency plans already in place. From the discussion, it was clear that navigating this crisis required careful consideration of several key factors. Attributing the attack definitively is crucial for any response. Building an international coalition to condemn China's actions and uphold space norms is vital. Asset redundancy is an essential component to consider in America's ability to compensate for any damages and maintain its strategic edge. Additionally, fostering communication with China and avoiding an arms race are important for long-term stability and to avoid inadvertent escalation. Finally, the council concluded that the administration needs to project control and maintain public confidence in American space capabilities.

## ASSESSMENT AND RECOMMENDATIONS

The National Space Council simulation highlighted a fundamental challenge in space crisis response: formulating effective policy without complete information. Attribution uncertainty initially constrained response options, but once Chinese involvement was established, the complexity of the situation demanded a carefully calibrated approach. The incident required balancing decisive action against significant economic interdependence and supply chain vulnerabilities with China. However, this crisis also presents a strategic opportunity to counter China's pattern of challenging the rules-based international order, similar to their militarization of the South China Sea. A coordinated response emphasizing this pattern of behavior could strengthen international coalitions, particularly with NATO and Asian space partners. While overt diplomatic and military measures are essential to protect U.S. assets, covert capabilities should be integrated into the response strategy. Additionally, the broader economic implications for the commercial space sector must be considered, as potential spikes in space insurance rates and market instability could hamper future private sector investment—a critical component of U.S. space leadership. These factors inform the following comprehensive response framework:

## *Immediate Term (0–90 Days)*
### Military & Strategic Readiness

- Reposition Geosynchronous Space Situational Awareness Program (GSSAP) inspection satellites and deploy rapid-response surveillance assets.

- Activate cyber-hardening measures.

- Conduct RF jamming attacks on adversary inspector satellites to assess vulnerabilities.

### Crisis Communication & Diplomacy

- Issue coordinated White House, DoD, and State Department statements affirming U.S. space resilience.

- Declassify and release select intelligence confirming adversary proximity to USA-2X7Y.

- Convene NATO and QUAD allies for a unified response and initiate NATO Article 4[63] consultations.

- Engage China through secure diplomatic channels while reinforcing deterrence posture.

**Legal & Economic Countermeasures**

- Document treaty violations and build a case for formal action at the UN.

- Announce targeted sanctions on adversary space and satellite manufacturers.

*Short Term (90–360 Days)*
**Military & Space Defense Measures**

- Launch a rapid-replacement GEO surveillance satellite under an expedited procurement model.

- Deploy additional U.S. inspection satellites to shadow adversary GEO assets as a deterrent.

- Strengthen cyber ISR capabilities and develop counter-space defense protocols.

- Conduct controlled counter-ASAT capability demonstrations.

**Strategic Economic & Industrial Actions**

- Expand export controls on dual-use space technologies to restrict adversary capabilities.

- Establish a public-private investment framework to enhance commercial space resilience.

- Develop rapid in-orbit servicing and satellite reconstitution capabilities.

### Global Space Security & Legal Initiatives

- Propose a "GEO Security and Stability Act" to codify norms for responsible behavior in space.

- Form the Allied Space Security Coalition (SSC) to enhance space domain awareness.

- Submit a formal case to the UN Security Council against adversary co-orbital operations.

### *Long Term Strategic Initiatives (1–5 Years)*
### Space Resilience & Technological Superiority

- Deploy a distributed GEO surveillance architecture with autonomous maneuverability.[64]

- Develop and field space-based directed-energy capabilities for orbital protection.[65]

- Expand AI-driven cyber defenses and integrate real-time threat analysis capabilities.

- Harden space communication and control systems against electronic warfare threats.

### International Leadership & Governance

- Lead negotiations on responsible co-orbital operations and non-interference agreements.

- Establish a Space Traffic Management System (STMS) for safe orbital operations.[66]

- Develop binding multilateral policies on orbital debris mitigation and long-term space stability.

**Industrial & Economic Security Measures**

- Strengthen U.S. domestic satellite manufacturing and space technology independence.

- Expand workforce development programs for space defense and cybersecurity.

- Foster innovation hubs to accelerate R&D in space resilience technologies.

## RISKS AND METRICS FOR SUCCESS

Based on the recommended actions and scenario conditions, we assess a moderate risk of counter-response from China with low probability of direct conflict. However, the importance of a firm and measured response cannot be understated. Failure to act decisively would significantly further degrade deterrence credibility, erode allied confidence, and potentially invite similar provocations from other actors. Success in the immediate term will be measured by three critical factors: maintaining comprehensive space domain awareness, deterring further aggressive actions, and restoring confidence among both public and commercial stakeholders. The metric for long-term success would be no additional attacks on U.S. space assets.

## SCENARIO 2: THE RED CELESTIAL GUARD—PRC'S CO-ORBITAL ASAT CONSTELLATION

While the previous scenario explored a single, provocative attack on U.S. space assets, the following scenario examines a systematic threat through China's deployment of a co-orbital ASAT constellation. This evolution from isolated incident to persistent threat poses new challenges for space security and deterrence.

*Note: This scenario was generated and played nearly a year before President Trump issued his executive order on The Iron Dome for America, where he directed the "Development and deployment of proliferated space-based interceptors capable of boost-phase intercept;"[67] this decision constitutes a major policy shift since the 1993 decision by President Clinton to abandon development of such a system.*

### SCENARIO RATIONALE

Until now, the PRC has fielded only direct-ascent ASATs and experimented only with on-orbit co-orbital counterspace systems. It has, however, demonstrated its ability to rapidly deploy approximately 260 reconnaissance satellites to LEO. Were China to deploy an equivalent-sized operational co-orbital counterspace constellation and associated in-space space domain awareness, it would be an unambiguous deployment of offensive space forces and represent a significant threat to U.S. critical space infrastructure for which the U.S. had no equivalent deterrent. The capability for rapid deployment and plans for a large constellation are underway, as evidenced in a *Cybernews* article stating, "Chinese researchers from the People's Liberation Army's Space Engineering University in Beijing say they're planning to build a powerful constellation network consisting of exactly 12,992 satellites to compete with Elon Musk's SpaceX program ... But—this is where it gets interesting—*China's satellites will be designed to detect, identify, track and catalog the details belonging to each and every satellite in the Starlink fleet.* What's more, the *satellites will be equipped with new AI weapons, including lasers and high-powered microwaves, developed for use to destroy Starlink satellites* that pass over China and other sensitive regions" (emphasis added).[68]

*The Scenario*

**The Daily Astronomer | Front Page**
*April 14, 2026*

In a bold and unprecedented move, the People's Republic of China (PRC) has rapidly deployed a fully operational constellation of approximately 260 co-orbital anti-satellite weapons (ASATs) into low Earth orbit (LEO). Unlike previous direct-ascent ASAT systems and experimental co-orbital counterspace activities, this latest development represents a fully operational and precision-targeted disruption capability aimed at U.S. and allied space assets. The orbital planes and altitudes of the ASATs have been deliberately selected to provide rapid access to critical National Reconnaissance Office satellites and the U.S. Space Force Proliferated Warfighter Space Architecture constellation, marking a significant escalation in China's counterspace strategy.

These co-orbital ASATs are equipped with advanced rendezvous and proximity operations capabilities, including robotic arms and dual-mode propulsion systems that allow for prolonged, rapid, and highly precise orbital maneuvers. The onboard satellite sensors enhance the PRC's in-space domain awareness, providing real-time tracking, monitoring, and identification of U.S. and allied space assets. This technological sophistication enables precise targeting and coordinated ASAT activities, significantly amplifying the potential threat to Western military and intelligence space infrastructure.

This deployment marks a clear, aggressive deployment of weapon systems into orbit by the PRC, signaling a definitive shift in Beijing's space policy. Moving beyond mere experimental activities, China has now fielded an operational and potentially aggressive space-based counterforce capability. The U.S. and its allies currently lack an equivalent deterrent to counteract this emerging threat, creating a dangerous imbalance between two nations. The presence of an operational PRC co-orbital ASAT constellation raises urgent concerns over the potential disruption or disablement of key Western space assets, with implications for global military, intelligence, and communications networks.

The international response has been one of alarm, with growing calls for urgent discussions on space security agreements to prevent further militarization of the domain. Concerns over potential space debris generation and the broader implications for the security of commercial and civilian satellites have fueled diplomatic tensions, as world leaders grapple with how to respond to China's provocative escalation.

*NOTE: The President saw this article and is concerned. He has asked the Vice President to convene a National Space Council to provide the President with options and recommendations for immediate response and long-term programmatic response options.*

## SIMULATED NATIONAL SPACE COUNCIL DISCUSSION

The deployment of the PRC's co-orbital ASAT constellation raised concerns about the potential threats to U.S. and allied space assets. The council recognized the need to craft a response that effectively deters China from attack, reassures allies, and safeguards U.S. space assets, all while considering long-term strategic implications and potential technological advancements.

There was a significant focus on understanding China's intent and capabilities. Council members considered the implications for Taiwan and broader regional security in the context of Chinese military capabilities, particularly in the timeframe leading up to 2027. While the co-orbital ASATs present a clear threat, the time required for these satellites to form a kill chain and their overall number may not suffice to substantially degrade U.S. capabilities. The U.S. commercial imagery market and diversified satellite constellations add resilience to U.S. space assets.

The Chinese view the U.S. as the destabilizer through its historical development of ASAT capabilities and attempts to deny space capabilities to China. Members noted that China's actions are not abrupt but part of a long-term strategic plan. The U.S. intelligence apparatus has been keenly aware of these developments for some time; however, U.S. politicians were caught off guard.

The council discussed at length the importance of establishing and adhering to international norms and legal frameworks. Members suggested considering historical precedents such as the nuclear arms race during the Cold War. The potential for initiating arms limitation talks similar to those between the U.S. and the USSR was discussed as a long-term strategy. The Secretary of State suggested that while crafting a response, it is crucial to navigate these norms without undermining the U.S.'s right and capability to defend its assets and ensuring that any international agreements do not disproportionately benefit adversarial powers like China. The strategic and tactical value of norms, particularly in scenarios like the South China Sea, was highlighted, stressing the need to consider how norms could be used as both a shield and a sword.

As a response, the Department of Defense and the Vice President advocated for resuming ASAT testing and showcasing U.S. capabilities to deter China. This could involve a measured demonstration without revealing everything. One option was to emphasize U.S. capabilities and resilience in space, reassuring both domestic and international audiences that the U.S. is not vulnerable and has the means to deter and respond to threats and preserve secrecy around U.S. covert space capabilities to maintain strategic advantage in potential future conflicts. The possibility of limited support from developing nations for certain actions against China was acknowledged, as was a more extreme option of using cyber operations to potentially neutralize China's overt ASAT capabilities.

Meanwhile, the Secretary of State and Secretary of Commerce stressed the importance of a coordinated international response, potentially including economic pressure and establishing new legal norms for space activities. They also suggested exploring non-kinetic responses such as opening up uncensored internet access to Chinese citizens via platforms like Starlink to challenge Chinese censorship and exert soft power.

## ASSESSMENT AND RECOMMENDATIONS

The space council rightfully viewed the Chinese co-orbital constellation as a major provocation in the space domain that threatens not just U.S., but international space activities in LEO—not to mention ruining a $3 trillion space economy. The unprecedented size and scale of the adversary constellation required a response to assert U.S. strength, but it also came with an opportunity to demonstrate leadership. The following action plan focuses on rapidly protecting U.S. assets, demonstrating capabilities for deterrence, and providing sustainable practices for international norms.

*Immediate Actions (0–30 Days)*
**Protect Assets (48 Hours):**
- Disperse critical satellites to safer orbits.[69]

- Activate cyber-hardening protocols and execute covert cyber operations against PRC ASAT systems.

**Communicate Strategically (72 Hours):**

- Issue coordinated White House, DoD, and State Department statements.

- Brief allies and industry and convene NATO Space Coalition.

**Enhance Monitoring (Week 1):**

- Surge space domain awareness (SDA) capabilities with allied and commercial data.

- Establish a 24/7 joint watch center for real-time tracking.

*Short-Term Actions (1–12 Months)*
**Military/Technical:**

- Accelerate deployment of proliferated constellations (for example, PWSA).[70]

- Launch rapid-replacement microsatellites and strengthen ground-based ISR alternatives.[71]

- Demonstrate counter-ASAT capabilities through controlled tests.

**Economic/Diplomatic:**

- Impose targeted sanctions on PRC space industries and enforce technology export controls.

- Coordinate allied industrial responses and incentivize private-sector resilience.

- Expand uncensored internet access in China (for example, Starlink).

## Long-Term Strategy (1–5 Years)
### Space Architecture:
- Build distributed constellations and deploy autonomous, AI-driven systems.[72]

- Develop on-orbit manufacturing and orbital debris removal programs.[73]

### International Leadership:
- Form a space security alliance and negotiate arms control agreements.

- Lead on space sustainability through orbital debris mitigation and verification protocols.

## RISKS AND METRICS FOR SUCCESS

While the comprehensive plan should position the U.S. well to respond to the Chinese manufactured crisis, it does carry some risks of escalation to the point of conflict. The U.S. could compromise the capability of ambiguity and there may be some commercial sector instability. A successful execution of the plan over the first six months would be enough deterrence such that no ASAT incidents occurred. Over the next 18 months if there is reduced PRC ASAT constellation activity and we have an established space alliance that would be an accomplishment. Ultimately, if a debris mitigation capability became operational because of this crisis, that would be a positive second-order effect.

Not discussed by the participants was rapidly fielding a comparative system because no such system was in development.[74] The second The Trump administration's Iron Dome executive order likely accelerates the U.S. ability to rapidly field a capable defensive system and should drive expanded response options to such scenarios. Moreover, this scenario is important to study because if the U.S. were the first to deploy a space-based Iron Dome, it would likely encounter a similar international dynamic.

## SCENARIO 3: GLOBAL TENSION ESCALATES AS NORTH KOREA AND IRAN SHOWCASE ANTI-SATELLITE MIGHT

Beyond direct military confrontation with peer competitors, the proliferation of space capabilities to second-tier powers and commercial actors creates new vulnerabilities and challenges to traditional security frameworks.

## SCENARIO RATIONALE

To date, only the U.S., USSR/Russia,[75] China,[76] and India[77] have demonstrated direct-ascent kinetic anti-satellite weapons tests. All these nations also have significant assets in space that they rely on. Lesser powers do not have such reliance on space, but they do have the missile capability or capability to reach orbit, as well as national security pressures that could lead them to conduct debris-causing tests. For example, both North Korea[78] and Iran[79] have succeeded in launching satellites into orbit. Orbital capability is not even required for a direct-ascent ASAT missile, as an ASAT missile does not need to achieve orbital speed, but merely a high enough altitude that a satellite will smash into it. Even sounding rockets can reach such altitudes,[80] and Pakistan and Saudi Arabia have more capable long-range missiles that can reach 2,750 km and 4,000 km, respectively. Under the Biden administration, the U.S. self-imposed a moratorium on the testing of debris-creating direct-ascent ASAT missiles.[81] Thus, proliferation of direct-ascent ASAT weapons by second-tier space powers may not likely to be well tolerated by the United States, even given the U.S. may be developing and fielding space-based interceptors for missile defense purposes, which many assert constitute an inherent kinetic (and debris-causing) anti-satellite capability.

### The Scenario

**The Daily Astronomer | Front Page**

*December 7, 2029*

In a striking demonstration of military capability, North Korea and Iran have simultaneously conducted kinetic anti-satellite (ASAT) weapon tests, joining the ranks of a select group of nations with such advanced capabilities. These tests not only serve as a bold challenge to U.S. space leadership but also as a deterrent against intervention, showcasing their ability to target critical space assets. Notably, both countries have undertaken measures to minimize space debris, mirroring India's responsible approach to ASAT testing, in an effort to position themselves as conscientious actors in the arena of space security.

This development has sparked a domino effect, with Pakistan and Saudi Arabia signaling their intentions to acquire similar ASAT capabilities, potentially altering the balance of power in space. The tests by North Korea and Iran, nations with a history of collaboration in rocket technology, underscore the proliferation of space warfare technology and the increasing number of states capable of engaging in such acts.

Further clarity has emerged regarding the technology behind these tests. Our investigative journalists have learned that both nations have utilized passive coherent tracking, leveraging commercial space situational awareness (SSA) radars to analyze signals from Starlink satellite constellations to locate and guide their ASAT missile to their targets. This technique, previously demonstrated by Germany for radar tracking purposes, highlights a sophisticated method of identifying and targeting satellites, emphasizing the growing accessibility of advanced targeting capabilities.

The cooperation between North Korea and Iran in their rocket programs has been well-documented, and these latest tests suggest a continuing partnership in developing military strategies that extend into space. This collaboration, combined with their efforts to minimize debris generation, suggests a nuanced strategy to assert their presence in space without drawing undue ire for irresponsible actions.

The international response to these provocations remains to be seen, but the implications for international space security are profound. With the potential expansion of ASAT capabilities to additional nations like Pakistan and Saudi Arabia, the urgency for diplomatic and regulatory efforts to manage space as a contested domain has never been higher. As the global community grapples with these developments, the traditional U.S. allies are looking to the U.S. to stem the proliferation and rebuke both the ASAT testers and would be testers. American defense hawks want the U.S. to give a show of force, while the broader world looks to the U.S. to develop a collective approach to prevent the further weaponization of space and ensure its peaceful use is underscored, amidst an increasingly complex geopolitical landscape.

*NOTE: The President saw this article and is concerned. He has asked the Vice President to convene a National Space Council to provide the President with options and recommendations for immediate response and long-term programmatic response options.*

## SIMULATED NATIONAL SPACE COUNCIL DISCUSSION

The council quickly identified that these ASAT tests signal a significant shift in the power dynamics of space, as second-tier actors like North Korea and Iran demonstrate their ability to destroy critical space assets. Both countries' efforts to minimize space debris, while responsible on the surface, reflect a nuanced strategy aimed at legitimizing their actions. This raises a key tension: how the U.S. should respond decisively to these provocations without appearing hypocritical, given its own history with ASAT testing.

One major concern voiced by the Secretary of Defense and the Director of National Intelligence is the potential for rapid proliferation of ASAT technology, with countries like Pakistan and Saudi Arabia signaling intentions to develop similar capabilities. This proliferation threatens to destabilize space security, allowing more actors to challenge U.S. dominance in low Earth orbit (LEO). The Secretary of Defense proposed a three-tiered strategy: deterring countries from acquiring ASAT technology, deterring their use, and implementing a clear response plan should ASATs be deployed. This plan, however, highlights another tension within the council—whether diplomatic efforts or military deterrence should be prioritized in the face of a growing space arms race.

Geopolitical implications also weighed heavily on the discussion. Both the Secretary of State and the CCP Subject Matter Expert pointed out that this could be part of a coordinated effort by larger adversaries like China and Russia, using North Korea and Iran as proxies to disrupt U.S. space assets. The Secretary of State emphasized the need to isolate North Korea and Iran diplomatically while ensuring that China and Russia are kept in check through global collaboration. However, this raises the question of how far the

U.S. should go in involving international allies like India and Israel without escalating tensions further. The Secretary of Commerce echoed this concern from an economic standpoint, warning that space-related industries could suffer if the proliferation of ASAT capabilities leads to more debris and disrupted satellite operations.

The NASA Administrator and Heavy Reusable Launch Expert were particularly focused on the threat of space debris. While North Korea and Iran claim to have minimized debris from their ASAT tests, even small amounts could pose significant risks to space operations, including the Artemis mission and commercial satellites. The council members debated the efficacy of the U.S. condemning ASAT tests when it has previously conducted similar operations, creating a potential diplomatic double standard. The NASA Administrator advocated for U.S. leadership in promoting space sustainability, calling for a global moratorium on kinetic ASAT tests while encouraging non-destructive alternatives, like electronic jamming. They also emphasized the need for resilient satellite architectures and In-Space Assembly and Manufacturing (ISAM) to mitigate long-term risks.

Domestically, there was concern about the American public's perception of these developments. The Assistant to the President for Domestic Policy and the White House Press Secretary both noted that public outcry could mount if commercial satellite services, GPS, or other space-based utilities are disrupted by debris or additional ASAT tests. This creates pressure on the administration to act swiftly and decisively, balancing a strong defense posture with a message of space sustainability. The Press Secretary warned that appearing hypocritical or weak could erode public trust and international credibility, urging the U.S. to emphasize its commitment to responsible space behavior.

## ASSESSMENT AND RECOMMENDATIONS

The scenario highlights a complex diplomatic challenge: responding to ASAT tests conducted by adversaries when the United States has historically performed similar tests. This creates a delicate balance between maintaining strategic deterrence and avoiding charges of hypocrisy in international forums. While the expert panel identified crucial technical and procedural responses, they did not fully address countermeasures to the sophisticated passive coherent tracking threat demonstrated through the exploitation of Starlink signals. A comprehensive framework must therefore integrate three critical elements: a nuanced public communication strategy that acknowledges historical context while emphasizing the evolution toward responsible space behavior, a robust program to enhance space architecture resilience, and an international collaborative approach that both strengthens alliances and creates meaningful disincentives for ASAT testing and proliferation.

### *Immediate Term (0-90 Days)*
**Deterrence Activation and Crisis Response**

- Implement targeted sanctions on ASAT developers and position rapid-response space assets.

- Establish a multilateral 24/7 Space Crisis Coordination Cell and activate terrestrial PNT alternatives.

- Create an emergency commercial space security fund.

- Implement enhanced signal protection measures for commercial satellite operators.

**Diplomatic Initiative**

- Acknowledge U.S. historical ASAT testing while emphasizing responsible space behavior.

- Launch a U.N.-centered dialogue on ASAT test bans and issue joint statements with allies.

- Engage China and Russia on shared space stability interests while maintaining deterrence posture.

*Short Term (90–360 Days)*
**Military & Technical Deterrence**

- Accelerate tactical responsive space (TACRS) program with 72-hour replacement capability and develop non-kinetic countermeasures.[82]

- Enhance satellite maneuverability systems and deploy multi-domain response capabilities.[83]

- Establish clear escalation protocols with allied nations.

**Economic Measures**

- Create a space insurance backstop program and develop public-private security partnerships.

- Launch space technology innovation initiatives and establish rapid certification processes for security upgrades.[84]

**International Framework**

- Draft an inclusive ASAT test ban treaty and create a debris monitoring consortium.

- Establish a shared early warning system and verification measures.

*Long Term Strategic Initiatives (1-5 Years)*
**Architecture Transformation:**

- Deploy distributed satellite networks and implement ISAM capabilities for in-space servicing and repair. [85]

- Develop rapid reconstitution abilities and redundant PNT systems to reduce vulnerabilities. [86]

- Build resilient command and control systems for continuity during crises.

**Security Framework:**

- Establish a binding ASAT treaty with enforcement mechanisms and verification protocols as the first step toward creating an enduring international space security regime to maintain stability.

- Build credible deterrence partnerships and shared response capabilities with allies.

**Industrial Base Development:**

- Strengthen domestic space security technology development through targeted incentives.

- Enhance supply chain resilience and establish innovation centers for advanced R&D.

- Develop a skilled workforce for space defense and commercial space resilience.[87]

## RISKS AND METRICS FOR SUCCESS

The actions outlined above are focused on ensuring the U.S. maintains a credible posture, while pursuing diplomatic agreements. However, ensuring independent verification of the international agreements through monitoring bodies adds a layer of complexity. This point is particularly salient when we consider recent failures trying to oversee Iranian nuclear facilities. It will be equally difficult for verification measures in the reclusive North Korean state. The risk of proliferation is real if the solutions are not executed in a timely fashion. Nevertheless, successful implementation of at least most of these recommendations is possible and hinges on a few factors. Offering resilience to our space infrastructure through operational PNT alternatives within 24 months and establishment of TACRS capability with 72-hour satellite replacement time would go a long way to enhancing security.

Moreover, implementing a universal ASAT test ban ratification and standing up an integrated international allied SSA network would be very effective.[88] Such a network would enhance international cooperation, reduce space security threats, and strengthen deterrence credibility. Alternately (and not explored in this simulation), a deployed space-based missile defense shield, such as ordered by the second Trump administration, could also intercept and prevent further direct ascent ASAT missile testing or employment.

## SCENARIO 4: ORBITAL TENSIONS—SATELLITE SABOTAGE SHOWDOWN

The demonstration of kinetic ASAT capabilities by emerging space powers represents one facet of proliferation. However, the next scenario illustrates that the commercialization of space introduces new vectors for conflict as corporate entities (and their respective governments) engage in orbital warfare.

### SCENARIO RATIONALE

Various U.S. officials have described space as a new "Wild West" with few rules, poor visibility, and no law enforcement. Historically, corporations beyond legal recourse have resulted in "self-help," employing dirty tricks and sabotage against their competitors and hiring their own private security forces. Such behavior in space, however, would be novel, and likely to shock the public. Moreover, if this occurred between companies of two adversarial states, the sponsoring states might be drawn into the conflict. These ideas are already being considered as "a group of Chinese researchers is suggesting China launch its own satellite constellation to 'suppress'

SpaceX's Starlink system. Researchers at China's Space Engineering University—which operates under the People's Liberation Army—floated the recommendation in a paper discussing 'countermeasures' against Starlink."[89]

## *The Scenario*

### The Daily Astronomer | Front Page
*September 22, 2028*

A sudden and alarming wave of malfunctions among Starlink satellites has raised urgent concerns about the security of commercial space infrastructure. Preliminary investigations indicate a pattern of sabotage, with digital forensics pointing to cyberattacks originating from SkynetComm, a major Chinese commercial space corporation. The revelation has ignited fears that space is now becoming a battleground for corporate warfare, with critical satellite networks caught in the crossfire.

The rapid expansion of private space enterprises has led to fierce competition for orbital slots and communication frequencies. SkynetComm, indirectly backed by the People's Republic of China (PRC), has struggled to compete with Starlink's dominant global network. In what appears to be a desperate bid to gain a competitive edge, the company has allegedly turned to cyber and electronic warfare tactics. According to intelligence sources, SkynetComm has employed a dual-pronged strategy—executing cyberattacks to degrade Starlink's network performance while deploying small satellites equipped with electronic warfare technology to jam signals and disrupt operations in orbit.

While covert, the sabotage has been effective, leading to widespread service outages and substantial financial losses for Starlink. The situation escalated dramatically when confidential documents leaked to the media exposed SkynetComm's involvement, fueling speculation that the attacks are part of a broader state-sanctioned economic warfare strategy by the PRC. The leaks have heightened fears over the vulnerabilities of space-based infrastructure, underscoring the potential for commercial entities to disrupt global stability.

Public reaction has been swift and intense. The revelation of a commercial space skirmish has sent shockwaves through industry and government circles alike. For years, space headlines have been dominated by technological breakthroughs and exploration milestones—now, the prospect of corporate sabotage in orbit has triggered widespread alarm. The idea of foreign interference targeting a U.S. commercial asset has led to mounting pressure for government intervention and protective measures.

As global leaders assess the implications of this escalating conflict, discussions on the militarization of commercial space enterprises are gaining traction. The incident has laid bare the urgent need for stronger cybersecurity measures, new regulatory frameworks, and potential countermeasures to safeguard vital space infrastructure. With tensions rising, all eyes are now on Washington as policymakers determine the appropriate response to this unprecedented challenge in the new era of space competition.

*NOTE: The President saw this article and is concerned. He has asked the Vice President to convene a National Space Council to provide the President with options and recommendations for immediate response and long-term programmatic response options.*

## SIMULATED NATIONAL SPACE COUNCIL DISCUSSION

Participants considered the situation a grave economic disruption, warranting a balanced response that spans cyber defense measures, public reassurance, and collaborative efforts to diplomatically isolate the threat. The importance of a strategic, cautious approach was noted, emphasizing restoration of affected services and warning against rash policy statements.

The council acknowledged that while the attack did not directly impact U.S. defense capabilities, it posed a severe risk to economic security and commercial satellite operations. This perspective reinforces the need for an economic rather than a military response. While SpaceX operators have demonstrated an aptitude in response to state-based threats during the Ukraine war, Elon Musk's readiness to launch his own countermeasures has raised concerns about the need for regulatory oversight to ensure private companies do not escalate conflicts on their own. This situation has drawn parallels with other international crises, suggesting a need for clearer guidelines on private-sector engagement in national security issues.

The economic dimensions of the incident loomed large, with the Secretary of Commerce emphasizing the imperative to react decisively to safeguard U.S. economic interests and global leadership in the space domain and prevent markets from crashing. Participants worried about the perceived reliability of Starlink, as its failure could lead allies and global users to question the U.S. capability in maintaining secure and reliable commercial satellite services.

There was a noticeable split between the Department of Defense and the intelligence community on whether the disruption was greenlit by the CCP. The prevailing assessment was that Chinese commercial space entities are inextricably linked to the state apparatus, raising doubts about the company's independence and autonomy in this matter. Proposals such as implementing unfettered internet access for Chinese citizens or blocking Chinese sovereign wealth fund investments in the U.S. were put forth as potential economic deterrents, albeit with risk of escalation. The council considered coordinating with international allies to impose sanctions on the Chinese company responsible, aiming to isolate it economically and diplomatically. While some members advocated for a forceful response to project strength and deter further aggression, others cautioned against overly provocative measures that could be perceived as existential threats by China, potentially prompting severe retaliation across multiple domains.

The incident was viewed by some as an opportunity to reassess the extent of government involvement in space infrastructure, drawing parallels to the debates surrounding Huawei and 5G technology, or to diversify its platforms to reduce dependency on commercial entities like SpaceX. One of the largest questions plaguing the group was whether the U.S. government or a U.S. commercial entity conducted any corporate or economic sabotage to precipitate a reaction from Skynet.

When considering public messaging, the significance of clear communication to the populace was underscored, highlighting the widespread impact on the economy and critical services. Lastly, there was an acknowledgment of the political dimension and the need for decisive messaging that supports the importance of space infrastructure, suggesting its designation as part of the nation's critical assets.

## ASSESSMENT AND RECOMMENDATIONS

The Chinese attack on Starlink through SkynetComm represents a new frontier in commercial space warfare. This unprecedented threat in the space domain challenges both economic and national security interests and needs to be addressed forcefully—as precedents will be set after this response. The incident demands a measured response that balances market stability, private sector autonomy, international cooperation, and most importantly, a deterrent component. The following framework provides immediate actions to restore services and confidence in Starlink, while establishing long-term mechanisms to protect commercial space assets and deter future aggression:

*Immediate Actions (0–72 Hours):*
**Operational Coordination:**
- Establish a unified command structure integrating SpaceX, U.S. Cyber Command, and Space Force to streamline communication and response efforts.

- Deploy advanced real-time cybersecurity monitoring systems in partnership with SpaceX and Cyber Command.

**Public Messaging and Stabilization:**
- Issue a unified public statement condemning the attack, ensuring transparency to reassure the public and allies.

- Privately communicate with Beijing to demand cessation of hostile actions while briefing Congress and key allies.

- Prioritize immediate restoration of Starlink services to mitigate service disruptions and restore public confidence.

- Activate market safeguards and support critical communications infrastructure to prevent financial instability.

**Policy Action:**
- Issue an executive order designating American commercial activity in every domain including commercial space systems will be designated as critical infrastructure, ensuring their prioritized protection and funding.

*Short-Term Measures (72 Hours - 30 Days):*
**Economic and Diplomatic Measures:**
- Impose targeted sanctions on SkynetComm and associated entities, coordinating with allied nations to apply economic pressure.

- Convene an international summit to establish shared norms for space security and build allied collaboration.

**Industry Resilience and Strategic Messaging:**
- Initiate a public-private partnership to develop secure technologies and shared protocols for mitigating cyber and electronic warfare threats. [90]

- Consider leveraging Starlink to provide uncensored internet access in China as a geopolitical countermeasure, assessing risks carefully.

*Long-Term Strategies (30+ Days):*
**Legislative and Regulatory Frameworks:**
- Draft and implement comprehensive legislation protecting commercial space assets, incorporating public-private partnership models.

- Advocate for international agreements to establish and enforce security norms and penalties for malicious space activities.

**Technological Advancements:**
- Invest in anti-jamming technologies, counter-electronic warfare capabilities, and distributed architectures to enhance satellite resilience. [91]

- Diversify reliance on single providers by supporting multiple commercial and government-led space systems. [92]

**Deterrence and Public Trust:**
- Develop clear response thresholds and integrate allied capabilities to strengthen deterrence against adversaries.

- Maintain sustained public messaging campaigns to reinforce trust in U.S. leadership and resilience in space.

## RISKS AND METRICS FOR SUCCESS

The crisis response strategy outlined herein must be deployed with consideration of potential for escalation and for continued or expanded patterns or interference among satellite services providers. There are a few metrics that will determine if the plan is executed successfully—first and foremost the Starlink services must be quickly restored and along with public trust. The markets will need to immediately be stabilized to ensure consumer confidence in space-based systems remains. Moreover, in the long-term commercial systems will need to demonstrate better resilience to these types of provocations.

Some independent reviewers judged that the scenario participants may have underestimated the traditional reaction of American strategic culture. Harassment of legitimate commercial activity has always been considered provocation sufficient to elicit military responses. From the Barbary Pirate campaign in the early years of the country to actions against Somali pirates in East Africa, the United States has often defended commerce through armed activity. Independent reviewers thought that the unique experience of space experts might have insulated them from the likely reactions in the broader American strategic culture. U.S. policy makers must be aware of this weakness of the American space policy intelligentsia.

## SCENARIO 5: CELESTIAL VANGUARD—PLA'S SPACEPLANE SQUADRON EMERGES

While both direct military threats and asymmetric challenges demand immediate attention, long-term space security depends on maintaining technological superiority. The following scenarios examine how Chinese advances in spaceplane and launch capabilities could fundamentally alter the strategic balance.

### SCENARIO RATIONALE

Spaceplanes have very different operational utility from satellites, enabling responsive space access, difficult-to-predict counterspace capabilities, and even the potential for orbital bombardment. China has been testing spaceplane concepts, but these experiments have not added up to an operational capability.[93] The U.S. has also only been experimenting. However, China has proved its ability to move rapidly from experiment to operations. The fielding of a spaceplane squadron would likely create a perception that the U.S. is significantly behind and offer the Chinese decided military advantages in space conflicts.[94] Were it to successfully demonstrate a landing capability in the American hemisphere with the same system, this would alarm the public with a potential novel mode of power projection or strike capability.

## *The Scenario*

### The Daily Astronomer | Front Page
*June 4, 2029*

China has officially announced the formation of the "Celestial Vanguard," an operational squadron of advanced spaceplanes under the command of the People's Liberation Army (PLA). This development marks a significant step in China's expansion of military capabilities in space, introducing a new class of assets capable of rapid deployment and versatile mission execution.

Unlike conventional satellites, these spaceplanes can perform a variety of operations, including on-demand satellite deployment, in-orbit repairs, and potentially deorbiting adversary satellites. The Celestial Vanguard is also believed to possess reconnaissance capabilities over global hotspots and, most notably, the potential for precision orbital strikes. The introduction of this squadron blurs the distinction between aerospace and space dominance, raising questions about the future balance of power in orbit.

The PLA Strategic Support Force (SSF)[95] recently conducted a public demonstration of one of these spaceplanes, executing maneuvers over key global military installations before landing in an international waters zone close to the American hemisphere. The flight profile is widely seen as a demonstration of the spaceplane's reach and capabilities.

The announcement of the Celestial Vanguard squadron has drawn widespread attention, particularly regarding its implications for strategic competition in space. Comparisons are already being made to Cold War-era concerns over nuclear-capable bombers and intercontinental ballistic missiles. U.S. allies have expressed concern over the power projection potential of the spaceplane fleet and its impact on global security.

As nations assess the significance of China's latest military development, discussions over space security and military posturing in orbit are expected to intensify in the coming months.

*NOTE: The President saw this article and is concerned. He has asked the Vice President to convene a National Space Council to provide the President with options and recommendations for immediate response and long-term programmatic response options.*

## SIMULATED NATIONAL SPACE COUNCIL DISCUSSION

As the discussion unfolded, a fundamental tension emerged—whether to view the spaceplanes as a provocative display of offensive capabilities or a potential platform for cooperation and peaceful exploration. The Secretary of Defense, echoing the Director of National Intelligence, painted a chilling picture: Spaceplanes could be Fractional Orbital Bombardment Systems (FOBS) capable of delivering devastating surprise nuclear attacks. The potential for the Chinese spaceplanes to carry nuclear weapons was seen as a game-changer, necessitating a complete reassessment of U.S. strategic, operational, and tactical policies. The council stressed the importance of preparing for a shift in nuclear deterrence and defense postures to address the reduced warning times and increased threat vectors.

To address this new class of weapons, there were recommendations for substantial investment in satellite surveillance, ground-based interceptor defense systems, and on-orbit attack capabilities—the financial implication of these developments could be substantial, with estimates reaching $150 billion over several years.[96] There were also perspectives that viewed the spaceplanes as an opportunity for the U.S. to catalyze its own advancements in spaceplane technology (expand on the X-37 program [or buy a squadron of Starships]) and to establish a clear lead in space through a combined approach of civil and military developments, akin to a modern-day Manhattan Project for space. Similar to the Sputnik challenge, it could be an opportunity to "catch up" on Chinese spaceplane technology, and NASA could lead a "project-level effort with a civilian face but with military capabilities."

In contrast, the Secretary of Commerce and Secretary of State dismissed this characterization, suggesting the spaceplanes were designed primarily for debris removal. Meanwhile, the Office of Science and Technology Policy thought China could use the space-planes for civilian LEO research. The China expert stated their rationale was that the PRC has been asymmetrically vulnerable to U.S. strategic strikes, which has harmed strategic stability. Having the spaceplanes enables the PRC to demonstrate a deterrence measure before hostilities arise and to establish mutual vulnerability.

The geopolitical dimensions of the spaceplane demonstration landing in Venezuela added further complexity to the council's considerations. Members considered engaging in further diplomatic and economic efforts in the Western Hemisphere to counter China's perceived influence in the region, particularly its collaboration with Venezuela. Leveraging international bodies such as the U.N. Security Council, particularly with the support of other Permanent Five members, like France and the United Kingdom, was discussed as a way to exert diplomatic pressure on China. The mixed responses from the American public to escalating tensions underscored the need for careful messaging and engagement.

The discussions also highlighted the need for clear communication and reassurance, both domestically and internationally. The White House Press Secretary emphasized the mixed response from the American public, while allies like NATO members and the Five Eyes nations, particularly Australia, sought clarity and affirmation of American resolve.

## ASSESSMENT AND RECOMMENDATIONS

If China were to successfully launch a squadron of spaceplanes capable of landing anywhere on the globe, this would represent a major strategic inflection point. The demonstration of precision landings in the Western Hemisphere near CONUS, coupled with potential nuclear payload capabilities, would fundamentally alter space domain and geostrategic dynamics. The draft framework below provides U.S. policymakers with a structured approach for developing an adequate response package.

*Immediate Actions (0-6 months)*

**Space Domain Awareness & Military Posture:**

- Deploy assets with the ability to track and monitor PLA spaceplane activity, including partnerships with commercial entities like NorthStar,[97] with a focus on the Venezuela and Cuba region.

- Deploy Aegis[98] assets strategically along known PLA flight paths and increase operational readiness of U.S. Space Command.

**Strategic Communications and Deterrence:**

- Conduct a high-profile demonstration of U.S. capabilities, emphasizing both civilian and military space applications.

- Rapidly implement a public communications strategy to address state and public concerns, emphasizing U.S. resolve and capability.

- Convene an allied summit to coordinate responses, issue a joint statement of deterrence, and establish unity among Western Hemisphere nations.

*Short-Term Actions (6-18 months):*

**Technology Development:**

- Launch a grant program for satellite defense and debris mitigation technologies, prioritizing commercial innovation.

- Fast-track deployment of the constellations used for comprehensive orbit monitoring.

- Accelerate development of the X-37 program with a focus on deterrent capabilities.[99]

**Regional Security**
- Establish a Western Hemisphere space security framework through the OAS and initiate intelligence operations targeting Chinese collaboration with Venezuela and Cuba.

*Long-Term Actions (18+ months):*
**Technology and Infrastructure**
- Establish a NASA-led "Manhattan Project" for spaceplane technology, with a civilian face and compartmented military applications.

- Develop methods for preemptive strikes (space domain awareness, targeting, and new interception methods) with an estimated cost of $100-$200 billion.

- Develop and deploy directed energy weapons, cyber-resilient satellite architectures, and advanced space situational awareness systems.

- Build out U.S. capabilities to interdict munitions and provide flexible deterrence, including advanced spaceplane programs.

### Capacity Building

- Expand STEM education, targeting aerospace innovation and defense technology fields to ensure a robust talent pipeline.

- Build a network of allied spaceports in the Western Hemisphere to counteract Chinese influence and strengthen regional resilience.

## RISKS AND METRICS FOR SUCCESS

Allowing a squadron of adversary spaceplanes to go unchecked will not fly. A bold move landing near CONUS must be met with a response that not only satisfies U.S. allies, but the general public to ensure confidence in the administration. Another primary risk will be for technical development delays for rapid development of the X-37 program and new SDA, detection and response assets. Success will be determined by demonstrating effective deterrence over time, maintaining cohesion with allies on space cooperation (the worry is how potential partners perceive China as a new leader in space), and keeping public confidence. However, the most crucial metric will be our ability to track and respond to PLA spaceplane maneuvers, while simultaneously developing our own capabilities and maintaining international partnerships.

## SCENARIO 6: CHINA'S GAME-CHANGER: LONG MARCH 9'S STUNNING DEBUT SIGNALS NEW ERA IN SPACE RACE

The military implications of China's spaceplane program highlight one aspect of technological competition. However, as the final scenario demonstrates, commercial space capabilities like advanced launch vehicles can have equally profound effects on national security and economic leadership.

### SCENARIO RATIONALE

The United States has enjoyed an advantage in space launch in both heavy lift and reusability. As of the time of writing, the Space Launch System (SLS) has demonstrated one successful mission. SpaceX Starship is making rapid progress, with a series of spectacular developmental launches already completed.[100] Once completed, Starship will be game-changing.[101] But the PRC has plans to develop a super-heavy lift Long March 9[102] capable of lifting 150 metric tons to low-Earth orbit, and targeting its first launch in the early 2030s. Recently the PRC has shifted the design to embrace Starship-like full reusability,[103] and is encouraging private sector companies to develop similar "chopstick" systems.[104] Should the PRC show itself equally capable with a SpaceX Starship-equivalent system, the U.S. would have to worry about losing global market share for launch, as well as the speed at which China could deploy space systems, including military systems.

## The Scenario

**The Daily Astronomer | Front Page**
*February 13, 2029*

On the first day of Chinese New Year, China has spectacularly launched the Long March 9, a super heavy-lift rocket, one year ahead of schedule, marking a monumental achievement with its first-time success of the entire reusable stack. This groundbreaking event not only demonstrates China's growing prowess in space technology but also directly challenges U.S. dominance in the sector, particularly at a time when American companies face regulatory hurdles slowing down commercial launch activities.

The successful deployment of the Long March 9 is a clear indication of China's ambitions to become a leader in space exploration and commercialization. With plans for mass production, the Long March 9 is set to play a crucial role in supporting China's Lunar base initiatives and constructing an ambitious solar power satellite program. This launch vehicle's capabilities mirror those of SpaceX's Starship, setting the stage for a competitive edge in heavy lift and reusability that the U.S. once undisputedly held.

Amidst increasing environmental and safety regulation that has beleaguered U.S. companies like SpaceX, Blue Origin, Relativity, and Stoke, China's strategic advance in space launch capabilities comes at an opportune moment. The Long March 9's debut and its implications for rapid deployment of space systems have raised concerns over the speed at which China could not only catch up but potentially outpace U.S. advancements in space technology.

Furthermore, China has articulated clear plans to commercialize the Long March 9, with a state-backed champion poised to recapture and expand its share in the global launch market. This move not only signifies China's intent to leverage its technological achievements for economic gain but also to assert its presence as a dominant force in the international space community.

In a stark warning that reverberates through the corridors of power and industry, leading U.S. rocket companies, including SpaceX, Blue Origin, Relativity, and Stoke, are sounding the alarm over the imminent threat posed by China's rapid advancements in space technology, notably the Long March 9's successful launch and reusability. These firms caution that without significant intervention from the U.S. government, they are on a precarious path towards financial instability that could lead to bailouts, bankruptcy, and the forfeiture of a critical market segment to Chinese dominance. U.S.

firms argue that the American government has not provided a comparable market drive or facilitation, leaving them at a competitive disadvantage. The stark warning outlines a grim future where, without prompt and decisive government action, the U.S. risks not only losing its commercial space edge but also jeopardizing the Space Force's secure access to space—a critical component of national security.

As the Long March 9 prepares for mass production and subsequent missions critical to China's space infrastructure, the global space race enters a new phase of heightened competition and strategic positioning. The United States, now facing a formidable challenge, must navigate its regulatory landscape carefully to maintain its leadership role in an increasingly contested outer space environment. Many analysts look to hear what the new administration will say in the State of the Union and Presidential Budget Request.

*NOTE: The President saw this article and is concerned. He has asked the Vice President to convene a National Space Council to provide the President with options and recommendations for immediate response and long-term programmatic response options.*

## SIMULATED NATIONAL SPACE COUNCIL DISCUSSION

The Long March 9 is not only a technological achievement but a clear signal of China's ambition to dominate both commercial and military space sectors. A primary tension that emerged during the discussion was the perceived narrowing gap between U.S. and Chinese space capabilities. While some members, like the NASA

Administrator, maintained that the U.S. still holds a lead in launch capability, others, including the Secretary of Defense, viewed this as a "watershed moment" with significant implications for national security, commerce, and energy sectors. This disparity in assessments highlighted the urgent need for a comprehensive evaluation of relative capabilities and a unified strategy to maintain U.S. leadership.

Many Council members identified the U.S. regulatory environment, particularly export controls like ITAR, as a significant barrier to maintaining competitiveness. These regulations are stifling innovation and pushing U.S. companies to either slow their development or look for alternative markets, which could ironically benefit adversarial nations. The Vice President and Secretary of Commerce both argued that unless the U.S. reforms its regulatory framework, American companies may lose their commercial edge, which would directly affect national security. The Secretary of Defense echoed this, noting that the U.S. has yet to fully exploit reusability in space technologies, even though its commercial space sector pioneered the concept. There is a clear consensus that without regulatory reform, the U.S. risks losing both its technological leadership and its strategic military advantage in space.

Workforce development also emerged as a critical area of concern. The NASA Administrator and several other members highlighted the aging U.S. space workforce and the country's relative lack of STEM (science, technology, engineering, math) graduates compared to China. This demographic challenge threatens the U.S. ability to sustain innovation and leadership in space technologies. In contrast, China is producing a large number of STEM graduates, giving it a potentially insurmountable edge in the technical expertise required to dominate space exploration, manufacturing, and commercialization. To address this, members recommended bolstering STEM education, reforming immigration policies to attract global talent, and creating incentives for young professionals to enter the space sector.

Another major point of contention involved the military implications of China's advancements. The Secretary of Defense and DNI raised concerns about China's potential to dominate Cislunar space and disrupt U.S. space operations. The ability to rapidly deploy space systems through reusable rockets gives China a strategic advantage that could undermine U.S. military and commercial activities in space. This led to recommendations for a whole-of-government approach to counter China's rising capabilities, with several members calling for better interagency collaboration and a clear national strategy that prioritizes space security, economic interests, and energy initiatives like space-based solar power.

In terms of diplomacy, several officials, including the Vice President and the Director of National Intelligence, advocated for sending a congratulatory message to China, framing it as a gesture of goodwill while signaling the expectation that China adhere to international norms in space. While there was a consensus on the need to strengthen international partnerships, particularly through initiatives like the Artemis Accords, there was also recognition of the need to maintain a competitive edge over China. This was particularly evident in discussions about engaging with non-aligned countries like India, where the U.S. must find ways to cooperate without ceding strategic advantages. These alliances are seen as critical to countering China's growing soft power in space, particularly as Beijing may seek to persuade other nations that its space program is superior. The CCP Subject Matter Expert's input further complicated this dynamic, highlighting China's integrated approach to commercial and military space applications and the limited options for the U.S. to hinder their progress without potentially harming U.S. interests.

Finally, the council grappled with the challenge of public perception and resource allocation. The White House Press Secretary noted that a significant portion of the U.S. population views space exploration as a waste of resources that could be better spent on earthbound issues like education. This creates a tension between the perceived need for increased investment in space capabilities and potential public backlash, particularly from communities that feel left out of the space economy.

## ASSESSMENT AND RECOMMENDATIONS

China's successful launch of the Long March 9 during Chinese New Year marks a pivotal shift in the global space landscape—particularly as U.S. launch providers struggle under regulatory constraints. The combination of this technological achievement and Beijing's strategy of subsidizing launch costs to increase market competitiveness poses an immediate threat to both U.S. economic interests and national security capabilities. This critical situation demands a comprehensive whole-of-government response spanning immediate regulatory relief, industrial base strengthening, and long-term strategic reforms to maintain U.S. space leadership.

### *Immediate response (0–6 months)*
**Expedite Regulatory Review:**
- Implement temporary regulatory waivers for critical launch activities.

- Establish rapid-response teams at FAA/EPA with dedicated funding to fast-track approvals.

- Create a metrics-based evaluation system to track regulatory reform impact.

## DoD Launch Support:
- Provide direct funding for commercial launches using a maritime model to stabilize U.S. providers against China's "friendship pricing."[105]

- Establish a joint DoD-NASA-Commerce technical assessment team for Long March 9 capabilities.

- Create an emergency space policy coordination office within the White House.

## Public Messaging Campaign:
- Frame space spending as critical to economic growth, renewable energy, and national security.

- Develop a specific congressional engagement strategy for funding support.

- Create a coordinated diplomatic response strategy to reassure allies.

## Intelligence Reform:
- Conduct a rapid assessment of intelligence gaps on Chinese space capabilities.

- Establish new collection priorities for monitoring advancements.

- Create an interagency coordination mechanism for space intelligence.

*Short-term strategy (6–18 months)*
**Structural Reform:**
- Draft legislation to create a Department of Space and centralize civil space funding.

- Establish a National Astronautics Strategy modeled on the Maritime Strategy.

- Create space technology transfer protocols with allies, addressing IP and dual-use concerns.

**Workforce Development:**
- Fast-track visas for space-sector talent.

- Expand grants for trade schools and technical education.

- Launch minority outreach programs.

- Develop a workforce succession planning framework to address STEM shortages.

**Industrial Base Support:**
- Create tax incentives for domestic space manufacturing and supply chain development.

- Establish space technology innovation zones to foster regional industry clusters.

- Develop counterstrategies for China's predatory pricing practices.

- Create an international regulatory framework for point-to-point transportation.

## *Long-term vision (18+ months)*
### Space Industrial Policy Board:
- Establish a board to oversee U.S. space industry health and align civil-military procurement strategies.

- Lead efforts like space-based solar power (SBSP).

- Develop an integrated civil-military space infrastructure plan for long-term sustainability.

### International Partnerships:
- Strengthen Artemis Accords with economic and technical incentives.

- Develop a special space partnership with India, focused on Lunar exploration and joint technology development.

- Establish permanent funding mechanisms for allied programs through multi-year appropriations.

### Education and Workforce Pipeline:
- Fund space-focused vocational programs and create manufacturing apprenticeships.[106]

- Expand workforce succession planning efforts to ensure long-term STEM capabilities. [107]

- Build a talent pipeline that makes full use of America's talent base. [108]

**Regulatory Modernization:**
- Reform ITAR to streamline export controls for space technologies while maintaining national security.

- Streamline environmental reviews for space activities with updated processes.

- Develop an allied export control framework to counteract Chinese exploitation of U.S. innovations.

- Create a comprehensive space traffic management infrastructure to prevent collisions and ensure orbital safety.

## RISKS AND METRICS FOR SUCCESS

The primary risk of China's reusable launch development, and U.S. inaction, will be the erosion of American launch market dominance and space industrial base. Absent coordinated action to boost manufacturing capacity, increase capital investment, and reduce regulatory barriers, there is significant risk to both U.S. economic competitiveness and national security capabilities. Success will be measured through market indicators including U.S. launch sector market share, provider stability, and industrial base strength metrics such as workforce growth and manufacturing capacity.

## EMERGING THEMES AND CONCLUSION

The scenarios demonstrated that in the not-too-distant future the space domain will see increased strategic competition, rapid technological development, and a fight for international dominance and influence. Several themes materialized throughout the discussions, which are useful to contemplate how to address these potential futures.

**Contingency Planning.** The novelty of the scenarios clearly posed a challenge to the space council participants—highlighting the lack of ready-made response options and demonstrating the need for comprehensive contingency planning. National leadership needs a menu of courses for action, which could be achieved by specifying the task for DoD to lead interagency contingency planning in the Joint Strategic Capabilities Plan (JSCP) to USSPACECOM.

**Crisis Communication.** Nearly all scenarios had a very strong component of communication to public, congressional, and allied stakeholders. However, the absence of a National Space Council crisis communications playbook represents a significant vulnerability—and this severely limits the USG ability to provide coherent and effective responses. Of note, the council is not organized for crisis management like the National Security Council (NSC) but rather for conversations and policy development. An executive committee or something similar should be developed that only includes those necessary for decision making in a rapid sense. All other options can be delegated to sub-committees for later discussion and decision.

**Capability Development.** One far too common theme was the U.S. being perpetually behind the eight ball in the scenarios— specifically because America did not have an equivalent technology or system in the pipeline capable of being fielded rapidly. Maintaining technological superiority in co-orbital counterspace capabilities, spaceplanes, advance launch and satellite internet is crucial for both deterrence and response options

**Strategic Narrative**. A key competitive strategy to mobilize public support and funding for space development was reframing of U.S. space efforts—both military and civilian—as critical to economic growth, renewable energy, and national security. This method is far more effective and compelling than traditional space exploration narratives alone.

**Foundational Investments.** All scenarios highlighted the need for the nation to invest in fundamentals that enable us to stay ahead, pre-empt, or rapidly respond. STEM and workforce development was a critical and limiting ingredient or a rapidly mobilizable tech and industrial base.

These themes paint a clear picture: success in achieving American space dominance and deterrence of attacks will require not just technological superiority, a communication strategy, the ability to adapt, and the benefit of being prepared and well-funded.

## CHAPTER 2 SUMMARY AND RECOMMENDATIONS

- **Introduction.** As space becomes increasingly contested, congested, and competitive, U.S. policymakers must prepare for a range of potential crises that could threaten American space supremacy and national security. Each scenario presented here explores different aspects of space competition, from direct military confrontation to technological rivalry, testing current response frameworks and highlighting areas requiring enhanced capabilities or policy evolution.

- **Scenario 1: Incident in the Cosmos—The Downing of a U.S. Satellite.** A Chinese inspector satellite destroys a critical U.S. space domain awareness asset in geosynchronous orbit, creating immediate public outrage and demands for response. Key recommendations focus on strengthening attribution capabilities, developing proportional response options, and building international coalitions to condemn such actions while avoiding uncontrolled escalation.

- **Scenario 2: The Red Celestial Guard—PRC's Co-orbital ASAT Constellation.** China deploys a constellation of 260 co-orbital ASATs capable of threatening U.S. space assets, representing a systematic challenge to space security. Recommendations focus on developing distributed architecture solutions, enhancing defensive capabilities, and establishing clear deterrence frameworks for constellation-level threats.

- **Scenario 3: Global Tension Escalates as North Korea and Iran Showcase Anti-Satellite Might.** North Korea and Iran conduct coordinated ASAT tests while minimizing debris, demonstrating sophisticated targeting capabilities and potentially spurring proliferation to other nations. Recommendations emphasize preventing further proliferation through diplomatic initiatives, enhancing space domain awareness networks, and developing international frameworks for responsible behavior in space.

- **Scenario 4: Orbital Tensions—Satellite Sabotage Showdown.** Chinese commercial entity SkynetComm conducts cyber and electronic warfare attacks against Starlink satellites, highlighting vulnerabilities in commercial space infrastructure. Response framework prioritizes public-private partnerships for cyber defense, international legal frameworks for commercial space activities, and enhanced protection for critical commercial space infrastructure.

- **Scenario 5: Celestial Vanguard—PLA's Spaceplane Squadron.** China demonstrates operational military spaceplanes with global reach, including provocative maneuvers near U.S. territory. Response strategy emphasizes developing counter-spaceplane capabilities, enhancing space domain awareness for rapidly maneuvering objects, and strengthening aerospace defense integration.

- **Scenario 6: China's Game-Changer: Long March 9's Stunning Debut Signals New Era in Space Race.** China's successful deployment of a fully reusable super-heavy launch vehicle challenges U.S. commercial space leadership and national security capabilities. Recommendations prioritize regulatory reform to enhance U.S. competitiveness, strengthening the domestic space industrial base, and maintaining technological advantages in critical space capabilities.

# CHAPTER 3

## China's Bid for Space Energy Dominance

### INTRODUCTION

As China seeks long-term energy security to fuel its economy, "the state has decided that power coming from outside of the earth, such as solar power and development of other space energy resources, is to be China's future direction."[109] The ability to generate and transmit power from space could reshape not just space exploration and commerce, but international energy geopolitics. If successful, the U.S. will have to deal with a new international energy supplier—potentially capable of providing nations across the globe with cheap clean energy, and one that harnesses nuclear power to transit Cislunar space. This chapter examines three scenarios of increasing technological sophistication: from a modest solar power demonstration to megawatt-class solar arrays, and ultimately to nuclear reactors in space. Each advancement could fundamentally alter the strategic balance in space and on Earth.

## SCENARIO 7: SOLAR SENTINEL—PRC'S LEAP IN SPACE-BASED POWER

Space-based solar power is a concept for a novel renewable energy system.[110] It would involve placing into orbit very large satellites that collect solar energy and beam it to the ground. Unlike terrestrial solar, the satellites collect sunlight 24 hours a day. As such, these satellites can beam through clouds and weather, overcome problems of intermittency, storage, and long-distance transmission to provide green, renewable power. This renewable power would be city scale, base-load appropriate, and dispatchable. In principle, it could scale to meet all global demand, offering a very low carbon alternative.

### SCENARIO RATIONALE

The PRC has been serious about energy security in space for a while. China announced an ambitious plan to develop space-based solar power, with a series of progressively impressive demonstrations building toward city-scale space solar power. Beginning in 2008,

The State Administration for Science, Technology and Industry for National Defense [SASTIND] officially began in-depth research and analysis of foreign space based solar power station development; subsequently, in 2013, President Xi received briefings on SBSP research and proposals, which he approved, and "the State Administration of Science, Technology and Industry for National Defense, united with 16 ministries and departments including the National Development and Reform Commission, the Ministry of Science and Technology, the Ministry of Industry and Information Technology, and an organization of 100 national experts, developed a national strategy and development pathway for space based solar power stations."[111] One of the near-term goals which China has announced is the deployment of a 500kW solar power station in 2028. This station represents an extremely consequential capability. Currently only the International Space Station has 100kW, with most high-power communication satellites being in the range of 5–20kW.

The ability to construct a 500kW platform is significant, as most terrestrial military lasers are in the range of 30–100kW, and even 15kW lasers can shoot down drones. Even if purely for microwave power beaming, a 500kW directed-energy platform in LEO that orbits overhead like Sputnik is likely to raise concerns among the American public. China is well aware of the benefits to space-based solar power and regardless of concerns by other nations, is continuing towards deployment of a demonstrator system in 2028.[112]

## The Scenario

### The Daily Astronomer | Front Page

*June 1, 2028*

China has achieved a major milestone in space-based energy technology, successfully activating its "Solar Sentinel"—a 500-kilowatt (kW) space-based solar power (SBSP) station in low Earth orbit (LEO). The breakthrough marks a significant step in the global pursuit of clean and sustainable energy, as the concept of harvesting solar power in space and transmitting it to Earth moves closer to reality.

This achievement is particularly notable given that most high-power communication satellites typically operate within the 5–20kW range. The Solar Sentinel, operating at 500kW, represents a substantial leap in power generation and transmission capabilities. Designed primarily for microwave power beaming, the platform has the potential to support high-power communication networks, space-based industrial operations, and other energy-intensive applications.

China has widely publicized the Solar Sentinel's activation as a peaceful milestone in space development, underscoring its commitment to advancing clean energy solutions. However, military analysts worldwide have taken note of the platform's broader implications. The same technology enabling efficient power beaming could, in theory, be adapted for directed-energy applications capable of targeting drones, satellites, or other space-based assets. The dual-use nature of the technology raises questions about its long-term strategic implications and the challenge of differentiating between civilian and military applications in orbit.[113]

The development has prompted discussions among U.S. and allied defense officials about maintaining the balance of power in space. As China continues to advance its capabilities in space-based energy systems, policymakers must weigh the potential need for similar advancements to ensure parity and deterrence in an evolving strategic environment.

*NOTE: The President saw this article and is concerned. The American public, on becoming aware of the Solar Sentinel's power capabilities, expresses concern over the potential use of this system as a weapon economically and militarily. The President has asked the Vice President to convene a National Space Council to provide the President with options and recommendations for immediate response and a long-term "get-well plan" with programmatic response options and resource implications.*

## SIMULATED NATIONAL SPACE COUNCIL DISCUSSION

The Vice President and other council members viewed China's deployment of the Solar Sentinel, the largest object in low Earth orbit (LEO) dedicated to high-capacity solar power generation, as a dual-use technological milestone with implications for the U.S.'s position in green energy and space-based power. While some saw it as an opportunity for collaboration and advancement in renewable energy, others expressed concern over strategic competitiveness and the military potential of such technology.

There were significant concerns about the practicality and perception of SBSP systems. A SBSP system based in geostationary orbit (GEO) was considered more viable than a LEO-based one due to constant visibility over target areas, which a LEO system lacks due to rapid orbital movement. The potential for weaponization, particularly through high-capacity microwave systems, was a concern that needed addressing to reassure both international partners and the U.S. public, who remain skeptical about the deployment of on-orbit military assets.

Discussion highlighted the Solar Sentinel's dual capabilities, particularly its potential for high-power communication and, more worryingly, its capability for space-to-space power beaming and directed-energy applications—for example, the development of future space-based laser systems capable of intercepting ballistic missiles in flight. The differentiation between RF and laser energy transfer systems was key, with experts noting that while RF systems require gigawatt levels to cause significant damage, laser systems at the megawatt level could achieve substantial destructive effects.

The council also grappled with the broader geopolitical implications of the Solar Sentinel achievement. The CCP Subject Matter Expert cautioned that China might view its technological leadership as a source of leverage, potentially limiting the incentives for collaboration with the United States. Conversely, the Secretary of State framed the development as an opportunity for diplomatic engagement, positioning SBSP as a tool for fostering climate resilience and enabling China's transition toward a non-fossil-fuel-based economy. Some framed China's achievement as a catalyst for collaboration and a "win-win" scenario. Proponents of this view, including the Secretary of Commerce, argued that China was merely following the lead of the United States in grappling with the climate crisis, presenting an opportunity for joint efforts and the involvement of American commercial entities in the burgeoning SBSP industry.

Domestic policy advisors and science and technology experts recommended leveraging the private sector's agility and creativity to expedite development, proposing indirect government support through subsidies and regulatory ease. The question of budget and resource allocation emerged as a critical point of contention, with estimates ranging from $2–5 billion to $200 billion over a decade-long timeframe. While some advocated for a private-sector-led model akin to the nuclear power industry, others envisioned a government-driven effort, like the Apollo program, spearheaded by agencies such as NASA and the Department of Energy, with significant support from the Department of Defense and the intelligence community. The Assistant to the President for Domestic Policy cautioned on public skepticism about the need for a massive U.S. program, especially in the absence of an immediate military threat. The White House Press Secretary echoed this concern, acknowledging the mixed public response to green energy investments.

## ASSESSMENT AND RECOMMENDATIONS

China's successful deployment of the 500kW Solar Sentinel platform in LEO is a strategic inflection point in SBSP technology. While Beijing frames this as green energy development, there is huge potential for military applications—including directed-energy capabilities and power-beaming to space and terrestrial assets.

*Immediate Actions (0-6 Months)*
**Surveillance & Threat Assessment**
- Deploy dedicated space-based intelligence assets to monitor PRC SBSP developments.

- Expand ground-based tracking of PRC's energy-beaming experiments.

- Establish an Interagency SBSP Intelligence Task Force (DNI, DoD, NASA, DOE).

**Public Messaging & Global Narrative Control**
- Proactively define the global SBSP narrative. Prevent China from framing this as a purely peaceful green initiative.

- Expose potential military implications to allies and the public.

- Launch a public-private initiative promoting U.S. space energy leadership.

**Diplomatic & Regulatory Frameworks**
- Block China from setting global SBSP norms.

- Launch a Multinational Space Energy Alliance with allies (Japan, NATO, India, UK, Canada).

- Propose a Space Energy Security Treaty—Establish clear international norms against weaponized SBSP and forced energy dependencies.

*Short-Term Actions (6-24 Months)*

**U.S. SBSP Demonstrator (Rapid Deployment)**

- Fund & launch a 100-500 kW U.S. SBSP prototype within 18-24 months.

- Public-private partnership model, leveraging NASA, DoD, DOE, and commercial players.

- Establish ground-based test facilities for high-power beam safety

**Economic & Industrial Strategy**

- Establish the U.S. SBSP Market Development Fund ($5B initial investment).

- Accelerate patent filings & IP protections for U.S. SBSP technology.

- Fast-track spectrum management & regulatory approvals for power beaming.

- Create distributed space power grid immune to single-point failure

**Military Readiness & Countermeasures**

- Develop hardened U.S. satellite defenses against directed-energy interference.

- Explore adaptive shielding & power redundancy solutions for space assets.

- Assess U.S. counter-SBSP capabilities for deterrence.

### *Long-Term Actions (2-10 Years): U.S. Space Energy Dominance*
**Deploying a Megawatt-Class SBSP System**
- Develop a 100MW SBSP system cost estimates range from $2-200 billion over a decade

- Establish a U.S.-led space-based energy infrastructure by 2032.

- Secure government and commercial integration for long-term sustainability.

- Create modular power relay network in various orbits and develop on-orbit power storage solution

**Countering PRC's Energy Leverage**
- Position SBSP as an alternative to China's Belt & Road energy dominance.

- Ensure U.S. allies are energy-independent and not reliant on PRC SBSP.

**Space Energy Governance & U.S. Rule-Setting**
- Define the legal & operational framework for space energy security.

- Expand the Multinational Space Energy Alliance into a governing body.

- Establish a Space Energy Transparency Initiative to prevent weaponization.

## RISKS AND METRICS FOR SUCCESS

Promptly responding to China's SBSP platform is essential for both economic competitiveness and national security. A delayed U.S. response could enable Beijing to dominate SBSP technology through patents, international standards, and global supply chains, potentially creating energy dependencies among both allies and neutral nations. Most critically, delayed action could make future market entry cost-prohibitive—leaving U.S. commercial interests unable to compete effectively in the SBSP sector. While the high initial capital investment may face public scrutiny, clear metrics for success can justify this expenditure: achieving deployment of a comparable 500kW SBSP demonstrator within 24 months, establishing a megawatt-class operational system within 5 years, and ultimately securing at least 50 percent of the global SBSP market by 2035. Success also means preventing any single nation from monopolizing space-based energy transmission technology or using it for coercive leverage.

## SCENARIO 8: PRC BEGINS CONSTRUCTION OF MEGAWATT-CLASS SOLAR POWER SATELLITE IN GEO

While China's 500kW Solar Sentinel demonstration proved their capability in space-based power generation, their ambitions extend far beyond this initial achievement. The next scenario examines China's bold move to scale up this technology by an order of magnitude, transitioning from low Earth orbit to geostationary orbit with implications that could reshape global energy dynamics.

### SCENARIO RATIONALE

China's real-world plan for Space-Based Solar Power includes multiple progressively larger demonstrations. The next announced goal is the deployment of a 1-megawatt (MW) solar power station (enough to power 1,000 homes) in 2030.

This represents an extremely significant capability.[114] Currently only the International Space Station has 120 kilowatts (kW),[115] with most high-power communication satellites being in the range of 5–20kW. In order to receive a megawatt on the ground, multiple megawatts must be robotically assembled in space. According to NREL, "these solar cells are currently produced in low volumes, typically on the order of 100's of kW/year to low MW/year."[116] Such a large order for space-qualified photovoltaics is likely to significantly distort the market, and may create learning curves for PRC suppliers that result in exceptionally low costs it would be difficult for U.S. industry to match.

Moreover, the ability to construct a 1-MW platform is significant. The Lockheed / Department of Defense IFPC-HEL at 300kW[117] is among the most powerful military lasers, and the U.S. Air Force airborne laser (which could shoot down ballistic missiles) was a megawatt-class laser.[118] The emplacement of such a high power directed energy platform is likely to raise concerns among the American public.

As China approaches commercial SBSP capability, it gains greater ability to integrate space-based energy systems into overseas infrastructure packages like the Belt and Road Initiative and BRI space corridor. Integrating space-based power with its broader strategy of providing all-up packages for infrastructure, space based GNSS, satellite broadband, smart cities, all meaningfully increase its ability to push turn-key surveillance and debt-trap diplomacy. As we have seen recently with Russia's use of its natural gas pipeline as a tool of coercion, the ability of an autocracy to provide and then threaten to turn off, or actually turn off energy sources, tightens the potential for autocratic control across the globe.

## *The Scenario*

### The Daily Astronomer | Front Page
*June 1, 2029*

In a groundbreaking move that has captured the attention of the global energy and space communities, the People's Republic of China has officially commenced construction on its first megawatt-class solar power satellite. The project, unveiled at a high-profile event in Beijing, marks a significant step forward in the nation's quest for sustainable energy sources.

The satellite, named "Tian Guang-1" (Heaven's Light), is designed to harness solar energy directly from space, where solar radiation is stronger and more consistent than on Earth's surface. This energy will then be converted into microwave (5.8Ghz) and optical frequency (1064nm) energy and transmitted back to ground-based receivers. These stations will convert the energy back into electricity, feeding it into the national power grid.

The satellite, estimated to cost upwards of 10 billion yuan ($1.5 billion USD), will be assembled robotically in space from sections launched from the newly expanded Wenchang Space Launch Center on Hainan Island. Once complete, it will measure a staggering 1 kilometer across, dwarfing any existing space structure at nearly 10 times the length of the ISS. Tian Guang-1 will orbit the Earth in a geosynchronous position, constantly bathed in sunlight.[119]

"This project is not just a technological leap; it is a bridge towards a greener future," said Dr. Li Wei, director of the China National Space Administration, during the satellite's unveiling. "We aim to provide a viable solution to our growing energy needs while reducing our carbon footprint."

The construction of Tian Guang-1 involves collaboration between China's top scientific institutions and several international technology firms, highlighting a new era of global cooperation in space technology and renewable energy.

At the core of the project is an array of high-efficiency solar panels spread over an area equivalent to ten football fields. This expansive design allows the satellite to capture sunlight with unprecedented efficiency. The innovative transmission system is expected to mitigate energy loss, a challenge that has historically plagued similar endeavors.

Experts suggest that the success of Tian Guang-1 could revolutionize power generation globally. "If China succeeds, it will be a game-changer. Imagine a future where energy could be harnessed and distributed anywhere on Earth, without the need for extensive infrastructure," explained Dr. Emily Rausch, a U.S.-based energy analyst.

However, the project is not without its critics. Concerns have been raised about the potential for weaponization of the energy transmission technology, and the environmental impact of constructing and launching the massive satellite.

Additionally, the economic feasibility of such an ambitious project remains a topic of intense debate.

As the construction progresses, the international community watches closely, eager to see whether China's bold venture into space-based solar power will soar to success or encounter turbulence. Either way, Tian Guang-1 represents a bold stride towards a future where space not only captures the imagination but also powers our homes.

Despite the concerns, China is forging ahead, and the Chinese government has committed significant resources to the project, viewing it as a cornerstone of their national energy strategy. Plans are already underway for additional satellites, pending the successful deployment and operation of Tian Guang-1.

The ambitious project is expected to take two and a half years to complete, with initial power generation slated for 2030. The success, or failure, of Tian Guang-1 will be closely watched by the international community, potentially ushering in a new era of space-based renewable energy or serving as a cautionary tale. China's bold actions on a project of such immense scale have called into question U.S. space leadership. While the idea of a solar power satellite was invented in the United States, it has failed to develop a program. Takeshi Nakamura, military analyst with the Sakura Security Institute expressed doubts the U.S. Space Force will be able to keep pace, "America has severely underinvested in space mobility and logistics and in-space servicing, assembly and manufacture, is it even possible to catch up?" The U.S. president is likely to receive many questions at the upcoming NATO and G7 summit.

*NOTE: The President saw this article and is concerned. He has asked the Vice President to convene a National Space Council to provide the President with options and recommendations for immediate response and long-term programmatic response options.*

## SIMULATED NATIONAL SPACE COUNCIL DISCUSSION

The Vice President opened the discussion by noting the U.S.'s lag in space-based solar power (SBSP) development, with China's apparent cost efficiency ($1.5 billion) raising suspicions of undisclosed technological advancements. While the United States has the capacity to compete, a lack of sufficient investment in SBSP and in-space manufacturing (ISAM) has left the U.S. behind, both technologically and strategically. The Secretary of Defense emphasized that China's achievements align with their long-term space plans, which the U.S. has consistently underestimated, signaling a need for more proactive strategic planning to avoid being caught off-guard in the future.

A central tension in the discussion revolves around the potential weaponization of China's SBSP technology. The Secretary of Defense, Director of National Intelligence (DNI), and the CCP Subject Matter Expert all raised concerns that the microwave energy transmissions designed for power generation could be repurposed for military applications. One member emphasized the need to develop countermeasures, such as megawatt-class Diode Pumped Alkali Lasers (DPALs). The limited intelligence on Chinese advancements and their dual-use capabilities heightens fears that the satellite could be used to disrupt global security. This uncertainty is compounded by China's lack of transparency, making it difficult for U.S. intelligence agencies to assess the full extent of the technological threat. The possibility of China leveraging this technology to gain energy independence—and extend that advantage to its allies—poses a significant geopolitical challenge, especially for the U.S.'s energy and defense posture.

Another key tension is the U.S.'s struggle to balance public and private sector involvement in SBSP development. The Secretary of Commerce and several other council members advocated for leveraging public-private partnerships to accelerate U.S. competitiveness. They suggested that companies like SpaceX or Virtus Solis could be crucial partners in building SBSP infrastructure, with government incentives needed to encourage private sector investment. However, there are concerns that traditional defense procurement processes will be too slow and inefficient, potentially undermining U.S. efforts. Moreover, the Assistant to the President for Domestic Policy raised concerns about potential political resistance, particularly within a Republican administration, which may face pushback from constituents and energy companies wary of investing in space-based solar technologies.

The question of U.S. space leadership also emerged as a critical issue. The Secretary of State and NASA Administrator warned that China's successful development of SBSP could severely undermine U.S. leadership in space. If China manages to integrate SBSP into its energy infrastructure, it could not only cement its technological superiority but also create new strategic partnerships with countries like the UAE, which would challenge the U.S.'s global influence. To counter this, the Secretary of State recommended that the U.S. pursue international partnerships with allies such as Japan, India, and ESA to develop a competitive SBSP program. A coordinated response could demonstrate U.S. leadership and reassure global allies about the future of space cooperation.

The NASA Administrator's proposal to focus on Lunar-based SBSP, as part of the Artemis program, introduces another angle of tension—whether to match China's GEO-based system or leapfrog it with more advanced technologies. Developing SBSP infrastructure on the Moon would reduce the risk of weaponization and serve as a more powerful demonstration of U.S. technological prowess. The Administrator's recommendation to revive NASA's On-orbit Servicing, Assembly, and Manufacturing (OSAM) program[120] was seen as essential for competing with China's ability to build large space structures,[121] though concerns remained about securing long-term funding and political support.

Finally, domestic political realities emerged as a potential roadblock. The White House Press Secretary and Presidential Policy Advisor highlighted the difficulty of framing SBSP development in a way that would garner bipartisan support. The administration needs to navigate opposition from big energy companies and secure buy-in from Congress, particularly with Republicans likely to oppose large investments in space-based solar technology. However, they also suggested that SBSP could be framed as a job creation initiative, leveraging clean energy momentum from previous Democratic administrations. This framing could help generate public and political support, but it remains uncertain whether it would be enough to counter China's rapid pace of development.

## ASSESSMENT AND RECOMMENDATIONS

The deployment of China's Tian Guang-1, the first megawatt-class solar power satellite, truly raises the stakes in the global space race. On the economic front, pioneering SBSP technology and developing a global network would position China to become the world's dominant energy provider. The U.S. must act swiftly to prevent China from achieving energy dominance in orbit and controlling space governance norms. This development requires a decisive and coordinated response from the United States to address the energy challenge.

## *Immediate Actions (0-6 months)*
### National Security and Intelligence Enhancement

- Frame as a critical national security issue to Congress and brief key Congressional committees.

- Establish an intelligence surge focused on Chinese space capabilities and direct a surge in space domain awareness assets.

- Closely monitor the development of the 1-MW laser technology for potential national security implications.

### Commercial & Industrial Mobilization

- Engage leading companies like Virtus Solis and SpaceX for rapid capability assessments and development.

- Direct EXIM Bank and U.S. International Development Finance Corporation (DFC)[122] to develop financing packages to support these initiatives.

- Invoke the Defense Production Act[123] for critical supply chains in space technology and solar energy sectors.[124]

**Diplomatic & Alliance Actions**

- Initiate a coordinated response with key partners such as Japan, India, and Australia.

- Call for an emergency session of the UN COPUOS to discuss and establish power transmission standards.

- Begin the formation of an international space energy coalition and strategically address these topics at upcoming NATO and G7 summits.

*Short-Term Actions (6-24 months)*[125]

**Dual-Track Technology Development**

- Develop terrestrial 100kW demonstration SBSP satellites and accelerate Lunar power beaming capabilities aligned with the Artemis program.

- Continue to develop and accelerate megawatt-class lasers[126] and other advanced space-based technologies.

- Explore Lunar rovers capable of energy transmission, propulsion systems powered by beamed energy, and the use of lasers for deflecting asteroids (e.g., laser ablation).

**Industrial & Education Development**

- Launch an extensive STEM education initiative focused on space manufacturing and renewable energy technologies.

- Create tax incentives for domestic solar and space technology manufacturing.

- Establish and standardize space manufacturing standards, especially for in-space assembly and operations.

## Regulatory and Safety Framework

- Streamline licensing for space-based power systems and develop comprehensive safety standards for power transmission.

- Create clear guidelines for commercial space assembly and operations to encourage innovation while ensuring safety and compliance.

## *Long-Term Actions (2-5 years)*
## Space Infrastructure and International Collaboration

- Establish robust orbital assembly platforms and develop a comprehensive space logistics network with standardized interfaces for in-space construction.

- Promote joint development projects with allies (including Japan, India, and ESA), focusing on shared technology development while maintaining U.S. leadership.

- Develop common standards and protocols for international space operations to ensure compatibility and interoperability.

## Defense and Security Enhancements

- Develop and deploy advanced space asset protection systems and counter-directed energy capabilities.

- Expand the space domain awareness network to ensure comprehensive monitoring and security of space assets.

**Funding and Support Structure**
- Immediate reprogramming of $2B for national security measures related to space.

- Secure new authorization of $5B for FY2030 and $8B annually from FY2031-2034, with provisions for private sector cost-sharing to foster innovation and deployment.

## RISKS AND METRICS FOR SUCCESS

The U.S. response to China's SBSP initiative faces several critical risks: potential loss of technological leadership, weaponization concerns of power transmission systems, and uncertain political/private sector support. It will be critical for the U.S. public to understand the nature of the threat and that it is not a wasteful green initiative. Success will be measured through clear technical milestones, including a 100kW demonstration within 18 months and Lunar power beaming capability by 36 months. Enduring success will be establishing key commercial partnerships and industrial base expansion with consistent congressional support and funding.

## SCENARIO 9: CELESTIAL CORE—PRC'S FIRST SPACE NUCLEAR REACTOR

As significant as China's advances in space-based solar power may be, they represent only one aspect of Beijing's comprehensive space power strategy. The following scenario explores China's parallel development of space nuclear power—a capability that could enable them to project power throughout Cislunar space and beyond. Space-based nuclear technology will not supplant SBSP but rather work in concert with it, providing China with a major strategic advantage in space energy if it remains unchecked.

### SCENARIO RATIONALE

The U.S. has flown only a single nuclear reactor in space (in 1965),[127] and the most recent reactor flown by the USSR was in 1988. Both the U.S. (NASA and DARPA) believe nuclear reactors offer significant spacefaring/space power advantage. The PRC likewise has announced plans for fission reactors in space and nuclear shuttles that can mine the asteroid belt at scale by 2040[128] within broader plans to build a solar-system-wide logistics network.[129] Were the PRC to fly a space nuclear reactor first, especially if it were of significantly high power (>100 kilowatts), this would likely create a perception the U.S. was behind in a space race and spark public concerns. This is a future that the U.S. should prepare for because the PRC is currently developing and testing a megawatt-class space nuclear reactor130 and published its specifications.[130]

## *The Scenario*

### The Daily Astronomer | Front Page
*July 10, 2029*

China has announced a major breakthrough in space nuclear power, successfully testing a high-powered space nuclear reactor exceeding one megawatt—far surpassing any previously known capabilities. The reactor, named "Heavenly Core," represents a significant leap in space power technology and is designed to support a range of ambitious applications, including long-duration crewed missions, deep space exploration, and asteroid resource extraction.

The successful deployment and operation of Heavenly Core marks a milestone in China's push for technological leadership in space. The People's Republic of China (PRC) has devoted substantial resources and intellectual capital toward developing an advanced space nuclear power system, viewing it as a critical step toward achieving strategic autonomy and long-term dominance in space operations. The initiative aligns with China's broader strategy to solidify its status as a preeminent spacefaring nation, capable of sustaining a permanent presence beyond Earth.

Heavenly Core is engineered for reliability, safety, and versatility, with a power output that fundamentally changes the scope of possible space missions. The reactor enables extended deep-space operations, supports off-world bases and industrial activities, and provides a foundation for more ambitious exploration initiatives. Equipped with advanced safety features and radiation shielding, the system is designed to protect space assets and crew, mitigating risks associated with nuclear energy in orbit.

The revelation of the successful Heavenly Core test has sent shockwaves through the global space community. Beyond its technological significance, the development alters strategic considerations and competitive dynamics in space exploration and utilization. The PRC's demonstrated capability in deploying such advanced technology raises new questions about the future balance of power in space and the long-term implications for international space policy.

As nations assess the broader impact of China's latest achievement, discussions on space power competition and the regulatory challenges of nuclear technology in orbit are expected to take center stage in global space diplomacy.

*NOTE: The President saw this article and is concerned. He has asked the Vice President to convene a National Space Council to provide the President with options and recommendations for immediate response and long-term programmatic response options.*

## SIMULATED NATIONAL SPACE COUNCIL DISCUSSION

The council discussed the implications of China's newly tested high-powered space nuclear reactor, acknowledging that while their own country had laid the groundwork for leadership in space nuclear power, they now faced a situation where they had been overtly surpassed.

One of the primary tensions that emerged during the meeting was the conflict between the U.S.'s vision of space exploration and China's ambitious plans. While the U.S. has been focusing on smaller-scale expeditions to the Moon and Mars, China appears to be aiming for a more expansive presence in the solar system, with the potential to exploit resources like asteroids and extend civilization beyond Earth. This dichotomy raised concerns about the long-term implications of China's techno-authoritarian values governing the solar system, as opposed to the liberal Western ideas championed by the U.S. and its allies. The development of nuclear-powered spacecraft could be enabling key technology for China to pursue a broader space vision. One member stated, "We are building ships to sail across the Mediterranean, while China is building ships to sail across the Atlantic."

As the council considered geopolitical implications, the disparity between our vision and that of China's could draw allies away from the U.S.—for example, France perceived the U.S. to be weak. Some members considered allying with Germany and Japan, who have turned away from nuclear power, while India's planned nuclear reactor launch added another layer of complexity. Additionally, the relevance of the internationally agreed upon Outer Space Treaty, in light of China's advancement, was another point of discussion. While some council members suggested exploring whether China's reactor could be framed as a violation of the treaty's ban on stationing nuclear weapons in space, others argued that the technology did not clearly fall under the treaty's prohibitions and that framing it as a weapon could rein in the U.S. nuclear space advancements.

The Secretary of Defense highlighted the potential military implications of China's enhanced capabilities, such as faster asset deployment, continuous maneuvering, and efficient station-keeping at Lagrange points. Defense concerns were emphasized, especially China's ability to take assets to Cislunar space and beyond, as well as expand their deep space exploration capabilities, which enable the exploitation of resources like asteroids.

Questions were raised about whether the U.S. had been caught by surprise and why, with calls for hearings to be conducted. NASA's investments in nuclear propulsion were scrutinized, and the agency's failure to communicate with colleagues was highlighted. China's higher investment compared to the U.S. was cited as the reason for their advancement along with the previous administration's role in putting the U.S. in this disadvantageous situation. There was no shortage of blame to go around as the lack of congressional appropriations was identified as an issue as well.

Amid these tensions and contradictions, the council explored various options for responding to China's progress. These ranged from increasing funding for NASA and DARPA programs to establish a presidential council focused on prioritizing nuclear propulsion and power in space. The Democratic administration's efforts in building on Space Policy Directive 6 (SPD-6),[131] which focuses on a 40-kilowatt Artemis base camp,[132] were recognized. The council considered advocating for a significant U.S. project to develop a near-term 100-megawatt system, paralleling China's ambitions but ensuring U.S. technological independence. Budget proposals ranged from $2 billion to $5 billion, reflecting a strong commitment to reestablishing U.S. leadership in space nuclear technology.

Finally, there was agreement that U.S. public anxieties about nuclear technology in space needed to be addressed, including the handling of nuclear material in space and the associated risks. The council agreed that the government needs to provide reassurance and a focus on the peaceful applications of space nuclear power as that is crucial to garner public support for the U.S. response.

## ASSESSMENT AND RECOMMENDATIONS

The Heavenly Core nuclear reactor is an important development because it signifies Beijing is thinking about space with a much broader vision than Washington. A megawatt-class nuclear reactor powered craft will allow China to more efficiently transit the space domain, which will have implications for U.S. national and economic security—as it allows them to more easily access and exploit space resources. The framework here will need to address how to accelerate American technological development and foster cooperation.

### *Immediate Actions (0-30 days)*
**Strategic Vision and Funding**
- Launch the Solar System Leadership Initiative to guide democratic values in space and secure an emergency funding request to Congress for $2.5B, plus reprogram $500M from existing budgets.

**Intelligence and Verification**
- Direct the intelligence community to provide daily updates on PRC's Heavenly Core capabilities and establish rigorous verification protocols.

**Diplomatic Engagement**
- Initiate strategic dialogues with key allies (France, India, Germany, Japan, UK) to align nuclear development programs and enhance nuclear cooperation.

**Public Communication**
- Implement a public education campaign to highlight U.S. commitments to safety, environmental safeguards, and the economic benefits of space nuclear technology.

*Short-Term Actions (1-12 months)*
**Technology Development**
- Fast-track development of megawatt-class reactors with specified milestones for design, testing, and prototype stages, supported by dual-track civilian and military applications.[133]

- Revise and expand Space Policy Directive-6 (SPD-6) to incorporate goals for MW class reactors.

**Regulatory Updates**
- Reform space nuclear regulations, update export controls for better international cooperation, and draft a comprehensive space nuclear legislation package.

**Industrial and Workforce Development**
- Launch public-private partnerships with incentives for space nuclear technology, establish a dedicated workforce development program, and bolster the domestic supply chain.

### International Frameworks

- Develop new international protocols for space nuclear operations and establish a multinational working group on space nuclear safety standards.

## *Long-Term Strategies (1-5 years)*
### Infrastructure and Capability Development

- Build diverse reactor types for different power needs, establish Earth and Lunar testing facilities, and create a framework for Cislunar infrastructure.[134]

### Economic and Commercial Initiatives

- Develop a commercial space nuclear marketplace, create economic incentives for private sector involvement, and establish markets for space-based power generation.

### International Leadership and Cooperation

- Lead an international consortium for space nuclear development, create a verification and monitoring regime, and develop shared infrastructure projects.

### Crisis Management and Safety

- Implement comprehensive accident response protocols, establish an international notification system for space incidents, and develop debris tracking and mitigation capabilities.

## RISKS AND METRICS FOR SUCCESS

While the framework aspires to position the U.S. ahead of China in space nuclear technology, there are significant risks to its execution. The most critical risks include technological feasibility, development timelines, sustained funding requirements, and maintaining public support. Success will be measured by three key outcomes: launching an operational megawatt-class reactor-powered spacecraft in a timely fashion, developing a robust industrial base with solid commercial suppliers, and establishing effective international cooperation on safety protocols and governance frameworks.

## EMERGING THEMES AND CONCLUSION

In-space energy for industrial-scale applications is an emerging area of strategic competition that is likely to require significant attention. As the PRC and others demonstrate progress in energy initiatives like space-based solar power and nuclear reactor technologies, we could witness a shift in global power dynamics. The scenarios highlight several alarming trends relevant for space energy.

**Dual-Use Technology Concerns.** Space-based energy production is a necessary precursor for next-level capabilities such as extractive industries, in-space manufacturing and deep space propulsion. However, such access to hundreds of kilowatts to gigawatts has significant national security implications as beaming energy could be used for directed energy weapons or powering long dwell drones, among other effects.

**Strategic Energy Independence.** Delayed action could make future market entry cost-prohibitive—leaving U.S. commercial interests unable to compete effectively in the SBSP sector, leaving our alliance partners open to energy coercion, and compromising our market and energy advantage in-space. China may emerge as the premier global energy superpower and be able to provide cheap clean energy—allowing Beijing unprecedented diplomatic and economic leverage over countries in ways that could eclipse current energy geopolitics.

**Public Perception Management.** Obtaining cost-effective energy sources in space will be crucial for development and economic progress, but this will not be possible without public support. Therefore, shaping public understanding and acceptance of space-based energy is critical. It will require a clear communication strategy to address concerns about the risks of beaming energy through the atmosphere or nuclear reactor safety in orbit.

**Industrial Base Readiness.** The absence of pre-existing programs makes attempts to match Chinese capabilities costly and difficult to accelerate to timescales of political and strategic relevance. Without strengthening domestic supply chains and ramping up R&D, the U.S. risks ceding critical market segments—and, by extension, national security advantages—to Chinese firms.

**Vision and Scale Disparity.** It should be fundamentally unacceptable for U.S. in-space power ambitions to be of such a smaller scale (20x smaller) than the PRC's ambitions (U.S.: 40kW; PRC: 500kW-1MW-1MW to Gigawatts)—America is sadly not even playing in the same league. America can't be a space power if it is second in in-space power. National mandates must set high bars (larger than a megawatt) for both solar and nuclear power sources.

As the U.S. considers its energy needs in space, the timelines for development need to be benchmarked against the PRC's timelines. National space strategy must prioritize the development of space-based energy sources.[135] Specific direction must be provided to DOE, USSF, and NASA. It should focus on the creation of commercial and commercially scalable public-private-partnership models that can rapidly close the capability gap while establishing sustainable long-term advantages.

## CHAPTER 3 SUMMARY AND RECOMMENDATIONS

- **Introduction.** As China seeks long-term energy security to fuel its economy, it has turned to the skies for space-based solar and nuclear power. The ability to generate and transmit power from space could reshape not just space exploration and commerce, but global energy geopolitics. If successful, the U.S. will have to deal with a new global energy supplier—potentially capable of providing nations across the globe with cheap clean energy, and one that harnesses nuclear power to transit Cislunar space. This chapter examines three scenarios of increasing technological sophistication: from a modest solar power demonstration to megawatt-class solar arrays, and ultimately to nuclear reactors in space. Each advancement could fundamentally alter the strategic balance in space and on Earth.

- **Scenario 7: Solar Sentinel (2028).** China successfully deploys a 500kW solar power station in low Earth orbit—five times more powerful than the International Space Station's capability. While presented as a green energy initiative, the station's power output matches that of military-grade lasers, raising dual-use concerns. Key recommendations include developing a comparable U.S. demonstrator within 24 months, establishing international power-beaming standards, and creating a Multinational Space Energy Alliance.

- **Scenario 8: Megawatt-Class Solar Power Satellite (2029).**
  China begins construction of a kilometer-wide solar power
  satellite in geostationary orbit, capable of providing constant
  power to terrestrial receivers. The $1.5 billion project's
  surprisingly low cost suggests undisclosed technological
  breakthroughs. Recommendations emphasize accelerating
  U.S. space manufacturing capabilities, forming international
  partnerships for competitive development, and establishing
  clear frameworks for space-based power transmission.

- **Scenario 9: Celestial Core Nuclear Reactor (2030).** China
  tests a megawatt-class space nuclear reactor, enabling
  extended operations throughout Cislunar space and
  asteroid belt missions. This capability dramatically expands
  China's reach in space and ability to exploit space resources.
  Recommendations focus on fast-tracking U.S. space nuclear
  development through a $2.5 billion emergency funding
  request, reforming regulatory frameworks, and leading
  international protocols for space nuclear operations.

# CHAPTER 4

## Conflicts on the Moon

### INTRODUCTION

Building on China's pursuit of space-based energy resources, we shift our focus to the race for Lunar industrialization—which is likely to reshape the geopolitical landscape beyond Earth. The Moon has become a critical frontier for economic and strategic competition, as evidenced by Beijing and Moscow teaming up to form the International Lunar Research Station (ILRS).[136] Meanwhile, the U.S. and its allies are seeking to advance their own Lunar ambitions via Artemis.[137] The ability to establish industrial capabilities on the Lunar surface—from 3D-printed structures to resource extraction—will determine not just energy security but also technological leadership in the space domain.

In the following five scenarios, we explore how clashes over settlement zones, resource extraction, and competing visions for Lunar development might unfold, revealing both the vulnerabilities and opportunities facing U.S. policymakers in this rapidly evolving domain.

## SCENARIO 10: PRC WOWS WORLD WITH
## 3D-PRINTED MOON STRUCTURES

The ability to 3D print on the Lunar surface—using Lunar resources—opens up the potential for a self-expanding industrial capability[138] that could scale independent of launch. A nation that does not have a comparable capability could be perceived as falling behind. The ability to build and launch things from the Moon may over time provide superior logistics and industrial depth. The potential of a self-replicating industrial capability on Lunar industrial development has been considered by NASA since 1983,[139] and was further developed by Johns Hopkins University in 2004[140] and Lewis-Weber in 2016.[141] A critical component of such systems is additive manufacturing, or 3D printing. The stark national security implications were recognized by NASA authors in 2016:[142]

The modeling also indicates a *significant national security risk*. On Earth, the industry of a nation is limited by its resources including real estate, energy, ores, and the education and size of its labor pool. In a robotic industry occupying a solar system, the resources and real estate are *a billion times greater*. Education and talents are learned once then transmitted electronically to all robotic laborers, which are mass produced by the industry itself. Until this industry begins to feel the limits of the entire solar system, it can grow exponentially. *If any nation initiates and controls such an industry first, then it will have a perpetual lead in industrial power over any other nation that initiates the same capability second.* [emphasis ours]

## SCENARIO RATIONALE

Beijing understands the potential of Lunar 3D printing. Harnessing this technology fits into its a broader strategy to create a solar-system wide logistics system,[143] build a $10 trillion dollar Moon-Earth Economic Zone,[144] and industrialize the Moon[145] to build kilometer-scale structures[146]—such as solar power satellites. China has also proposed expansive autonomously constructed and additively manufactured Lunar bases.[147]

It is within this broader context that the PRC has announced an ambitious program to develop and demonstrate 3D printing on the Moon[148] to build bricks[149] and habitats,[150] and published a vision of how it could enable an ambitious Lunar base.[151] Starting with Chang'e 8 in 2028, China will first begin to demonstrate this technology for the world.[152]

## The Scenario

**The Daily Astronomer | Front Page**

*February 19, 2028*

The People's Republic of China has taken a giant leap forward in Lunar ambition, showcasing a stunning series of robotically 3D-printed structures on the Moon's surface. Robotic arms, orchestrated by Chinese engineers, have been constructing igloo-like edifices out of Lunar regolith, streamed live for an enraptured global audience. This display of technological might has brought China's Lunar base from a concept to a burgeoning reality, overshadowing NASA's plans with an awe-inspiring vision of extraterrestrial architecture.

Amid this celestial construction boom, the United States finds its own space efforts under scrutiny. NASA's plans for an eventual Artemis Base Camp, once the pinnacle of American space ambition, now appear less vibrant, almost anemic, when cast against the dynamic backdrop of China's proactive Lunar construction efforts. This has stirred a wave of discontent among Americans, who question their invest- ments in NASA. "What are we paying for? Why can't NASA do any of this stuff?" echoes across social media and news forums, as the public demands more tangible results.

The European Space Agency (ESA), Japan Aerospace Exploration Agency (JAXA), and the Canadian Space Agency (CSA) have taken keen notice of these developments. While not shifting allegiances, they are openly questioning whether NASA can truly fulfill the Artemis Accords' vision.

Their concerns reflect a broader international unease about the current pace and direction of U.S.-led Lunar exploration.

Meanwhile, nations such as Brazil, Nigeria, and Argentina, all signatories to the Artemis Accords, are now expressing renewed interest in China's International Lunar Research Station (ILRS). Their engagement with the ILRS signifies a possible pivot toward what is perceived as a more immediate and ambitious Lunar future.

American commercial space firms argue that they have the capability to match and exceed China's achievements. Yet they express frustration at a perceived lack of NASA's drive to innovate in kind. In response to the public outcry and the commercial sector's readiness, space advocacy organizations are pushing Congress to hold hearings, seeking to rekindle the pioneering spirit within NASA and ensure America's place at the forefront of Lunar exploration.

The PRC's 3D-printed Lunar structures not only have redefined what's possible in space architecture but also have stirred a strategic reassessment among America's partners and allies. As the Lunar landscape begins to bear the marks of human ingenuity, the United States is now at a crossroads, facing the imperative to inspire and execute a vision of space exploration that rises to meet the challenges and opportunities of our time.

**Note:** *The President saw this article and is concerned. He has asked the Vice President to convene a National Space Council to provide the President with options and recommen-*

*dations for immediate response and long-term programmatic response options.*

## SIMULATED NATIONAL SPACE COUNCIL DISCUSSION

One of the primary tensions highlighted during the discussion was the balancing act between the necessity for a swift response and the risk of appearing overly reactive to China's achievements.[153] While some NSpC members viewed the situation as an emergency requiring immediate action, others, like the Secretary of Defense, urged caution and warned against being too reactive. The Vice President expressed concern about how the media would frame the situation, while the Press Secretary emphasized the importance of controlling the narrative and acknowledging China's progress while highlighting U.S. commitments and capabilities.

The council members also grappled with the role of the private sector in countering China's state-led program.[154] The Secretary of Defense and the NASA Administrator both advocated for leveraging the capabilities of American commercial space firms. They highlighted the past administration's failures in fostering effective public-private collaborations—though they did not cite any specific examples—and stressed the need for a unified approach to leverage the private sector's innovations. This stance was supported by the Lunar and Asteroid Mining Subject Matter Expert, who emphasized that free enterprise should be the cornerstone of the U.S. response, arguing that the U.S. could not counter a state-led program with another state program. However, this approach raised concerns about the need for decoupling from U.S. corporations active in China.[155]

Several controversial options were put forward during the

meeting. The Secretary of State suggested reconvening and updating the Artemis Accords to show a united front among allies and partners, while also proposing the establishment of economic trade zones on the Moon to align with U.S. economic policies and involve allies. The Assistant to the President for Domestic Policy recommended putting the country on a "war footing" to emphasize the importance of U.S. values and focus on the Lunar challenge.[156] The Director of National Intelligence proposed declassifying information to prove that China is polluting the Lunar environment while highlighting U.S. efforts to maintain a clean presence.[157]

Throughout the discussion, council members acknowledged the need to reassure allies, demonstrate U.S. capabilities through tangible actions on the Moon, and set ambitious goals to overshadow China's achievements. NSpC participants expressed concerns about nations like Brazil, Nigeria, and Argentina showing renewed interest in China's International Lunar Research Station. They warned that this could lead to unspecified long-term strategic repercussions if the U.S. failed to present a compelling alternative. The NASA Administrator suggested showcasing the ability to turn Starship into a Lunar base within 180 days,[158] while the Secretary of Commerce recommended highlighting the work of students at universities to demonstrate the U.S.'s ongoing commitment to Lunar exploration and technology development.

However, the meeting also brought to light the political challenges faced by the administration, particularly in light of the upcoming elections and public opinion. The Presidential Policy Advisor emphasized the need to consider the electoral implications of any actions taken and suggested creating noise around the Moon issue, such as establishing an economic free trade zone, to boost the administration's standing. The Assistant to the President for

Domestic Policy also raised concerns about the administration's polling numbers and the potential pushback from companies heavily invested in China.

## ASSESSMENT AND RECOMMENDATIONS

After walking on the Moon over half a century ago, it is hard for Americans to fathom why there has not been much progress on returning humans there. China's demonstration of advanced Lunar construction capabilities represents both a public relations challenge and a direct threat to U.S. economic and national security interests in space. The erosion of American leadership in Lunar development risks not only public confidence but also our strategic position in the emerging Cislunar economy. This framework presents actions to revitalize the Artemis Accords, accelerate commercial innovation, strengthen our industrial base, and reassert U.S. leadership in space exploration and development.[159]

*Immediate Actions (0 to 6 months)*
**Executive Order for a Lunar Innovation Fund**

- Establish a fund that includes fast-track approvals for space-related projects, emphasizing university research and development in sustainable Lunar technologies.

- Create a Lunar Innovation Showcase Program to highlight innovative research and applications from universities and private sectors.

**Strategic Declassification and Communication**

- Direct the DNI to prepare and release a declassification package showcasing the negative environmental impact of China's Lunar activities, emphasizing U.S. adherence to sustainable practices compared to international counterparts.

- Launch a public affairs strategy, titled American Space Innovation, which includes curated footage of U.S. advanced manufacturing and space capabilities. Revamp leadership in public messaging to align with the narrative that space exploration is a key driver for the 21st-century economy, innovation, and scientific discovery.

**Security and Monitoring Enhancements**
- Create a Cislunar SDA plan that uses USSF surveillance satellites for tracking activities in Cislunar space and conduct assessments of foreign Lunar tech transfer attempts and the establishment of a joint Defense-Commerce task force to review U.S. companies with significant ties to the Chinese space sector.

*Short-Term Actions (6 months to 2 years)*
**Lunar Security and Innovation Legislation**
- Pass the Lunar Security and Innovation Act of 2028 with appropriations adjusted to foster state and university-level research, including specific tax incentives for companies reducing exposure to foreign space sectors.[160]

**International Cooperation and Standards**
- Host the Artemis Accords Evolution Summit to update and expand the accords, focusing on creating economic development zones on the Moon, setting environmental

protection standards, and establishing a Trusted Lunar
Partner certification program.

## Industrial and Supply Chain Strategy

- Establish the Lunar Industrial Base Protection Program
  to incentivize companies to shift space supply chains from
  high-risk areas to the U.S. and develop criteria for trusted
  versus restricted space technology partners.

- Unleash private sector capabilities by facilitating
  public-private partnerships, particularly focusing on the
  development and deployment of the Starship Lunar base, to
  demonstrate U.S. technological superiority and dismiss the
  significance of China's Lunar constructions.

### *Long-Term Actions (2 to 5 years)*
## Comprehensive Lunar Development Strategy

- Enhance the Space States Initiative by engaging state-
  level resources and facilities for a robust space industry
  base, focused on environmental monitoring and talent
  development through a university-focused program.

## Industrial Base Transformation

- Implement the Space Industrial Base Act focusing on
  supply chain resilience, domestic production incentives, and
  providing preferential treatment for allied nations.

## Expanded International Framework

- Broaden the scope of the Artemis Accords to include
  detailed frameworks for Lunar environmental protection,

economic development zones, resource utilization, and technology transfer protocols.

- Promote a clear narrative internationally that the construction of sovereign territories or "islands" by any nation on the Moon is unacceptable, reinforcing U.S. commitment to upholding international space laws and American values regarding the use of outer space.

## Public Messaging

- Frame Lunar program initiatives as crucial for national security, job creation in key states, environmental leadership, and maintaining economic competitiveness.

## RISKS AND METRICS FOR SUCCESS

The framework faces several key implementation risks, with public interest volatility being primary among them. Effectively communicating the rationale to spend funds supporting Lunar initiatives along with allied support will be essential. Metrics for success will hinge on several predictable factors including the level of sustained public interest, the successful deployment of a Starship Lunar base, and ability of the U.S. to either expand the Artemis Accords' membership or prevent key nations from aligning with China's ILRS initiative. Additional success indicators include establishment of Cislunar space monitoring capabilities, increased private sector investment in Lunar technologies, and development of a robust space industrial base.

## SCENARIO 11: CHINA BEATS THE U.S. BACK TO THE MOON

While China's demonstration of advanced manufacturing capabilities through 3D printing marked a significant technological milestone, the next scenario explores an even more dramatic development: China places human boots on the Moon *before* the U.S. can return. As manufacturing capabilities lay the groundwork for sustained presence, the symbolic and strategic value of achieving the first crewed landing of the new space age arrives.

### SCENARIO RATIONALE

An early human landing, ahead of U.S. efforts, would change the perception of global leadership and whether the U.S. can keep up. It could either increase pressure on NASA or put NASA's funding in jeopardy.

China has articulated an ambitious plan for the Moon, including as a supplier of energy for sustainable development, since as early as 2002.[161] China's crewed mission is not an end in itself but is meant to enable a permanent sustained presence[162] from which to develop a Lunar industry[163] and a Moon-Earth economic zone.[164] Toward that end, China is already signing up international partners to participate in its International Lunar Research Station (ILRS)[165] and launched a number of robotic precursors.

In 2019, following China's successful Change'4 landing on the Lunar far side, Vice President Mike Pence addressed NASA, stating,

> Now, make no mistake about it: We're in a space race today, just as we were in the 1960s, and the stakes are even higher. Last December, China became the first nation to land on the far side of the Moon and revealed their ambition to seize the Lunar strategic high ground and become the world's preeminent spacefaring nation ... And I'm here, on the President's behalf, to tell the men and women of the Marshall Space Flight Center and the American people that, at the direction of the President of the United States, it is the stated policy of this administration and the United States of America to return American astronauts to the Moon within the next five years. And let me be clear: The first woman and the next man on the Moon will both be American astronauts, launched by American rockets, from American soil ... But to accomplish this, we must redouble our efforts here in Huntsville and throughout this program. We must accelerate the SLS program to meet this objective. But know this: The President has directed NASA and Administrator Jim Bridenstine to accomplish this goal by any means necessary ... If our current contractors can't meet this objective, then we'll find ones that will. If American industry can provide critical commercial services without government development, then we'll buy

them. And if commercial rockets are the only way to get American astronauts to the Moon in the next five years, then commercial rockets it will be.[166]

Though NASA was tasked formally in the National Space Policy to "[l]ead a program to land the next American man and the first American woman on the Moon by 2024, followed by a sustained presence on the Moon by 2028,"[167] NASA has already missed the first goal, and almost certainly will miss the second as well. The first human return is now projected to be no earlier than 2027.[168] NASA's "Moon base" in the mid-2030s consists of just a small habitat, small ISRU experiment, a pressurized rover and an unpressurized rover. Moreover, NASA's plans do not even include a permanent presence but only a small habitat for short-duration stays, building slowly from 6.5 days in 2027 to a week in 2030, and only 60 days for four crew by 2033.[169] The anemic base and short stay is hardly responsive to the top-level goal of the National Space Policy which states, "Extend human economic activity into deep space by establishing a permanent human presence on the Moon, and, in cooperation with private industry and international partners, develop infrastructure and services"[170] or the National Cislunar Strategy to "enable capabilities for large-scale ISRU and advanced manufacturing at the Moon."[171] However, despite such laudable policy statements, fiscal priorities do not seem logically connected to these ends. NASA's current Artemis strategy and architecture are unaffordable, behind schedule, and cannot accomplish the national purposes set out in the national space policy. Even to accomplish the first goal of returning an American astronaut to the Lunar surface, NASA has faced delay after delay. NASA chose to bet on an expendable shuttle derived launch system rather than leverage existing or in development commercial space efforts. This proved much more expensive and much longer to develop than anticipated. The supporting ground infrastructure including the towers (which cost more than Burj Khalifa skyscraper in Dubai)[172] and the crawler transports The Orion capsule is underpowered and required NASA to first construct a gateway space station placing a Lunar landing further in the queue.[173] Early underfunding of the Human Landing System (HLS) has placed it behind schedule—it also experienced further delays due to contract protests from competitors, Federal Aviation Administration licensing issues, and environmental concerns from the Fish and Wildlife Service.[174] Moreover, the lack of adequate space suits provided an additional delay.[175]

In contrast, China articulated a desire to land taikonauts (Chinese astronauts) before 2030[176] with the possibility of its spacecraft being ready as early as 2027,[177] and is reporting progress on its lander and rover.[178] Thus, the combination of NASA delays and PRC acceleration make it possible that NASA will fail to execute the U.S. policy goal that the next human landed on the Moon will be an American.

### The Scenario

*In a high-stakes race to the Moon, the United States faces a pivotal moment that could redefine its global leadership in space exploration. With China's recent successes and ambitious Lunar plans, the question looms: Can the U.S. keep up?*

**The Daily Astronomer | Front Page**
*November 10, 2029*

In an era when space exploration has taken center stage, recent developments in Lunar exploration are rapidly reshaping the landscape of global space leadership. The United States, traditionally at the forefront of space exploration, now finds itself in a race against time and geopolitical rivals to maintain its dominance beyond Earth's atmosphere.

### *China's Lunar Leap*

The catalyst for this renewed race is none other than China. The China National Space Administration (CNSA)[179] has orchestrated a series of breathtaking Lunar missions, culminating in their groundbreaking achievement of landing taikonauts on the Moon, ahead of the U.S. return. Their Chang'e series, including Chang'e 7 and Chang'e 8, have captured the world's attention with their successful Lunar landings, Lunar sample returns, and the robotic site preparations for a permanent Lunar base.

But it's not just their Lunar conquests that have the world talking. China's announcement of its intent to establish a semi-permanent Lunar base to develop new industrial technologies within five years has sent shockwaves through the global space community. This ambitious plan signifies a tectonic shift in Lunar exploration and geopolitical power dynamics.

### Global Partnerships Emerge

Recognizing the strategic importance of Lunar presence, other spacefaring nations are racing to catch up and collaborate. India and Russia, both space titans in their own right, have declared their Lunar aspirations and extended their hands in partnership. The international space arena is buzzing with discussions of joint Lunar missions and cooperative Lunar bases.

Intriguingly, China has not closed the door on collaboration, extending invitations to join its Lunar endeavors. With newfound alliances forming, the global community is contemplating the merits of cooperation versus competition in the final frontier.

### The Great Divide: Cancel or Continue Artemis?

Meanwhile, NASA, the U.S. space agency that once planted the Stars and Stripes on the Lunar surface, is facing a peculiar divide. Under the Artemis program, NASA is striving to put American astronauts back on the Moon. However, the debate within the nation is intense and incongruous.

Some argue passionately for the continuation of Artemis, believing it is essential for maintaining U.S. space leadership and scientific exploration. Others, however, advocate for canceling the program, citing budget constraints and the need to focus on more pressing domestic issues. The world watches as the U.S. grapples with its Lunar identity crisis.

*Note:* *The President saw this article and is concerned. He*
*has asked the Vice President to convene a National Space*
*Council to provide the President with options and recommen-*
*dations for immediate response and long-term programmatic*
*response options.*

## SIMULATED NATIONAL SPACE COUNCIL DISCUSSION

The Vice President opened the discussion by stressing the importance of maintaining the U.S.'s technical leadership in space. Concerns were raised about the public's perception of these events, the
financial implications of competing with China, and the role that
allies might play in this new space race.

One of the primary points of contention was how to balance
public-private partnerships with government-led initiatives. The
consensus was that the U.S. cannot rely solely on NASA or military
programs to regain its footing. Instead, leveraging the innovative
capabilities of the private sector was seen as crucial. This included
suggestions for creating economic incentives, such as tax holidays
and commercial orbital transportation services (COTS), to encourage private companies to invest in Lunar and space exploration.

Economic strategy and the role of defense were also hotly
debated. While some participants argued for a stronger military
presence to protect U.S. interests in space, others cautioned against
militarizing the issue, suggesting that economic and technological leadership would be more effective. The suggestion to create
economic trade zones on the Moon[180] and to demonstrate rapid
advancements through programs like SpaceX's Starship were
highlighted as ways to reassert American dominance and attract
commercial interest.

Geopolitical implications also loomed large in the discussion. There was a shared anxiety about China's potential to reshape global power dynamics through its Lunar presence, particularly if it succeeded in establishing a semipermanent base. The need to form and strengthen international alliances was emphasized, with some advocating for new treaties and norms to govern space activities, ensuring that China does not set the rules unilaterally. The idea of expanding the Artemis Accords and involving more international partners was proposed as a means to counterbalance China's influence.[181]

Tensions arose as the discussion turned to security matters, with the Defense Secretary urging caution over China's potential military intentions on the Moon. The CCP expert echoed these worries, likening China's approach to its strategic creep in the South China Sea. Others maintained a more optimistic economic view, insisting that space activities were critical for driving long-term technological progress.

Despite the differing perspectives, a few common threads emerged. Many pushed for accelerated timelines measured in *months rather than years* to regain momentum. Others called for expanded international partnerships and coalitions to establish norms governing space activities before China dictated them unilaterally. The importance of effective public messaging was a central theme, with ideas ranging from comprehensive strategic reviews to reframing space endeavors as vital economic necessities.

## ASSESSMENT AND RECOMMENDATIONS

China's successful Lunar landing and its plans for a permanent base are not just technological milestones—they are a direct challenge to American leadership in space. For years, the U.S. has wavered between Lunar and Mars ambitions, plagued by delays and set-backs that have yielded little tangible progress. Now, with global space dominance at stake, America must move decisively to reclaim its position as the world's leading space power. This will require a full-spectrum approach—combining rapid action, sustained invest-ment, and strategic vision.[182]

## *Immediate Actions (0-60 Days)*
### Executive Order: Strategic Lunar Initiative (SLI)

* Combines Lunar industrialization, defense ISR, and commercial incentives into a single national space directive.

* 14-day emergency review of all space-related acquisitions.

* Establish Lunar Economic & Trade Zone within the Artemis Accords.[183]

* Direct NASA to redirect $5B from non-critical programs toward SpaceX and Blue Origin for immediate Starship/ Blue Moon Lunar lander acceleration.

### Military & ISR Actions

* Deploy X-37C[184] & Space Force/NRO ISR satellites for real-time Cislunar monitoring.

* Initiate Lunar Security & Stability Operations—Space Force is not "militarizing the Moon," but monitoring space traffic & ensuring safe operations.

* Establish Cislunar Rapid Deployment Concept for Space Force/NASA cooperation.

## Commercial Space Acceleration

Lunar COTS and beyond[185] program launched within 30 days. Guaranteed government purchase of Lunar propellant & water.

- Establish tax holiday & regulatory fast-track process for Lunar economic activity.

### *Short-Term Actions (60-180 Days)*
## Pass Space Enterprise Act of 2030

- The act should have funding line items for Lunar infrastructure acceleration,[186] Cislunar defense ISR & rapid response,[187] commercial space incentives (tax incentives, subsidies, space banking),[188] and international cooperation and Artemis partner expansion.[189]

## Defense & ISR Upgrades

- Joint Cislunar Task Force established (NASA, Space Force, NRO, commercial partners).

- Cislunar Early Warning Network (CEWN) deployed for detecting space-based threats.

- Lunar communication/navigation architecture begins construction.

## Commercial & Economic Policy

- Lunar trade agreements established under Artemis Accords.

- Expand Commercial Lunar Base Development Program (C-LBDP) for private sector Lunar habitats.

## *Long-Term Actions (180+ Days)*
### Lunar Infrastructure & Industrialization
- Artemis Enterprise Zone (AEZ) established for commercial Lunar development.

- Guaranteed Lunar resource contracts for U.S. & allied companies.

- Permanent refueling depots & space-based industry launched.

### Cislunar Security & Space Force Integration
- Full Lunar ISR & Space Domain Awareness system operational.

- Rapid response capabilities expanded via U.S. Space Force/ Artemis partnership.

- Military space logistics network created—focused on support, not occupation.

### Global Space Governance & Economic Expansion
- Free World Space Alliance created as a counter to China's space influence.[190]

- Orbital energy development programs and space-based solar power initiatives begin.[191]

- Lunar trade and resource extraction policy codified in international agreements.

## RISKS AND METRICS FOR SUCCESS

Failing to respond effectively to China's Lunar ambitions risks ceding not just prestige, *but control over critical space resources,* industrial pathways, and strategic orbital positions. The U.S. is in danger of being excluded from key economic and security opportunities in Cislunar space—allowing authoritarian China to set the rules. Success will be measured by tangible milestones: accelerated Artemis timelines, operational Lunar infrastructure, robust international partnerships, and a self-sustaining space economy.

## SCENARIO 12: CAN A PRIVATE COMPANY CLAIM THE MOON?

As national space programs compete for Lunar achievements, private sector actors introduce another layer of complexity to Lunar development. The following scenario examines how commercial entities might challenge traditional space governance frameworks, forcing policymakers to balance private enterprise with national interests and international obligations.

## SCENARIO RATIONALE

The Artemis Accords[192] have championed the idea of safety zones on the Moon to prevent harmful interference but provided no guidance as to their size. If an actor was to declare a safety zone of such size and expanse that it appeared to be excessive and exclude others, it might trigger a wide range of responses, from demarches, to nonrecognition, to rapid counterclaims.

Many observers see the non-appropriation clause as untenable in the face of space mining.[193] Already multiple attempts at commercial Lunar landings have been made by SpaceIL,[194] Astrobotic,[195] and a partial success by Intuitive machines in 2024.[196]

Certain U.S. companies have far more ambitious plans for large-scale development (for example, Lockheed, Bechtel, Blue Origin, Cislune, Lunar Resources, OffWorld, Startpath and Ethos Space).

While the U.S. enjoys a launch advantage, other nations—friendly or neutral—may provide a more favorable route to securing space resources. Luxembourg, the United Arab Emirates (UAE), Japan, and India all have pro-space resource laws or policies. Several years ago, the UAE even contemplated a $18 billion sovereign wealth fund to industrialize the Moon.

Several island states are known to be favorable locations for international off-shore banking, tax havens,[197] and money laundering and are willing to provide "flags of convenience" for international shipping.[198] [The Commerce Department under the first Trump term and Kevin O'Connell, Director of the Office of Space Commerce (OSC), were pushing for the U.S. to be the flag of choice for all commerce in space] Of note, several island states are not signatories to the Outer Space Treaty (OST)[199] and have not given up their sovereign right to claim territory in space. A claim originating from a non-OST state would provide an interesting legal challenge to the OST. Early claims could enable an advantage, and it is not clear how the world would react to a commercial claim.

## *The Scenario*

### The Daily Astronomer | Front Page
*October 20, 2030*

In a groundbreaking move poised to reshape the dynamics of space exploration and Lunar development, Starlight Ventures, under the visionary leadership of CEO Jason Morrow, has successfully planted its privately funded lander, the *Lunar Pioneer*, on the Moon. While the Federal Aviation Administration facilitated this achievement with a launch license, Starlight Ventures argues that existing legal frameworks fall short of governing their activities on the Lunar surface comprehensively. The company claims to be at the forefront of establishing safety and operational zones on the Moon, aligning with the Artemis Accords' principles for ensuring safe and sustainable space exploration.

Strategically headquartered in Vanuatu, known for its tax sheltering benefits and liberal use of flags of convenience for company and vessel registrations, Starlight Ventures leverages the island nation's non-signatory status to the Outer Space Treaty to its advantage. This positioning allows the company a unique flexibility in navigating the complexities of international space law. Vanuatu's prompt recognition of Starlight Ventures' Lunar claim, following the *Lunar Pioneer*'s landing, underscores the strategic use of Vanuatu's global financial system stance to bolster the company's ambitions on the Moon.

The claim over the Lunar Peaks of Eternal Light, regions valued for their continuous sunlight, crucial for the energy needs of future Lunar bases, highlights the strategic importance of this move. With the Lunar Exploration Corporation (LEC) of China set to launch a competing mission in just weeks, the race for these invaluable Lunar territories underscores the urgency of securing strategic Lunar locations. The implication is clear: Had Starlight Ventures not acted, LEC or another competitor would likely have claimed this critical Lunar site.

This bold initiative by Starlight Ventures has ignited a global debate on the need for modernized space law, sovereignty, and the shared heritage of outer space. Establishing a safety zone on the Moon, the company not only challenges existing international norms but also sets a controversial precedent that could redefine the future of Lunar governance and exploration, amid concerns over tax sheltering and the use of flags of convenience.

This situation places the U.S. administration in a dilemma. As suggested by one think tank pundit, "Does the U.S. preserve its strategic foothold and leadership on the Lunar frontier with its own commercial actor, setting a concerning precedent for others and allowing the company to 'speed' unchecked, or does it constrain Starlight Ventures and risk losing its foothold to China?" This conundrum underscores the intricate balance between fostering innovation and maintaining strategic leadership in the new era of space exploration.

*Note: The President saw this article and is concerned. He has asked the Vice President to convene a National Space Council to provide the President with options and recommendations for immediate response and long-term programmatic response options.*

## SIMULATED NATIONAL SPACE COUNCIL DISCUSSION

The Vice President and several council members emphasized the importance of maintaining a first-mover advantage in Lunar exploration and development. The council members grappled with the challenge of balancing U.S. strategic leadership in space with the potential consequences of allowing private companies to operate unchecked, particularly in light of Starlight Ventures' claim of extraterrestrial self-sovereignty. The risk of losing strategic Lunar locations to other countries, especially China, and the implications of non-signatory nations like Vanuatu circumventing the Outer Space Treaty were significant concerns.

The lack of clarity regarding Lunar governance, enforcement mechanisms, and the potential for territory division on the Moon, as well as the complexities surrounding citizenship, manufacturing, and legal issues in space, were also major points of discussion. Another key tension that emerged during the meeting was the U.S. government's apparent unpreparedness to address private space company governance and the public perception of its authority in the face of rapidly evolving space exploration dynamics.

Economic and security pressures on private companies

emerged as a critical issue. There were concerns about the potential for companies like Starlight Ventures to come under economic or security stress, which could lead to strategic vulnerabilities. This included the risk of such companies being co-opted by other nations, potentially compromising U.S. interests.[200] The importance of gathering intelligence on the backgrounds and motives of company principals was underscored, alongside the need to identify and ensure the essential functions required in space.

Several notable ideas and recommendations were put forward during the meeting. These included streamlining the U.S. licensing regime to provide more specifics on commercial space activities, using this case to establish norms and advocate for a new treaty that includes international coordination. Asserting U.S. responsibility and authority over U.S.-originated entities like Starlight Ventures while enabling appropriate commercial activities and considering alternative governance models like seabed or Antarctica treaties was also suggested. Working with allies to convene experts and establish rules for commercial Lunar activity, using multinational penalties to influence behavior and create an alternative to Chinese dominance, was also proposed.

Some council members suggested treating the commercial claim like a U.S. "island" and considering granting the U.S. government some shares in the company, ensuring U.S. leadership via the licensing regime and strategic points of control on the Moon. Developing a legal framework for economic activities on the Moon, with enforcement mechanisms potentially involving a space force or international body, and mandating landing pad positioning to reduce dust spread were also put forward as potential solutions.

## ASSESSMENT AND RECOMMENDATIONS

The United States has a historic opportunity to shape the future of Lunar development through private sector innovation. Recent commercial activities on the Moon present both a challenge and an opportunity to establish precedent-setting frameworks for space governance. This comprehensive licensing framework establishes clear rules of the road that protect U.S. interests, incentivize responsible commercial space activities, and secure strategic Lunar locations and resources. By acting decisively now, the U.S. will create a sustainable architecture for commercial space operations that advances national security, economic leadership, and international cooperation while ensuring American primacy in the next frontier.[201]

*Immediate Actions (0–3 months)*
**Unified Space Licensing Framework**
- Adopt a tiered licensing system
  - **Tier 1:** Basic launch and operation rights to operate on the Moon
  - **Tier 2:** Enhanced rights with authority over specific safety zones
  - **Tier 3:** Strategic partner status that includes U.S. government (USG) protection and possible equity participation.

**Emergency Regulatory Measures**
- Implement immediate safety and environmental standards (for example, minimum safety zones and dust mitigation plans) as part of the licensing requirements. This ensures all operations meet baseline safety and sustainability criteria.

**Strategic Communication Plan**

- Develop a communication plan that not only emphasizes the U.S. commitment to protecting commercial rights but also clearly outlines the governance framework and the benefits of operating under U.S. jurisdiction.

*Short-Term Actions (3–12 months)*

**Space Enterprise Protection Act of 2031**

- Establish the U.S. Space Development Corporation to oversee and support licensed commercial activities, including benefits like priority access to Lunar landing sites and tax incentives for U.S.-flagged operations, enhancing the attractiveness of operating under U.S. regulations.

**Security and Surveillance Enhancements**

- Implement a CONOP titled Licensed Zone Protection that incorporates Space Force surveillance and rapid response capabilities, alongside integration with allied space forces. This would enhance security for all U.S.-licensed operations on the Moon.

**International Licensing Recognition and Cooperation**

- Initiate the Washington Space Commerce Initiative to negotiate licensing recognition agreements and mutual defense provisions, incorporating small nation participation to broaden international support and cooperation.

## Long-Term Actions (1-3 years)
### Comprehensive Licensing Infrastructure
- Work towards establishing a network of U.S.-licensed Lunar landing pads and creating Lunar economic zones that facilitate organized development and resource rights allocation.

### Security Architecture
- Develop a permanent Cislunar presence under the Licensed Operations Protection Program, which includes an international surveillance network and emergency response systems, ensuring a sustained and secure environment for space activities.[202]

### Economic Development Framework
- Launch a Space Commerce Development Program that not only supports public-private investments but also establishes an international Lunar development bank to finance infrastructure and resource extraction ventures,[203] providing crucial financial backing for Lunar development.

## RISKS AND METRICS FOR SUCCESS
The proposed framework for U.S. Lunar activities holds significant promise, but it carries material risks in execution and enforcement. Primary concerns include international resistance to U.S. jurisdictional claims, Space Force capacity to effectively monitor vast Lunar territories, and challenges in enforcing compliance across multiple sovereign entities. Success metrics will focus on three key areas: international adoption rates of the U.S. licensing framework,

demonstrated capability to monitor Lunar activities in real-time, and commercial compliance with safety and environmental standards. Early warning indicators include the rate of partner nation participation, development of effective Cislunar surveillance capabilities,[204] and the percentage of U.S.-origin companies seeking alternative jurisdictions.

## SCENARIO 13: ARE CHINA'S MOON SAFETY ZONES A MASSIVE LUNAR LAND GRAB?

While private claims to Lunar territory present one challenge to space governance, the next scenario explores how state actors might use seemingly legitimate safety measures to establish de facto control over strategic Lunar locations. China's approach to claiming Lunar territory bears striking parallels to its terrestrial territorial assertions, raising concerns about the potential for similar patterns of expansionism beyond Earth.

## SCENARIO RATIONALE

While the Moon itself has more land area than the entire continent of Africa, there are certain unique regions, such as the Peaks of Eternal Light,[205] that are quite small yet strategic because of their simultaneous access to constant sunlight as well as to the permanently shadowed regions that hold large reservoirs of ice and volatile resources.[206] Early, uncoordinated occupation might be perceived as a land grab. It is already clear that the U.S. and China are looking at the same landing sites,[207] and some observers anticipate a scenario not unlike China's actions in the South China Sea[208]—including the current NASA administrator, who stated, "And it is true that we better watch out that they don't get to a place on the Moon under the guise of scientific research. And it is not beyond the realm of possibility that they say, 'Keep out, we're here, this is our territory.'"[209] On Earth, China has declared administrative control of areas in the South China Sea[210] and declared air defense identification zones (ADIZ) in the East China Sea,[211] challenging the status quo and U.S. leadership.

## *The Scenario*

### The Daily Astronomer | Front Page
*July 1, 2031*

In a landmark address to the United Nations, a spokesperson for the Chinese government declared China's intent to establish safety zones for its burgeoning Lunar operations. While this announcement was presented as a necessary measure to ensure the security and stability of China's Lunar missions, it has ignited a celestial conundrum with far-reaching implications.

Experts and scholars from prominent think tanks around
the world were quick to scrutinize China's proposed Lunar
safety zones. Their analysis unveiled a startling revelation:
These claimed operating areas encompass a staggering 60
percent of the coveted Peaks of Eternal Light, a Lunar region
celebrated for its perpetual sunlight and proximity to vital
water resources. Furthermore, the declared zones overlap
significantly with the territorial claims of not one but two
fellow Artemis Accords signatories, India and Japan.

This revelation has sent ripples of concern across the international community. Critics argue that while ensuring the
safety of Lunar operations is paramount, the extent of China's
claimed safety zones raises questions about equity and access
in the rapidly expanding arena of space exploration.

U.S. commercial companies, feeling the squeeze of this celestial standoff, are adding pressure to policymakers, expressing
their concerns. They are eager not only to safeguard their
own Lunar ambitions but also to make comparable claims
to protect their interests or seek the protective mantle of the
U.S. Space Force. Investors are equally jittery, fearing that the
outcome of this Lunar dispute could significantly impact the
stock market, as the fate of numerous space-related enterprises hangs in the balance.

While the United States is not directly impacted by these
contested zones, the issue has triggered a reevaluation of
several critical aspects. In addition to assessing freedom of
navigation concerns and territorial access, American poli-

cymakers are weighing the importance of supporting their allies in the Artemis Accords, such as India and Japan. Both nations have already signaled their intentions to permit international commercial operations within their Lunar territories, raising the prospect of potential access for U.S. companies.

As the debate surrounding China's Lunar safety zones intensifies, the world watches with bated breath to see how the United States and the international community will navigate this complex celestial dilemma. How might the U.S. cope with the intricate interplay of Lunar diplomacy, space governance, and strategic partnerships in the face of this Lunar land grab?[212]

*Note: The President saw this article and is concerned. He has asked the Vice President to convene a National Space Council to provide the President with options and recommendations for immediate response and long-term programmatic response options.*

## SIMULATED NATIONAL SPACE COUNCIL DISCUSSION

The NSpC grappled with the economic impact of China's actions, as American companies and investors heavily involved in Lunar operations could face significant losses. The potential for market volatility and the need to protect and support affected businesses emerged as a key concern.[213] Some officials suggested bold measures, such as temporary trading pauses, market intervention, and economic sanctions against China, to mitigate the financial fallout.

Beyond the economic sphere, China's Lunar safety zones were seen as part of a broader strategy to exploit existing norms and establish new ones in their favor. Drawing parallels to China's approach in the South China Sea, officials expressed apprehension about allowing Beijing to control critical Lunar territories, particularly the valuable Peaks of Eternal Light.

The council emphasized the importance of international cooperation in addressing the situation. With the territorial claims of key allies like India and Japan also affected by China's safety zones, joint action and international support were considered crucial. Some officials suggested taking China to international court, arguing that their claims violate the Outer Space Treaty. However, the legal challenges surrounding Lunar territorial disputes remain complex and largely untested.[214]

The role of the military in responding to China's actions emerged as another point of tension. While some officials advocated for a strong military presence to challenge China's claims, others cautioned against the optics of a heavy-handed approach. The deployment of the U.S. Space Force, which is not currently equipped for Lunar operations, was met with skepticism.[215] Covert operations and a reevaluation of the Space Force's role were proposed as alternatives to overt military action.

Alternatively, one member suggested an innovative "Operation Throw-Shade" approach to negate the value of China's claimed terrain through technological means, as a nonmilitary approach to addressing China's exploitation. Officials acknowledged the challenge of garnering public support for Lunar operations, particularly among progressive groups wary of militarization and the use of public funds to support private interests. To counter this, some suggested emphasizing the economic and strategic importance of the

Moon, as well as its potential to support climate and environmental research on Earth.[216] Developing a narrative that resonates with both investors and the general public was seen as key to building support for a strong response to China's actions.

## ASSESSMENT AND RECOMMENDATIONS
Beijing's unilateral claim to Lunar territory mirrors its aggressive territorial assertions on Earth, from the South China Sea to Belt and Road infrastructure. Their declaration of "safety zones" encompassing 60 percent of the Peaks of Eternal Light—areas critical for sustainable Lunar operations due to their constant solar power and proximity to water ice—directly threatens U.S. commercial interests, challenges our Artemis Accord partners' claims, and risks establishing dangerous precedents for space governance. This strategic framework provides specific, actionable measures across diplomatic, economic, and security domains to uphold international space law, protect U.S. and allied interests, and sets out to ensure sustainable Lunar development remains open to all responsible spacefaring nations.[217]

### *Immediate Response (0–30 days)*
**Economic Protection Measures**
- Establish market "circuit breakers" for space-related stocks to trigger at a 7 percent daily decline, stabilizing financial markets and protecting investments.

- Create an emergency lending facility through the Export-Import Bank to support affected companies, ensuring they have the necessary financial resources to withstand initial shocks.

- Implement sanctions targeting entities operating in unauthorized Lunar safety zones.

**Diplomatic and Legal Actions**
- File a joint legal challenge through UNOOSA with India and Japan, solidifying an international front against unilateral territorial claims on the Moon.

- Initiate a strategic communications campaign to highlight China's environmental and regulatory irresponsibility in their Lunar operations, shaping global public opinion and increasing diplomatic pressure.

- Ban the sale and import of minerals extracted from disputed Lunar zones.

**Operational Deployment**
- Deploy surveillance and reconnaissance assets to monitor Chinese activities, using existing Cislunar capabilities to ensure continuous intelligence and situational awareness.

- Begin freedom of navigation operations using NASA and commercial missions to assert rights under international space law and demonstrate commitment to free Lunar navigation.

*Short-Term Actions (30-180 days)*
**Legislative and Policy Development**
- Submit the Space Resources Protection Act of 2031, which includes tax incentives for rapid Lunar infrastructure

deployment, creating a Space Development Bank for commercial funding, and setting environmental standards for Lunar operations.

- Develop an integrated NASA-DoD Cislunar presence plan, ensuring that civil and military space operations are synergized for better protection and utilization of space assets.

### Military and Security Enhancements
- Establish a joint civil-military Lunar monitoring center to oversee all operations and ensure compliance with international laws and agreements.

- Create a Lunar Coast Guard[218] function within the Space Force[219] to manage security and assist in maintaining free navigation and operations on the Moon.

### Commercial and International Collaboration
- Establish an international Lunar resource tracking system and develop a mineral certification program to prevent resource laundering and ensure transparency in resource extraction.

### *Long-term Programs (180+ days and beyond)*
### Infrastructure and Strategic Development
- Accelerate the deployment of an international Lunar power grid in remaining Peaks of Eternal Light, ensuring sustainable energy resources for all Lunar operations.[220]

- Establish shared scientific outposts at strategic locations to facilitate international cooperation and scientific research, enhancing the collective understanding of Lunar resources and environment.[221]

## Economic and Cooperative Frameworks
- Launch an international Lunar Development Bank with Artemis partners to fund and support multinational Lunar development projects.

- Create Lunar economic zones with environmental protection provisions and establish international resource sharing agreements, promoting a balanced and equitable utilization of Lunar resources.

## Environmental and Traffic Management
- Develop capability for passive denial operations, including innovative concepts like Operation Throw-Shade to counter overreach physically without escalating conflicts.

- Establish an international Lunar traffic management system and an environmental monitoring network to oversee activities and ensure compliance with sustainable practices.

## RISKS AND METRICS FOR SUCCESS
China's territorial claims carry significant risks of economic retaliation and further escalation—potentially destabilizing both the emerging space market and international partnerships. Success of this framework will be measured through specific metrics: (1) effective deployment of Cislunar surveillance capabilities and sustained

freedom of navigation operations, (2) preserved access to strategic Lunar territories, particularly the remaining Peaks of Eternal Light, (3) establishment of internationally recognized safety zone parameters that prevent excessive territorial claims, and (4) maintained competitive access for U.S. commercial entities to

Lunar resources despite Chinese pressure. Importantly, any response must avoid setting precedents that could legitimize excessive territorial claims while protecting U.S. and allied interests.

## SCENARIO 14: CHINA'S LUNAR FACTORY CRUSHES U.S. AMBITIONS

From territorial claims through safety zones, we now turn to perhaps the most consequential development: the establishment of industrial-scale manufacturing capabilities on the Moon. This scenario examines how achieving practical Lunar industrialization could definitively shift the balance of power in space, presenting both economic opportunities and potential security threats that demand careful consideration.

## SCENARIO RATIONALE

Commencement of actual Lunar regolith mining and Lunar-manufactured solar cell deployment would be a significant departure from past exploration. It would likely change perceptions about the strategic importance of the Moon, as well as trigger new environmental concerns. High-level PRC leaders have articulated their desire to create a "Moon-Earth economic zone" generating a continent's worth of economic activity (\$10 trillion/year in 2050)[222] and proposed an ambitious initial plan for a base.[223] The PRC's military leadership has announced its intention to industrialize the Moon to build solar power satellites.[224]

U.S. policy has articulated the importance of leading in the space economy and pursuing a Lunar industrial base across the past two administrations,[225] and has even become part of at least one party's platform.[226] More recently, the *National Cislunar S&T Strategy* states, "U.S. government organizations will leverage collaborations with private entities to enable capabilities for large-scale ISRU and advanced manufacturing at the Moon"[227] and the *National Cislunar Science and Technology Action Plan* directs NASA, USGS, DOD and NSF to "begin assessing the natural resources of the Moon"[228]—though no timeline or funding was identified and the administration did not identify that such objectives needed to stay ahead of adversary timelines. These goals are reflected in NASA's "Moon to Mars Objectives"[229] and have been the subject of a DARPA program to develop a Lunar economy in 10 years, Luna-10.[230]

Moreover, the U.S. Space Force, Air Force Research Laboratory, Defense Innovation Unit "State of the Space Industrial Base" report identified "space manufacturing and resource extraction for terrestrial and in space markets" as one of the "six areas most vital

CONFLICTS ON THE MOON

to . . . US national power in space" and as areas "most likely to be at the center of gravity in great power competition."[231]

The U.S. originated the concept of mega-scale industrial development to build solar power satellites circa 1979–1985,[232] updated in 2016.[233] The potential of a self-replicating industrial capability on Lunar industrial development has been known by NASA since 1983[234] and was further developed by Johns Hopkins University in 2004.[235] Moreover, its national security implications were recognized by NASA authors in 2016.[236] Currently, multiple U.S. firms—including Lockheed, Bechtel, Blue Origin, OffWorld, ICON, Lunar Resources, Cislune, Starpath and Ethos Space— have major industrial ambitions, and are developing the necessary in-space industrial capabilities such as metal refining, volatiles extraction, structure building, and photovoltaic cells. American allies in Europe have likewise examined an industrial base to build solar power satellites[237] and provided a vision video.[238]

Past studies of using Lunar materials to build solar power satellites and space habitats have often preferred the use of mass drivers,[239] whose dual-use applications have been explored in fiction (a mass driver is essentially an electromagnetic "rail" or "track" that uses powerful magnets or coils to accelerate payloads—like chunks of rock or processed materials—off a planetary surface and into space).[240] In August of 2024, the PRC published its first public paper on a nuclear-powered rotating Lunar mass driver.[241]

The importance of a clear advance in industrial extraction and processing on the Moon is likely to be taken very seriously, as evidenced by this recent exchange in the House Natural Resources Committee on "The Mineral Supply Chain and the New Space Race:[242]

**Congressman Collins:** "Well, let's look at a worst-case scenario then Dr. Autry and Dr. Hanlon really quick—I know I'm running out of time—what's the worst case if China wins the race for space mining and how would that negatively impact the United States, and Dr. Autry you want to start with that?"

**Dr. Greg Autry:** "I don't want to be hyperbolic here, but if China wins the race in space, we've ceded the strategic high ground militarily and we've ceded the entire economic future, and the United States will be relegated to a backwater position for the rest of human history. I honestly think that this is an existential point."

**Dr. Michelle L.D. Hanlon:** "I agree with Dr. Autry . . . if the Chinese will have the ability to not only block us to the Moon but to all of space, and humanity's future lies in space."

An early success in space industrialization is likely to trigger concerns about the U.S. falling behind.

*Note:* We privately informed the Director of National Intelligence player that there was evidence of military R&D paper designs for mass driver–launched weapons—common in conceptual explorations—with low confidence that any decision to pursue them had been made. However, some indications of potential stockpiling of component materials suggested that the mass driver could eventually be developed as an Earth-strike weapon. This input was meant to be deliberately ambiguous to see how the players would respond.

## *The Scenario*

### The Daily Astronomer | Front Page
*October 1, 2031*

In a striking display of extraterrestrial industrial might, China has "stolen the march" on the United States by commencing large-scale Lunar regolith mining and deploying solar cells manufactured on the Moon. This initiative, directly utilizing techniques first proposed by U.S. universities and companies, including Blue Origin[243] and Lunar Resources,[244] has positioned the PRC at the forefront of sustainable development and green energy production in space.

The PRC's swift and visually impactful Lunar advancements have not only accelerated General Zhang Yulin's ambition to "industrialize the Moon to build solar power satellites" but have also unsettled the global perception of American leadership in space and sustainability. With megawatts of power expected to flow from these solar cells, the implications extend far beyond mere energy generation. This power surge sets the stage for operating a Lunar "mass driver," an ambitious project that would facilitate the transportation of materials from the Moon to Earth or other space destinations, revolutionizing space logistics and commerce.

China's Lunar surge seeks to claim leadership in the critical global agenda of sustainable development, green energy, and combating climate change. The PRC asserts that harnessing solar power on the Moon is a giant leap toward a carbon-neutral future, as it offers a continuous and emission-free energy source. The stunning pace of China's achievements on the Moon—laid out for the world to see in daily broadcasts—contrasts starkly with the slower, more methodical progress of U.S. efforts, casting doubt on America's position as a space leader.

The framework for an expansive Lunar power grid is now materializing and, with it, the potential to power a mass driver, a concept that could transform Lunar materials into a powerhouse of space-based industry and commerce. Such a tool would be a game-changer for in-situ resource utilization, presenting a novel approach to off-world development.

As China's Lunar program unfolds with remarkable speed and scale, it challenges the United States to reevaluate its strategic priorities in space. American stakeholders, from the halls of Congress to Silicon Valley, are now compelled to respond with renewed vigor and vision. The race to secure a sustainable future has extended beyond Earth, and the next move will determine the balance of spacefaring leadership in the decades to come.

*Note: The President saw this article and is concerned. He has asked the Vice President to convene a National Space Council to provide the President with options and recommendations for immediate response and long-term programmatic response options.*

## SIMULATED NATIONAL SPACE COUNCIL
## DISCUSSION

One major point of contention was the timeline for China's achievements. While some participants believed China's progress was overstated, others expressed concern about the potential for rapid advancements. This disagreement highlighted the difficulty of assessing China's true capabilities and intentions.

Another area of tension was the severity of the threat posed by China's Lunar activities. Some participants emphasized the potential for military applications, such as weaponizing mass drivers or using Lunar resources for offensive purposes. This military focus, however, was met with caution by other members, who warned against overreaction. They argued that framing China's Lunar factory as an inherent military threat could stifle international commercial development in space, potentially hindering the growth of U.S. private industry—particularly through overly restrictive regulations like ITAR. Furthermore, some argued that mass drivers were impractical as weapons due to their predictable trajectories and long travel times. Instead, they advocated for increased R&D investments and the development of comparable capabilities by U.S. companies, not just on the Moon but in free space as well, to ensure a balanced and economically driven approach to space competition.[245]

Diplomatic and public communication strategies also surfaced as critical areas of concern. On the diplomatic front, disagreements arose over the most effective approach to engage with China and the international community. The Secretary of State proposed aggressive measures, including potential sanctions and the revocation of China's permanent normal trade relations (PNTR) status.[246] The White House Press Secretary, by contrast, stressed the importance of transparency in public communications, especially given the lingering mistrust from past intelligence failures like the WMD controversy in Iraq. The need to provide concrete evidence before making any claims about the weaponization of Lunar infrastructure was seen as essential to maintaining public trust and avoiding unnecessary escalation.

The council also considered long-term strategies to counter China's influence. The proposal to create a CHIPS-type act for space emerged as a viable solution to accelerate U.S. technological and industrial capabilities. This initiative, alongside the recommendation to involve international monitors for Lunar mass drivers, reflected a desire to combine economic growth with global diplomatic engagement, ensuring that U.S. actions were both effective and internationally supported.

## ASSESSMENT AND RECOMMENDATIONS

Gauging the timeline of China's Lunar advancements remains uncertain, but once they achieve operational resource extraction and energy production capabilities, the U.S. must respond decisively. This framework proposes a three-pronged approach: accelerating U.S. commercial development, establishing robust monitoring of Chinese Cislunar activities, and implementing rapid response options to preserve American space leadership.

### *Immediate Actions (0–90 Days)*
**Executive Order: Centralized Lunar Licensing & Streamlined Regulation**

- Designate the Office of Space Commerce as the *single licensing authority* for all Lunar activities.

- Impose a 60-day maximum review period for commercial Lunar applications, ensuring rapid approvals and clarity.

- Protect Commercial IP with a streamlined framework and provide narrow ITAR exemptions for critical Lunar technologies (for example, in-situ resource utilization, non-offensive mass driver R&D).

**Cislunar Intelligence & Transparency**
- Deploy/redirect at least one dedicated monitoring satellite to Cislunar orbit, with a public-facing dashboard for non-sensitive data—boosting public trust and deterrence through transparency.

- Direct the DNI to produce an unclassified threat assessment summarizing potential dual-use risks, so policymakers and the public have a clear baseline.

**Diplomatic Engagement & Code of Conduct Talks**
- Launch preliminary discussions on a "Mass Driver and Lunar Infrastructure Code of Conduct" with core U.S. allies (Artemis Accords signatories, EU, Japan, Canada).

- Hold classified congressional briefings to align lawmakers on the scope of the challenge and the immediate regulatory changes.

*Short-Term Actions (6–18 Months)*
**Legislative Push: "Cislunar Innovation and Resource Security Act" (CIRSA)**
- Seek a multibillion-dollar appropriation to fund:

- R&D matching grants for Lunar ISRU, mass driver tech, and space-based solar power (SBSP).[247]

- Tax incentives to attract private investment in Lunar manufacturing and commercial exploration.

- A legal framework clarifying property/resource usage rights on the Moon, consistent with Outer Space Treaty obligations.

### Technical & Operational Programs

- NASA/Commercial ISRU Pilot: Aim to demonstrate small-scale regolith extraction and on-site solar panel manufacturing by ~2035.[248]

- Joint NASA–USSF Cislunar CONOPS: Develop comprehensive procedures for emergency response, rapid launch (2–4 weeks), and on-orbit servicing to protect U.S. and allied interests.

### Allied Intelligence & Verification Initiatives

- Establish an international Lunar Observer data-sharing platform, open to allies and potential third parties for consistent monitoring of Lunar surface operations.

- Develop verification protocols (pre-launch notifications, payload declarations) to reduce surprises and build confidence in peaceful uses of mass drivers and other dual-use infrastructure.

### Long-Term Strategy (2–5+ Years)
### Multinational Lunar Resource & Energy Consortium

- Convene a NASA-led, multinational partnership (including commercial players) to co-develop:

- Shared Lunar infrastructure (power grids, comm networks).

- A safe corridor approach for mass driver operations.

- Collaborative standards for ISRU scaling (extraction, refining, manufacturing).

**Space-Based Solar Power Demonstrations**
- Commit to at least one 1–5 MW SBSP pilot by ~2038, testing wireless power beaming to Earth or Cislunar installations.[249]

- Establish a Space Energy Development Fund, possibly tied to carbon-credit revenue or public–private partnerships, to sustain R&D in advanced energy systems.

**Mass Driver Code of Conduct & Treaty Mechanisms**
- Transition the initial code of conduct talks into a formal multilateral agreement:

- Require pre-launch notifications, payload/velocity parameters, and inspection rights.

- Provide a clear dispute resolution mechanism for alleged violations.

- Integrate these norms into broader Cislunar traffic management (similar to maritime codes) so that all major spacefaring nations have consistent rules of engagement.

**Lunar Special Economic Zone (Optional Exploration)**

- Evaluate the feasibility of a Lunar Special Economic Zone under the consortium model, offering:

- Tax breaks and streamlined regulations for commercial operators.

- Legal certainty for resource extraction while adhering to treaty obligations.

- Ensure robust international dialogue to avoid contravening the Outer Space Treaty's non-sovereignty principles.

## RISKS AND METRICS FOR SUCCESS

Industrializing the Moon is necessary for U.S. economic growth and scientific progress—and Beijing seems poised to benefit first without intervention. However, while arresting Chinese progress (and/or at least ensuring the U.S. keeps pace), we must be careful not to risk overregulating and inadvertently stifle U.S. commercial innovation. Measuring success in this environment requires clear benchmarks: establishment of streamlined licensing processes, deployment of dedicated Cislunar monitoring, securing congressional funding, and development of U.S. resource extraction capabilities by 2035. Additional metrics include the number of U.S. companies receiving Lunar operating licenses, successful demonstration of space-based solar power capabilities, and establishment of international verification protocols with key allies.

## EMERGING THEMES AND CONCLUSION

Lunar development and industrialization are rapidly emerging as critical areas of strategic competition that demand immediate policy attention. These scenarios highlight that the stakes of Artemis and licensing of novel space activities have far greater economic and national security implications than prestige points for getting to the Moon first. The current focus of Artemis appears to narrow to compete, placing too much emphasis on science and prestige, and placing insufficient emphasis on developing extractive and productive industry.

**Strategic Resource Control and Economic Security.** American space leadership and future economic security will hinge on access to and control of key Lunar resources and locations, particularly the Peaks of Eternal Light, on the Moon. The ability to extract and utilize Lunar resources will determine not just economic success, but also operational capabilities beyond Earth orbit. Early positioning in strategic locations could create lasting advantages— particularly if the U.S. expects to be relevant in the projected trillion Cislunar economy.

**Insufficient Funding and Investment.** The scenarios consistently revealed the need for massive funding increases ($65B and $150B) and national-level initiatives (a national space directive, a space commerce development program, a Washington space commerce initiative) to close the capability gap. The scenarios prompted proposals of comprehensive legislation (Lunar Security and Innovation Act of 2028, Space Resources Protection Act of 2031, Space Industrial Base Act, Cislunar Innovation and Resource Security Act (CIRSA) [modeled on the $52.7B CHIPS act[250]]. This included broader economic development models: a *single licensing authority (Department of Commerce)*, Lunar economic zones or Lunar

Special Economic Zones with Licensed Zone Protection, Lunar Industrial Base Protection Program) and special funds (Lunar COTS and beyond, Space Energy Development Fund). In addition to legislation, there was a push to create novel institutions—such as a Space Development & Security Bank (SDSB), U.S. Space Development Corporation, Lunar Development Bank, or something akin to a port authority—for the special economic development zones.

**NASA's Limited Mandate.** While the 1958 NASA Charter states, "The Congress declares that the general welfare and *security* of the United States require that adequate provision be made for . . . space activities. The Congress further declares that such activities shall be the responsibility of, and *shall be directed by, a civilian agency exercising control over . . . space activities sponsored by the United States*, except that activities peculiar to or primarily associated with the development of weapons systems, military operations, or the defense of the United States,"[emphasis ours].[251] NASA's surrendering of its Cold Warrior identity to win great power competition, and cultural aversion to industrialization and economic development—anything that is not exploration and science for curiosity or glory—mean that Congress and the administration will likely have to look beyond NASA to mobilize or create new institutions with sufficient focus and will to develop and secure American interests on the Moon. Finding institutions with sufficient focus on the development of space resources—beginning on the Moon—may be of existential importance.

**Rapid Response Required.** All of the scenarios require the rapid development of a narrative for the public and allies to mobilize a response—and that the basis of such narrative is always about prosperity, relative economic advantage, and the need for agreed upon norms which enable the private sector to engage fruitfully in rapid but responsible economic development. However, success in Lunar development requires not just government funding, but also effective public-private partnerships and regulatory frameworks that encourage innovation while protecting national security interests.

As the U.S. considers its Lunar strategy, development time-lines must be accelerated to match or exceed competitor capabilities. National space policy must prioritize Lunar industrialization through clear directives to NASA, the Space Force, and commercial partners.

**CHAPTER 4 SUMMARY AND RECOMMENDATIONS**

- **Introduction.** The Moon has become a critical frontier for economic and strategic competition, as evidenced by Beijing and Moscow teaming up meanwhile the U.S. and its allies advance their own Lunar ambitions. The ability to establish industrial capabilities on the Lunar surface— from 3D-printed structures to resource extraction—will determine not just energy security but also technological leadership in the space domain.

- **Scenario 10: PRC Wows World With 3D-Printed Moon Structures.** China demonstrates advanced Lunar manufacturing capabilities through live-streamed 3D printing of structures using Lunar regolith, challenging U.S. leadership in space technology. Recommendations focus on establishing a Lunar Innovation Fund, enhancing public-private partnerships, and developing strategic communication to showcase U.S. capabilities while protecting the industrial base.

- **Scenario 11: Global Tension Escalates as China Achieves Early Human Landing.** China's successful crewed Lunar landing ahead of NASA's Artemis program triggers international realignment and domestic debate about U.S. space leadership. Recommendations emphasize rapid commercial acceleration through programs like Lunar COTS enhanced Cislunar monitoring capabilities, and establishment of economic incentives to maintain U.S. competitive advantage.

- **Scenario 12: Private Company Claims Lunar Territory.** A U.S.-originated but foreign-registered company stakes claim to strategic Lunar locations, exploiting legal gaps in space governance. Recommendations propose a unified space licensing framework, enhanced security monitoring, and development of international protocols for commercial activities while protecting U.S. interests.

- **Scenario 13: China's Moon Safety Zones Raise Concerns.** China's declaration of extensive safety zones encompassing 60 percent of the Peaks of Eternal Light challenges international access to strategic Lunar resources. Recommendations include implementing freedom of navigation operations, establishing international monitoring systems, and developing countermeasures while supporting allies affected by Chinese claims.

- **Scenario 14: China's Lunar Factory Development.** China's achievement of industrial-scale Lunar manufacturing and energy production capabilities, including mass drivers, presents both economic and security challenges. Recommendations focus on accelerating U.S. commercial development, establishing robust monitoring of Chinese activities, and implementing international protocols for dual-use technologies while maintaining U.S. technological leadership.

# CHAPTER 5

## Space Safety and Rescue

### INTRODUCTION

"On my last mission to space, my crew and I traveled far-
ther from Earth than anyone in over half a century. I can
confidently say this second space age has only just begun.
Space holds unparalleled potential for breakthroughs in
manufacturing, biotechnology, mining, and perhaps even
pathways to new sources of energy. There will inevitably
be a thriving space economy—one that will create opportunities for countless people to live and work in space. At
NASA, we will passionately pursue these possibilities and
usher in an era where humanity becomes a true spacefaring
civilization."

– Jared Isaacman, Commercial astronaut[252]

As Lunar industrialization accelerates, the risks associated
with American space activity grow—as evidenced by Blue Origin,

SpaceX, and Virgin Galactic who were the first private companies to pioneer space tourism. While American presence in space is a welcome development, it will bring with it challenges. In this chapter, we examine how policymakers must navigate the complexities of spaceflight disasters, rescue capabilities, planetary defense, and the potential consequences of adversarial actions in space. Through four scenarios, we explore the urgent need for preparedness in an era where space is no longer just a frontier—but a domain of real-world risk and responsibility.

## SCENARIO 15: TRAGEDY IN ORBIT: CALL FOR TIGHTER REGULATIONS AFTER FATAL COMMERCIAL SPACEFLIGHT INCIDENT

Even though a small orbital tourism market has developed with a laudable (at least at the time of writing) safety record, rockets are dangerous, and spaceflight is still experimental. The recent stunning success of Jared Isaacman's Polaris Dawn all-commercial mission and the first commercial spacewalk suggests a possible bright future.[253]

## SCENARIO RATIONALE

So far, the FAA Office of Commercial Space Transportation (AST) has overseen some 500 safe flights,[254] including recent orbital tourism spaceflights. More are on the horizon. SpaceX hopes to fly eight crew around the Moon[255] and eventually perhaps as many as 100 tourists via Starship.[256] To date, Congress has asked the FAA to take a hands-off approach to regulation[257] of space worthiness for the astronauts themselves (who are treated as adventurers with informed consent) and to protect only the public. But a significant in-space accident with loss of life is likely to shock the public and demand some sort of action—and potentially an over-reaction—that might reduce U.S. advantage, competitiveness, and ability to meet national goals. Such an accident might also create a serious hazard to navigation as well as a public spectacle.[258]

*The Scenario*

**The Daily Astronomer | Front Page**
*January 27, 2029*

In a harrowing event that has sent shockwaves through the world, a commercial spaceflight operated by GalaxyZ ended in catastrophe, resulting in the loss of 30 lives, including prominent citizens from Japan, Korea, Norway, Brazil, and Nigeria. The MarsShip, which had embarked on an orbital tourism mission, encountered a fatal thruster malfunction during a live-streamed refueling operation just prior to reentry, leading to a collision with the refueling tanker. The incident, broadcast live, resulted in a devastating explosion and the creation of a massive debris field in space, witnessed by millions around the world.

This tragedy marks the first significant loss of human life in the era of commercial space tourism, a sector that had seen over 500 safe flights[259] under the oversight of the Federal Aviation Administration Office of Commercial Space Transportation. Until now, the FAA and Congress have maintained a relatively hands-off approach[260] to spaceflight regulation, focusing on public safety rather than the space worthiness of the spacecraft or the safety of the astronauts,[261] who are considered adventurers providing informed consent. The debris—including large fragments of the MarsShip and its tanker, both exceptionally large—further draws condemnation for the hazard to navigation it presents to all actors in low-Earth orbit, with some space sustainability thought leaders, such as Kwame Nkrumah of the African Space Agency, stating that "as a would-be responsible spacefaring state, the U.S. should hasten to clear the hazard."

The public outcry following the incident has been swift and loud, with many calling for the U.S. government and the FAA to implement stricter regulations on commercial spaceflight. Critics argue that the current regulatory framework, which prioritizes innovation and market growth over stringent safety measures, may have contributed to the tragedy. The call for action comes at a critical juncture, as GalaxyZ's ambitious plans for orbital tourism, including flying up to 100 tourists per MarsShip mission and conducting a crewed Lunar flyby,[262] now hang in the balance.

The timing of the disaster could not be more inopportune for the U.S., as GalaxyZ was gearing up to begin refueling operations for the Human Landing System (HLS)[263] in preparation for the first American landing on the Moon in decades. The return, already delayed[264] from 2024 to 2025, then 2026, and now 2029, means that any further delay or setback now not only threatens the future of U.S. Lunar exploration but also provides a window of opportunity for the People's Republic of China (PRC) to surge ahead in the new space race with its planned human landing in 2030.[265]

As the nation grapples with the aftermath of this unprecedented tragedy, the debate intensifies over the balance between fostering innovation in the burgeoning space tourism industry and ensuring the safety of its passengers. With the PRC's space program hot on its heels, the U.S. faces a delicate dilemma: how to respond to public demand for greater safety without stifling the competitive edge that has positioned it as a leader in commercial spaceflight. The decisions made in the wake of this incident could reshape the future of space exploration and commercialization for years to come. The President will be meeting with the families later this week.

*NOTE: The President saw this article and is concerned. He has asked the Vice President to convene a National Space Council to provide the President with options and recommendations for immediate response and long-term programmatic response options.*

## SIMULATED NATIONAL SPACE COUNCIL DISCUSSION

The central tension in the NSpC discussions revolved around balancing the need for greater regulation in space tourism with the imperative to maintain U.S. leadership in the commercial space sector. The Vice President and others emphasized that GalaxyZ's reusable, low-cost spaceflight capabilities provide the U.S. a significant strategic advantage over China. Yet they also acknowledged the serious risks posed by incidents like this one, which could cause damage to critical infrastructure, including the International Space Station and adversarial space assets.

Concerns about over-regulation were voiced by the Secretary of Commerce and Heavy Reusable Launch Expert, who argued that an overly aggressive regulatory response could stifle innovation and undermine the competitive edge of U.S. companies in the international launch market. They pointed out that the commercial space sector has operated relatively safely thus far and that this incident, while tragic, should not lead to reactionary policies that could damage the industry. At the same time, there was a recognition that maintaining public trust and demonstrating responsible governance would require some regulatory recalibration. The Vice President proposed an investigation into the root cause of the malfunction, while other members suggested a review of current safety protocols to prevent future accidents, without unduly hindering the industry's growth.

International relations and diplomatic fallout formed another major point of tension in the discussion. The Secretary of State highlighted the delicate task of managing relationships with the countries whose citizens were killed in the disaster, including Japan, South Korea, Norway, Brazil, and Nigeria. Although the U.S. has strong relationships with these nations, the incident would require careful handling to prevent strains in diplomatic relations. The Secretary of Defense and the Director of National Intelligence, by contrast, raised concerns about adversaries exploiting the tragedy for propaganda or surveillance purposes. Both urged caution in messaging, recommending the U.S. project confidence in its ability to manage the crisis, while avoiding the appearance of complete control—given the inherent risks involved in debris management.

Debris mitigation and the potential threat of a Kessler Syndrome scenario were seen as critical issues, especially by the Director of National Intelligence and Director of the Office of Science and Technology Policy. With the growing satellite population and the importance of military constellations in low-Earth orbit, the evolving debris field posed both immediate and long-term risks to U.S. assets and global space operations. The Secretary of Defense saw this as an opportunity for the U.S. to take proactive leadership in debris management, leveraging its military capabilities to clear the field and prevent future collisions. There was consensus on the need for thorough tracking and real-time updates on the debris field, but the council wrestled with the question of how aggressively the U.S. should pursue debris-clearing operations in collaboration with commercial actors like GalaxyZ.

A central theme in the discussion was the political ramifications of the incident, particularly in relation to the broader U.S. space program. The Presidential Policy Advisor warned of significant fallout for the Human Landing System (HLS) program, which had already seen multiple delays. Any further setbacks could diminish U.S. leadership in the race to return to the Moon, especially with China's planned human landing on the horizon. Managing the public narrative was also crucial, with the White House Press

Secretary stressing the need for swift, coordinated messaging that reassured both domestic and international audiences. This included holding a press conference to convey condolences, take responsibility, and outline the U.S. response plan to mitigate the damage and prevent future accidents.

Ultimately, the council recognized that while the disaster demanded a serious response, it needed to strike a careful balance between fostering continued innovation in commercial spaceflight and implementing tighter safety regulations. Suggestions for an international space safety summit and a blue-ribbon safety panel of U.S. experts aimed to position the U.S. as a leader in both space safety and innovation.

## ASSESSMENT AND RECOMMENDATIONS

There is no limit to what can be accomplished in space and humans are only beginning to scratch the surface of the potential opportunities. Unfortunately, as technology advances there will be problems and, in this case, a tragic loss of life. However, as incidents occur, the U.S. must demonstrate both leadership and responsibility by taking immediate action to address the situation, mitigate damages, and establish robust frameworks for crisis management.

### *Immediate Actions (0–3 Months)*
### Executive Order: Commercial Spaceflight Stand-Down & Safety Review

- Narrow Suspension of purely orbital tourism flights for 60 days—exempt NASA, DoD, and cargo flights to keep Artemis/HLS on schedule.[266]

- Commercial Space Safety Review Board: Led by FAA and NASA, with participation from industry and NTSB, to release preliminary findings on the incident.

**Operation LEO Shield: Debris Mitigation & Tracking**
- Space Force CONOP: Rapid debris assessment and partial removal of largest fragments.[267]

- 24/7 Tracking & Alert Center (integrated with NASA and Commerce) providing near-real-time warnings to satellite operators.

- Diplomatic Data-Sharing: Offer continuous updates to foreign ministries whose citizens were lost or at risk from orbital hazards.

**Press & Diplomatic Engagement**
- High-Level Press Conference: Express condolences, outline steps to prevent future incidents, and underscore the inherent risks of spaceflight.[268]

- Secretary of State Outreach: Immediate calls to allied nations that lost citizens; invitation to observe or cooperate in the debris response.

*Short-Term Actions (3–12 Months)*
**Legislative Proposal: Commercial Space Safety Act of 2029**
- Accelerate End of FAA "Learning Period" and establish mandatory safety standards for orbital tourism.

- Certification for In-Space Refueling: Introduce docking and thruster-control requirements for crewed vehicles.

- Liability & Insurance Reforms: Increase coverage mandates for operators and set minimal abort-system standards.

**National Space Incident Response Center**
- Expanded Interagency Hub: Formalize a permanent incident response capability within the existing or newly chartered center, coordinating NASA, Space Force, FAA, and Intelligence Community for rapid crisis management.

- Mandatory Reporting: All U.S.-licensed operators must notify the center of major anomalies or close calls.

**Artemis/HLS Program Updates**
- Safety Protocol Integration: Incorporate new lessons learned (for example, redundant fueling systems, improved software tests) into HLS contracts.

- Secondary Provider: If budget permits, accelerate an alternative lander option or parallel refueling architecture to safeguard the Moon landing timeline.

**International Space Safety Summit**
- Commerce-Led Event with State Department support, inviting key allies and commercial stakeholders.

- Voluntary Guidelines for collision avoidance, fueling operations, and debris prevention—laying groundwork for future binding accords.

## *Long-Term Strategy (12+ Months)*
### Space Commerce & Security Act of 2030

- Commercial Space Safety Agency: Evolve FAA's Office of Commercial Space Transportation into a standalone entity overseeing human-rating, system audits, and licensing renewal.

- Debris Removal Incentives: Expand grants, tax credits, or procurement of commercial services to tackle large debris objects.

- Space Traffic Control System: Centralize orbital data under Commerce, with advanced collision-avoidance tools and transparent public dashboards.

### Institutionalizing National Security & Commercial Integration

- Permanent "Guardian Space" Operations: Establish a Space Force-led debris patrol/satellite-servicing capability in close coordination with NASA and private industry. [269]

- Cislunar Domain Awareness: Fund next-gen sensors for beyond-LEO tracking, protecting both military and civil exploration assets.[270]

### Sustaining U.S. Leadership & Innovation

- Public-Private Partnerships: Continuous R&D for debris mitigation, heavy-lift improvements, and safe fueling tech.

- Global Norms & Treaties: Translate summit guidelines into formalized international space safety agreements, ensuring

U.S. remains the principal architect of responsible space governance.

## RISKS AND METRICS FOR SUCCESS

In times of crisis, action is necessary, but it's equally important not to overreact and risk harming future space engagement. However, not acting decisively risks undermining the public trust in U.S. space leadership and overregulation could stifle commercial space innovation and space exploration. One major risk is creating more debris during debris removal operations. To positively ameliorate the catastrophe, success will be measured by swift and comprehensive debris cleanup, updated safety protocols, and renewed confidence in U.S. leadership.

## SCENARIO 16: LUNAR ODYSSEY STRANDED: IS RESCUE POSSIBLE?

"As civil organizations from the international community expand human presence further into the AOR [Area of Responsibility] in the name of peaceful exploration, the need to recover astronauts in distress will become more complex and far-reaching. Currently, U.S. Space Command is charged with human space-flight support and actively supports launch and recovery operations of U.S.-based crewed spaceflight. As humankind continues to travel further out from the most special place in the cosmos, the command will be ready to execute its responsibility for the human space-flight support mission"

–Lieutenant General John Shaw, former Deputy Commander of U.S. Space Command[271]

While the previous scenario explored the implications of a major disaster for orbital space tourism, the next scenario examines what happens when a private Lunar flyby goes wrong—and whether the U.S. is prepared to mount a deep-space rescue.

## SCENARIO RATIONALE

Until recently, the only crewed spaceflight was by NASA astronauts, with only NASA having significant on-orbit responsibilities. However, the U.S. has now begun its first orbital tourism flights by SpaceX with plans for Cislunar tourism. What happens if something goes wrong and they need rescue? Historically, the U.S. military has assisted in the rescue of American citizens in frontiers and difficult environments. Moreover DoDI 5100.10 specifies that it is a common function of the military services to "organize, train and equip forces to conduct . . . personnel recovery operations" and to "conduct the . . . functions across all domains, including . . . space."[272] We now have both a U.S. Space Command with operational responsibility to protect and defend U.S., allied, partnered, and commercial space capabilities[273] and a U.S. Space Force (USSF) with responsibilities to "protect American interests in space."[274] But at present they both have very little capability to respond. The inability of NASA, USSPACECOM, and the USSF to rescue American citizens would likely create significant public outcry.

There has been a significant increase in orbital space tourism, with plans by SpaceX for Cislunar cruises for tourism.[275] While the industry and Congress have good reasons for wanting to extend the regulatory learning period,[276] incidents such as the *Titan* submersible disaster[277] have brought home that such adventures can be dangerous and may require significant resources to be mobilized for attempted rescue. More recently, troubles with Boeing Starliner showed that commercial crewed systems can encounter problems.[278] Both the Aerospace Corporation[279] and RAND Corporation[280] have examined the gap in a space rescue capability, which has become a subject for public debate.[281] The USSF Space Futures Workshop and "State of the Space Industrial Base" report[282] both forecast a future need for space rescue. Even the former deputy commander of USSPACECOM, Gen. John Shaw, said that "as humankind continues to travel further out from the most special place in the cosmos, the command will be ready to execute its responsibility for the human space-flight support mission."[283] In connection with the anticipated increase in human activities in space, the community has begun to explore the issue. Beginning with the Air University Space Horizons Task Force in 2015, various DoD authors have explored the topic of "personnel recovery in space"[284]—most of the authors have been Air Force personnel, likely because the Air Force is specifically tasked to "conduct global personnel recovery operations including theater-wide combat and civil search and rescue"[285] and has an organizational and cultural familiarity with the mission.

Space search and rescue has received increased attention in the last two years. The Aerospace Corporation's Center for Policy and Strategy published The In-Space Rescue Capability Gap.[286] Subsequently RAND and Aerospace jointly held a Space Rescue Workshop.[287] The U.S. is not alone in addressing this gap. Various institutions have begun to explore the need for search and rescue or personnel recovery specific to the Moon and Cislunar space. The International Association for the Advancement of Space Safety (IAASS) and the Beijing Institute of Technology (BIT) held the first international Lunar search and rescue conference in Hainan (China).[288] Concurrently, an Air Force Institute of Technology–led interagency working group has even explored the need for Lunar search and rescue[289] and its lead author also explored the geopolitical implications of China winning the race to a space rescue capability.[290]

In the following scenario, we examine how an incident involving a circum-Lunar private spaceflight mission which encounters trouble might appear in the public consciousness and for the National Space Council, and how we might respond.

## *The Scenario*

### The Daily Astronomer | Front Page

*June 12, 2029*

In a harrowing event that has gripped the world, the *Lunar Odyssey*, a commercial spacecraft on a pioneering Lunar tourism mission, suffered a catastrophic collision during an in-space refueling operation. With the crew stranded in Lunar orbit, questions are mounting about the capabilities of the U.S. Space Force or NASA to conduct a rescue operation, and whether international assistance from other spacefaring nations will be necessary.

The accident has thrown a spotlight on the nascent space tourism industry, touted for its ambition to make Lunar travel accessible to private citizens. The *Lunar Odyssey* mission, the brainchild of a leading space tourism company, promised an unprecedented journey around the Moon for private citizens. It was a testament to human ambition and technological prowess, relying on a sequence of complex maneuvers including a critical in-space refueling to ensure the space-craft's return journey. However, the collision, occurring during docking with the refueling station, has precipitated a crisis, highlighting the precarious nature of space operations and the dire consequences of miscalculations in the unforgiving vacuum of space.

The commercial space industry, once buoyed by the allure of space exploration, is now confronting a moment of truth. The *Lunar Odyssey* mishap has prompted a reevaluation of the risks associated with space tourism and sparked a conversation about the collective responsibility of the global community to protect those who venture beyond our planet.

The ensuing emergency has prompted urgent deliberations over the potential roles of the U.S. Space Force and/or NASA in orchestrating a rescue mission. Established with the aim of safeguarding U.S. interests in space, the Space Force now finds itself at the center of an international policy conversation about its operational scope and the extent of its capabilities in responding to spaceflight crises.

As the world watches, the predicament of the *Lunar Odyssey* has catalyzed a broader discourse on the necessity for international collaboration in space. Analysts and the public alike are questioning whether the U.S. will seek the assistance of other spacefaring nations to aid in the recovery of the stranded tourists. This situation highlights not only the complexities of space rescue operations but also the imperative for a cooperative approach to space exploration and safety.

*Note: The President saw this article and is concerned. He has asked the Vice President to convene a National Space Council to provide the President with options and recommendations for immediate response and long-term programmatic response options.*

## SIMULATED NATIONAL SPACE COUNCIL
## DISCUSSION

At the heart of the discussion lay the fundamental question of the government's role in rescuing civilians in space. While the Vice President and the Secretary of Defense emphasized the importance of private-sector involvement, with companies like SpaceX and Blue Origin potentially capable of conducting the rescue, they also acknowledged the emotional nature of the situation and the public's expectation for the U.S. to lead a competent and effective response. This sentiment was echoed by others stressing the need for the government to demonstrate its willingness to help those in need, drawing parallels to the age-old tradition of mariners assisting one another at sea.

However, the question of financial responsibility for the rescue operation loomed large, with some pointing out the potential burden on taxpayers in footing the bill for rescuing billionaires. This concern was compounded by the lack of proper insurance for space tourism missions, highlighting the need for a more robust regulatory framework to ensure that private companies are adequately prepared to handle emergencies.

International collaboration emerged as a critical theme, with the Director of National Intelligence highlighting the geopolitical risks, particularly if China were to lead the rescue. The director advocated for a U.S.-led coalition, involving entities like NASA and the European Space Agency, to harness all available capabilities. This was echoed by the NASA Administrator, who proposed an *international rescue authority* to standardize fuel interfaces, docking adapters, and rescue protocols. The emphasis was on creating a framework that would ensure interoperability and effective responses to future space emergencies.

Public perception and emotional impact were recurrent concerns, with some members emphasizing the need for clear communication about the U.S. Space Force's readiness for search-and-rescue operations. Others underscored the importance of saving lives, particularly given that one of the stranded individuals was a significant donor to the President's campaign. One participant advocated for a private contractor–led approach, with governmental augmentation as a backup, suggesting that this crisis could serve as an opportunity to enhance NASA's capabilities and leadership in space rescue operations, however the private contractors were reticent to assume the additional risk to their crews and vehicles. The fact that the stranded spaceflight participants were livestreaming their plight to the public added significant pressure to the discussions.[291]

## ASSESSMENT AND RECOMMENDATIONS

What started as suborbital flights at or approaching the Karman line unsurprisingly blossomed into Moon expeditions for private astronauts or space tourists. An unfortunate private sector accident triggered the urgent need to determine who should be relied upon to conduct the complicated and costly rescue missions in space. The following recommendations provide specific, actionable steps to enhance U.S. space rescue capabilities while promoting commercial innovation and ensuring American leadership in space safety and emergency response.[292]

### *Immediate Term (Next 0–96 hours)*
**Private-Sector Rescue, Government Support**
- Contract SpaceX/Blue Origin for immediate rescue; NASA provides Deep Space Network and mission-planning support; Space Force offers tracking and security; State coordinates with Japan/UK.

- Politely decline Chinese offers unless no other option remains.

**Crisis Communications**
- Emphasize private sector leadership with U.S. government support; use "spaceflight participants" to avoid tourist stigma.

- Maintain public focus on international collaboration and rescue urgency, while underlining U.S. leadership.

**Joint Command Cell**
- Form a Rescue Task Force led by NASA, with Space Force, FAA, and commercial reps, to streamline decisions and coordinate technical solutions.

*Short Term (1–6 Months)*
**Executive Order: Space Transportation Safety and Response Framework**
- Office of Commercial Space Transportation Safety (OCSTS) within DOT/FAA to oversee licensing, rescue readiness, and coordination.

- Mandates for Commercial Operators:

- Standby rescue capability for crewed missions.

- Minimum $500M rescue insurance requirement.

- Standardized docking adapters for emergency operations.

**Legislative Proposal: Commercial Space Safety Act**

- Proof of Rescue Capability required for FAA license.

- Liability caps and tax incentives for companies developing rescue solutions.

- Joint Emergency Response Center staffed by FAA, NASA, and Space Force.

**Clarify Space Force vs. "Space Guard" Roles**

- Space Force remains focused on national security.

- Study establishing a "Space Guard" under the Coast Guard model for rescue, safety inspections, and hazard response.

*Long Term (6+ Months and Beyond)*
**Space Ports and Safety Act**

- Formally create a U.S. Space National Guard (with Coast Guard type authorities as well as Title 10 and 32) to manage search & rescue and Lunar port operations.

- Establish Lunar port zones with rescue shelters, fuel depots, and standardized interfaces.

**International Collaboration: Artemis Rescue Accords**

- Universal docking/refueling standards among signatories.

- Clearly defined cost-sharing and liability frameworks for multinational rescues.

- Create a global space rescue training center in Houston (or Huntsville).

**Commercial Incentives & Infrastructure**

- Tax credits and R&D grants for rescue-tech developers.

- Guaranteed government contracts for proven rescue capabilities.

- Expand emergency communication relay infrastructure and annual international rescue drills to refine protocols.

## RISKS AND METRICS FOR SUCCESS

Cultivating a swift response to the crisis is imperative, with the primary risk being mission failure due to technical challenges—a failed rescue attempt would be catastrophic both for the lives at stake and future space operations. Immediate success means demonstrating U.S. leadership through a safe rescue operation. Long-term success requires the U.S. to leverage this event to drive specific investments in rescue capabilities and lead the international community in adopting standardized safety protocols, emergency response procedures, and rescue mission requirements.

## SCENARIO 17: GLOBAL ANXIETY SWELLS AS APOPHIS PREPARES FOR CLOSE EARTH APPROACH IN 2029

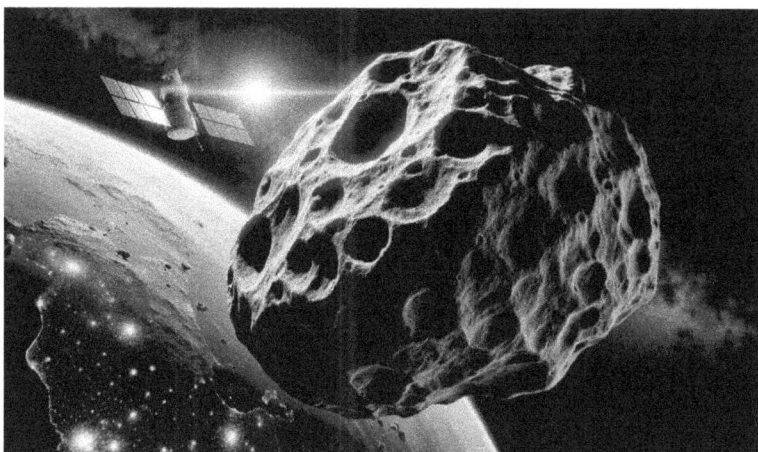

"Asteroids represented God's Intelligence Test for us: Fail and you go the way of the dinosaurs; pass and you get to occupy the solar system."

–John S Lewis, space scientist and prolific author

Rescue operations in deep space are only one challenge in an increasingly crowded and dangerous environment. But natural threats, like asteroids, pose an even greater existential risk. With Apophis set to make a historic close pass, the world must confront the reality of planetary defense—and the geopolitical tensions that come with it.

## SCENARIO RATIONALE

Recently we have had several close approaches of asteroids[293] that were detected quite late, as well as several bolide events,[294] one of which (Chelyabinsk 2013)[295] caused damage and injuries. However, we have not yet encountered a large potentially hazardous asteroid that passes close enough to be visible to the naked eye while also posing concerns for space traffic management. A sizable object such as Apophis,[296] which will pass very close to Earth—inside the geostationary orbit—on April 13, 2029, and be visible to the naked eye, is likely to raise concerns with the public and bring attention to whether the United States, NASA, or Space Force can deflect an asteroid for homeland and planetary defense.

*The Scenario*

**The Daily Astronomer | Front Page**
*April 7, 2029*

As the asteroid Apophis edges closer to its highly anticipated close encounter with Earth in 2029,[297] global anxiety is surging over the potential consequences of its proximity. Apophis, a 370-meter-wide asteroid, has been a subject of intense scrutiny since its discovery due to its size and the nearness of its approach, sparking fears reminiscent of the Chelyabinsk meteor[298] that exploded over Russia in 2013.

Countries around the world are concerned about the possibility of similar events occurring, given the extensive damage and injuries caused in Chelyabinsk, where over 1,500 people were injured by the blast. Leading the public awareness campaign is CosmoGuard, an international advocacy group.

CosmoGuard spokesmen, Dr. Irina Volkova, a planetary scientist who herself was injured in the Chelyabinsk event, stated, "The thought of something even larger looming so close to Earth is a sobering reminder of our vulnerability."

Further compounding the anxiety are worries about Apophis disrupting satellites as it crosses inside geostationary orbit, a band where many critical satellites reside. The potential for collisions is considered low but could have serious implications for satellite communication and weather forecasting services. "Even a small piece of debris traveling at such high speeds can disable a satellite, and the cascade effect from one collision could lead to more, crippling our orbital infrastructure," explained Dr. Mei Ling Tan of Singapore University's Orbital Sustainability Center.

These fears have intensified calls for enhanced planetary defense capabilities. Nations around the world are responding, with major powers like China, Russia, and India taking significant steps. China Planetary Defense Program[299] has recently announced the expansion of its space surveillance network, aiming to track Apophis's trajectory with unprecedented precision. Meanwhile, Russia has been conducting simulations to assess the asteroid's potential impact on its satellite systems and exploring strategies (including the use of a "peaceful nuclear explosion")[300] for deflection should the need arise. India is not far behind, having launched its own asteroid tracking system and collaborating internationally to research potential defense technologies. "The approach of Apophis must be a wake-up call for all of us," said Dr. Rajiv

Desai, head of India's Planetary Defense Coordination Office. "It underscores the urgent need for a comprehensive global strategy to address these celestial threats."

The increased focus on planetary defense has also led to calls for a united international response. Experts argue that a collaborative approach[301] would pool resources and expertise, increasing the chances of successfully averting a catastrophic event. "This is a global challenge that knows no borders. Only by working together can we hope to protect our planet," Dr. Desai emphasized.

As the April 13, 2029 close approach draws nearer, the world watches, waits, and prepares, hoping that when Apophis finally makes its close pass, Earth will be ready to face it head-on. The efforts made today could well determine our planet's resilience to the celestial dangers of tomorrow.

This week, America's newly re-elected president heads to give a speech at the United Nations. Sources have confirmed the UN Secretary General has asked him to speak on Planetary Defense, and even if he chooses not to, he's likely to be confronted by reporters who will greet him with a number of questions on the subject.

*NOTE: The President saw this article and is concerned. He has asked the Vice President to convene a National Space Council to provide the President with options and recommendations for immediate response and long-term programmatic response options.*

## SIMULATED NATIONAL SPACE COUNCIL DISCUSSION

At the heart of the discussion was the growing anxiety surrounding the asteroid's trajectory, which, though not expected to impact Earth, could disrupt global satellites and spark public fear. The Vice President and several council members emphasized the importance of conveying a calm, unified message to the public. The fear was that media sensationalism, driven by dramatic headlines, could trigger panic reminiscent of the COVID-19 supply chain disruptions, leading to stockpiling and market instability. Clear, coordinated messaging was seen as crucial to avoid such scenarios while reinforcing public confidence in government plans.

A key tension emerged around the issue of international leadership. While the U.S. must take charge in planetary defense efforts, there was concern that China and Russia, with their more aggressive approaches, might outpace the U.S. and seize the narrative. Russia's and China's talk of using nuclear deflection methods, under the guise of protecting Earth, was viewed with deep skepticism. The Secretary of Defense and Director of National Intelligence highlighted the dangers of allowing adversaries to push the boundaries of acceptable space activity, including the possible placement of nuclear weapons in orbit. This tension underscored the need for the U.S. to balance strong leadership with international cooperation, as highlighted by the Vice President's suggestion to work through the UN's Committee on the Peaceful Uses of Outer Space (COPUOS) to craft a global planetary defense framework.

Public perception and the possibility of mass panic were another major concern. The Secretary of Commerce and the White House Press Secretary both warned that fear-mongering around Apophis could lead to economic instability, with financial markets reacting to exaggerated threats of satellite damage or doomsday scenarios. The need for clear communication was echoed by multiple council members, including the NASA Administrator, who urged a science-based approach to inform the public that the likelihood of catastrophe was low. However, the concern remained that even the perception of risk—such as potential satellite collisions—could trigger real-world economic fallout. The council debated how to ensure transparency without inflaming public fears, advocating for a coordinated press conference that included NASA, the Department of Defense, and FEMA to reassure the public.

A particularly sensitive topic was the role of nuclear weapons in space. The Secretary of Defense and Director of National Intelligence both raised alarms about Russia and China potentially using Apophis as a pretext to place nuclear weapons in orbit under the banner of planetary defense.[302] While there was consensus that nuclear deflection should be avoided, the idea of preparing for a worst-case scenario lingered in the background. The NASA Administrator cautioned that a nuclear explosion in space could have devastating side effects, including electromagnetic pulses (EMPs) that would wreak havoc on satellite systems.[303] This created a delicate balance—how to deter adversaries from taking dangerous steps while avoiding the perception that the U.S. might need to resort to similar measures.[304] The Director of National Intelligence stressed the importance of getting ahead of the narrative by promoting non-nuclear deflection methods, such as the DART mission.

The council also explored opportunities to leverage current space technologies for planetary defense. The Heavy Reusable Launch Expert proposed examining how heavy-lift rockets could be used not only for asteroid deflection missions but also for placing large telescopes in space to enhance asteroid detection. This idea resonated with the council as a way for the U.S. to demonstrate leadership in planetary defense technology without resorting to nuclear options. Similarly, the Assistant to the President for Domestic Policy suggested establishing a Space Coast Guard to focus on space situational awareness, debris removal, and advanced warning systems. This would create jobs and position the U.S. at the forefront of planetary defense infrastructure.

## ASSESSMENT AND RECOMMENDATIONS

Hollywood has released several thrillers of asteroids hurtling toward Earth (*Armageddon*, *Deep Impact*, and more recently *Greenland*, among others) spurring people to band together and attempt a deflection or survive the aftermath. The reality is that at some point this fiction could become reality and while Apophis may not actually impact Earth it still has potential to wreak havoc by provoking public anxiety and disrupting satellites. The scenario certainly helps act as a forcing function to make the U.S. prepare for a prospective crisis.

### *Immediate Term (Next 0–30 Days)*
**Joint Crisis Communications Center**
- Establish a daily briefing hub co-led by NASA and FEMA, incorporating DoD and state-level coordination.

- Provide unified messaging to mitigate panic, dispel misinformation, and reassure the public about Apophis's low impact risk.

**Economic Stabilization Measures**
- Direct Treasury and Commerce to monitor and address any abrupt market reactions; deploy short-term credit or interest rate adjustments if needed.

- Activate the Defense Production Act for critical satellite infrastructure and create a Supply Chain Monitoring Task Force to preempt scarcity or hoarding.

**Emergency Space Coordination Cell**
- Have NASA and the U.S. Space Force operate a 24/7 cell focusing on immediate satellite protection, real-time debris tracking, and geostationary orbit adjustments.

- Coordinate with commercial satellite operators to reduce collision risks and maintain global communications.

**Operation Market Shield**
- Instruct the U.S. Space Force to secure vital national security and commercial satellites, plan orbital realignments if necessary, and ensure continuity for communications and data services.

*Short Term (1–6 Months)*
**Stand Up a U.S. Space Guard**[305]
- Create a dedicated entity (under DHS in peacetime, transitioning to DoD in crisis) to address debris removal, orbital emergencies, and potential asteroid deflection activities.

- Provide an initial operating budget, standard training protocols, and clear jurisdictional guidance.

**Economic and Workforce Development Programs**

- Introduce tax incentives and research grants for companies pursuing planetary defense technologies (for example, advanced propulsion, asteroid detection).

- Launch education and training initiatives in partnership with universities and community colleges to build specialized space and STEM career pathways.

**Quad Space Defense Initiative & COPUOS Collaboration**

- Strengthen ties with key allies (for example, India, Japan, Australia) to coordinate data sharing and develop nonnuclear deflection methods.[306]

- Lead a U.N. Committee on the Peaceful Uses of Outer Space (COPUOS) working group to prevent adversarial weaponization under the guise of asteroid defense.

**Space Security Act of 2029**

- Advocate a legislative package to establish the U.S. Space Guard,[307] offer industry incentives, and fund NASA/DoD planetary defense projects.

- Include mechanisms for education, workforce expansion, and mandated nonnuclear deflection research.

**Enhanced Space Domain Awareness**

- Expand the Space Fence network with new tracking stations and coordinate internationally on data-sharing protocols.

- Improve detection of near-Earth objects and address collision risks in geostationary and low Earth orbits.

## Long Term (6+ Months and Beyond)
### Permanent Planetary Defense Institutions

- Fully develop the U.S. Space Guard with an annual budget sufficient for rescue, debris mitigation, and planetary defense exercises.[308]

- Establish a dedicated NASA Planetary Defense Center to spearhead advanced deflection R&D and coordinate with allied agencies.

### Education & Workforce Pipeline

- Invest in degree programs and technical training grants for asteroid detection, orbital mechanics, and advanced materials engineering.

- Foster public-private partnerships that strengthen both national security and commercial space innovation.

### International Architecture & Norms

- Expand Quad-based coordination, integrate NATO space defense frameworks, and maintain a global tracking network under a permanent COPUOS subcommittee.

- Advance nonnuclear planetary defense principles to deter potential militarization efforts by adversaries.

### Comprehensive Space Security Act

- Enact long-range legislative authorization covering continuous R&D, recurring deflection test missions, workforce development, and deeper international collaboration.

- Sustain momentum for new technologies, stable funding, and integrated multinational response measures.

## RISKS AND METRICS FOR SUCCESS

If there are no plans in place to attempt an intercept for this or future asteroids, it could end human civilization—a true extinction event. In the case of Apophis, not adequately quelling public panic could set off a chain of events that triggers market volatility and causes supply chain issues. Moreover, if the U.S. does not show leadership adversaries could justify prepositioning nuclear weapons in space. Success would show stabile markets, safe satellite operations during and following Apophis approach, and legislation forming a U.S. Space Guard and internationally agreed upon nuclear/nonnuclear methods for asteroid deflection.

### *Postscript*

It is worth mentioning that since this scenario was designed and gamed, an asteroid, 2024YR4, 40-90 meters in size, has been discovered which has a 2% chance of striking Earth in 2032.[309] To mitigate the threat, China's State Administration of Science, Technology and Industry for National Defence (SASTIND) has begun recruiting "young loyal graduates focused on aerospace engineering, international cooperation and asteroid detection" for a "planetary defense force."[310] Moreover, the PRC has planned a DART[311]-like mission in 2027, targeting asteroid 2015 XF261 to test its deflection technology.[312]

U.S. space policy is generally enabling, but the DoD is not pulling its weight. Consistent with prior administrations, the Biden Space Priorities Framework stated, "The United States will lead, in cooperation with commercial industry and international allies and partners, in efforts to enhance warning of and mitigation against potential near-Earth object impacts"[313] and the Biden Strategic Framework for Space Diplomacy stated the U.S will "Pursue cooperative space situational awareness in civil, security, and comprehensive space dialogues. We will work with USG interagency partners and the U.S. commercial sector, as appropriate, to . . . Continue to support international consultation mechanisms for planetary defense" and "showcase U.S. transparency and engagement on coordination with other States on…planetary protection and defense."[314]

The most current 2020 National Space Policy (issued by Trump 1.0 and still in effect) also prioritizes planetary defense, stating, that appropriate agencies and federal laboratories should, "develop options, in collaboration with other agencies, and international partners, for planetary defense actions both on Earth and in space to mitigate the potential effects of a predicted near Earth object impact or trajectory" and tasks DoD specifically to "Provide to the Department of Commerce and other agencies, as necessary, SSA information that supports national security, civil, and human space flight activities, planetary defense from hazardous near-Earth objects."[315][316]

For nearly a decade, successive White House administrations have released interagency planetary defense strategies: in 2016,[317]

2018,[318] and 2023.[319] These documents tasked multiple agencies including NASA, DOD, USSPACECOM and U.S. Space Force. NASA has responded with its own Planetary Defense Strategy[320]—in fact NASA published its supporting strategy in the very same month as the national strategy was released.

The DoD has not published any similar document in the ensuing two years. This is quite astonishing, since these are specified taskings from the commander in chief—for example, the most recent strategy includes specified taskings to the DOD such as to identify offices and POCs, develop rapid response, reconnaissance options, develop, test, and implement NEO reconnaissance mission systems.[321] Equally astonishing, the October 15, 2024 update to DoD 3100.10 Space Policy incorporates the *National Cislunar Science & Technology Strategy* (dated November 2022 and barely mentions DoD), but failed to incorporate the *National Preparedness Strategy & Action Plan for Near-Earth Îbjåct Hazards and Planetary Defense[322]* even though it contained multiple specified tasks to DoD. It is also worth noting that very late in the Biden administration, the White House *National Cislunar Science & Technology Action Plan* tasked the Department of Defense as the *lead agency* to "Identify and prioritize research and development needed to support extension of U.S. SSA capabilities into Cislunar space, to include aiding planetary defense."[323] The DoD has not advanced material planetary defense capabilities since SDIO executed the 1994 Clementine 1 mission[324] (intended to visit asteroid 1620 Geographos[325]) and proposed the 1995 Clementine 2 mission (which would have tested kinetic impactors against 433 Eros and 4179 Toutatis[326]).[327] The U.S. Space Force has proposed no similar missions. This level of disengagement by the DoD should not be tolerated by the administration or the Congress.

## SCENARIO 18: CHINA'S ASTEROID RETURN: A SCIENTIFIC TRIUMPH OR PUBLIC SAFETY NIGHTMARE?

An Apophis close approach highlights the need for U.S. readiness and international coordination on planetary defense. But what happens when a major power, like China, takes matters into its own hands? The next scenario explores how Beijing's plan to return an asteroid to Earth is reshaping the debate over space safety, governance, and U.S. strategic interests.

### SCENARIO RATIONALE

China has articulated a long-term goal of mining asteroids by 2040.[328] Toward that end, China is pursuing heavy-lift rockets, advanced in-space nuclear power and propulsion, and asteroid reconnaissance and planetary defense missions. Distinct from its 2025 Tianwen-2 Asteroid Sample Return,[329] and its 2030 Asteroid Deflection mission,[330] China has discussed plans to send a mission in 2029 to capture an entire asteroid and *bring it back to Earth's surface in 2034.*[331] While any such returned asteroid would likely be small, the precedent and newsworthiness of returning an asteroid to Earth is likely to raise significant questions about safety and regulation, and renew interest in asteroid mining.

## *The Scenario*

### The Daily Astronomer | Front Page
*September 20, 2029*

The People's Republic of China (PRC) is on the verge of accomplishing an unprecedented space feat: the return of a small asteroid to Earth.[332] Launched in early 2029, the PRC announced today that its mission, known as Tian Kuang (Heavenly Miner), had succeeded in capturing its target with a huge bag, affixed the re-entry heat shield, and accomplishing its departure burn to return to Earth.

The mission has been celebrated by the PRC as a milestone in space exploration and a leap forward in the quest for resources beyond our planet with the potential to return tons of precious metals such as iron, nickel, copper, gold and platinum group metals.

The target asteroid, nicknamed "Xīng Guī" (Returning Star) is about 10 meters in diameter, and weighs between 1,047 and 2,618 metric tons. The asteroid is currently about 100 million km from Earth, with its anticipated re-entry into Earth's atmosphere in early 2034. If all goes as planned, the heat shield will slow the asteroid from 12.5 kilometers per second to 140 meters per second for its touchdown in north China's Inner Mongolia Autonomous Region.

Public concerns over safety and regulation have surged, along with a renewed interest in the potential of asteroid mining. "A controlled re-entry of a sample is one thing, but bringing back an entire asteroid presents a multitude of risks," stated Dr. Haruto Nakamura, a leading astrophysicist at Asia-Pacific Regional Space Agency Forum (APRSAF). "What measures are in place if the trajectory changes? The potential for impact could have disastrous consequences," said South Korean defense analyst Dr. Min-seok Choi. Public forums and social media are abuzz with debates over the international space treaties and the need for more robust regulatory frameworks. Many have called for greater transparency from the PRC and international bodies on the protocols established to ensure the safe handling of such missions. Simultaneously, the promise of asteroid mining has come back into the spotlight, reigniting discussions about the economic and environmental implications. The potential for extracting rare minerals and metals from asteroids could transform industries and economies but also raises ethical questions about space exploitation and environmental stewardship.

In the United States, the upcoming asteroid return has triggered reflections on its own space priorities. "Are we behind in the new space race for resources?" asked a recent op-ed in *The Washington Post*. The National Aeronautics and Space Administration (NASA) has assured the public that its efforts in space resource utilization are well underway, pointing to the Artemis missions and the ongoing Lunar Gateway project.

As the Tian Kuang mission approaches its next critical moment, the world holds its breath, not only for the safety implications but also for the glimpse into a future where space could become humanity's next frontier for mining. The outcome of this mission may very well set the stage for the next chapter in space exploration and international space policy.

"The safe return of Tian Kuang could herald a new age," said former ISRO chairman Dr. Patel adds optimistically. "But it must be approached with caution, respect for international concerns, and a collective commitment to the responsible use of space." As the countdown continues, all eyes turn skyward, waiting for history to be made—or, perhaps, for lessons to be learned.

The issue has become entangled with the annual U.S. defense authorization bill, which is about to go to Congress. House Intelligence Committee Chair, House Speaker, and House Resources Chair have been "concerned for weeks" about "the national security threat posed to the U.S. homeland, and U.S. satellites by anything less than perfectly controlled re-entry" and have sent an open letter the President asking about the competency of the USG to assure the safety of the Chinese operation, "how do we know this won't land on Washington D.C. or Houston?" and "what steps the U.S. is taking to keep pace on asteroid mining?"

*NOTE: The President saw this article and is concerned. He has asked the Vice President to convene a National Space Council to provide the President with options and recommendations for immediate response and long-term programmatic response options.*

## SIMULATED NATIONAL SPACE COUNCIL DISCUSSION

While China has framed the mission as a breakthrough in space exploration and resource utilization, U.S. officials expressed deep concerns about the safety, geopolitical implications, and potential national security risks of such an ambitious operation. With the asteroid's re-entry slated for 2034, the Council was divided between viewing the mission as an opportunity for technological competition and fearing the catastrophic consequences of failure.

The discussion revealed a stark contrast between the perceived capabilities of the U.S. and China in asteroid mining and space resource exploitation. The Secretary of Commerce and NASA Administrator expressed concern about the U.S. being on its "back foot" in this area, while the Heavy Reusable Launch Expert questioned China's ability to execute such a complex mission safely. This disparity in assessments pointed to a broader tension: how to accurately gauge and respond to China's space advancements without overreacting or underestimating their capabilities. There was clear anxiety that if the U.S. didn't act quickly, China could establish international norms and rules for space resource utilization, further undermining U.S. influence.

Concerns over China's ability to safely execute the asteroid re-entry added another layer of tension. The Secretary of State pointed out China's poor track record with uncontrolled rocket re-entries, warning that this asteroid mission could have even more dire consequences if mishandled. The Heavy Reusable Launch Expert went further, doubting China's technical capability to pull off such a complex operation, given their lack of experience with such large-scale space missions. These members argued that the U.S. must prepare for worst-case scenarios, including the potential need to intercept or divert the asteroid if China's plans fail. There was a prevailing sense that while the mission could be a scientific triumph, the global risks were simply too great to ignore.

Public perception and education emerged as critical factors, with several members highlighting the American public's lack of understanding about space resources and potential risks. The Assistant to the President for Domestic Policy and the Presidential Policy Advisor stressed the need to educate the public to garner support for more aggressive space policies. This revealed a tension between the urgency felt by the council and the time needed to build public understanding and support for major space initiatives.[333]

The council also grappled with governance issues, both domestically and internationally. The lack of a centralized U.S. authority for space policy decisions was contrasted with the need to establish international rules and standards for space resource utilization. The suggestion of creating a Space Czar role highlighted the tension between current decentralized decision-making and the perceived need for more unified leadership in space matters.

## ASSESSMENT AND RECOMMENDATIONS

China's propensity for uncontrolled reentry of their rockets makes controlled reentry of an asteroid a tough first for China to accomplish—not to mention there is nearly no room for error. While it's an impressive technology feat to capture an asteroid, returning it to

Earth at such a high speed is a challenging endeavor. Experts doubt China's ability to safely execute the mission by 2031–2034, but the possibility of success by 2035–2045 raises urgent questions about space governance, economic competition, and national security risks. This is particularly critical as the U.S. tries to shape norms for asteroid mining and space resource exploitation.[334]

## Immediate Term (0–6 Months)
### Executive Leadership and Coordination
- Appoint a National Space Security Advisor (Space Czar) jointly to the National Security Council (NSC) and National Space Council (NSpC) with authority over a cross-agency space security budget and a dedicated interagency staff drawn from NASA, DoD, and the Intelligence Community.[335]

### Defense and Space Monitoring
- Establish a Joint Interagency Task Force for Space Object Response and Tracking (JIATF-SORT), integrating commercial space tracking data, liaising with Indo-Pacific allies (Japan, Australia, South Korea), and providing real-time public trajectory updates.

- Accelerate U.S. Space Force tracking asset deployment in the Pacific region to monitor Tian Kuang's trajectory and potential future large object returns.

### Public Communication and Crisis Preparedness
- Launch a Space Security 2030 public education campaign focusing on U.S. space leadership, planetary defense, and space resource competition.

- Develop classified and unclassified asteroid risk assessments for congressional leaders and public messaging.

- Establish regular National Security Council briefings on space resource competition and a crisis communication strategy for potential asteroid reentry scenarios.

## *Short Term (6–18 Months)*
### Legislative and Policy Actions
- Introduce a legislative package (for example, Space Development Act of 2030) to expand NASA's asteroid redirect/intercept capabilities, provide tax incentives for commercial space tracking and debris removal, and establish a Space Resources Laboratory to advance asteroid mining technologies.

### International Space Governance and Security Agreements
- Propose a Responsible Space Resource Return Protocol at the United Nations Committee on the Peaceful Uses of Outer Space (COPUOS) to mandate transparency for all asteroid reentry missions.

- Establish bilateral space security dialogues with Japan, South Korea, and Australia to coordinate tracking, emergency response protocols, and planetary defense planning.

### Space Surveillance and Planetary Defense Capabilities
- Begin Phase 1 of an integrated operation (for example, Operation Skyshield or Operation Skywatch) to deploy early-warning tracking satellites, set up ground stations in

strategic locations (Alaska, Guam, Australia), and initiate development of interceptor or deflection technologies for planetary defense.

**Private-Sector and Commercial Space Acceleration**

- Expand public-private asteroid prospecting programs with SpaceX, Blue Origin, and Lockheed Martin, focusing on asteroid mining and in-space manufacturing.

- Direct NASA and DARPA to accelerate R&D on in-situ resource utilization (ISRU) technologies for space-based material processing.

- Remove regulatory barriers for private companies pursuing asteroid capture and space resource extraction.

*Long Term (18–36 Months and Beyond)*
**Infrastructure and Industrial Development**

- Establish a Space Resources Development Center as a public-private hub for asteroid processing and space manufacturing.

- Provide government-backed loans and research grants to companies investing in space mining and material extraction technologies.

- Develop a Space Commodities Exchange to commercialize and standardize the trade of off-world resources.

**Military Space Domain Awareness and Planetary Defense**

- Complete full deployment of Operation Skywatch, integrating planetary defense systems with the Space Force's Space Domain Awareness Command Center.

- Establish a dedicated planetary defense unit within the U.S. Space Force to monitor large-object threats and adversarial space operations.

- Deploy initial asteroid deflection capabilities using non-nuclear kinetic impactors and directed-energy technologies.

**International Space Leadership and Rulemaking**

- Expand Quad (U.S., Japan, Australia, India) space defense partnerships to strengthen multilateral planetary defense cooperation.

- Formalize an international planetary defense coalition, modeled after NORAD, for global early warning on asteroid threats.

- Integrate space resource utilization policies into the Artemis Accords, ensuring that U.S. and allied leadership sets the global rules for asteroid mining.

## RISKS AND METRICS FOR SUCCESS

The first mover advantage in a situation can be very impactful (no pun intended). Making the unilateral decision to capture an asteroid and attempt a highspeed controlled reentry could have a devastating effect if not conducted properly. The U.S. and the international community will need to decide whether it will risk trusting Chinese scientists or take matters into their own hands. Since a failed entry would be catastrophic, success would be a well-controlled reentry or deflection, internationally recognized protocols for asteroid capture, and a renewed focus on U.S. space mining and capability development.

## EMERGING THEMES AND CONCLUSION

Space safety and rescue capabilities are rapidly emerging as critical areas requiring immediate policy attention. While there are several agencies that handle space issues, like NASA, the Space Force, and FAA, they have overlapping jurisdictions making it difficult to understand who should be coordinating reactions to these complex space emergencies.

**Budgetary Impact and Legislation.** Like the previous chapter, the lack of preparedness necessitated the creation of new initiatives with substantial budgetary impact ($175M, $1.2B, $2.1B, $25B). Furthermore, the scenario responses resulted in new legislation (Commercial Space Safety Act of 2029, Space Security Act of 2029, Space Commerce & Security Act of 2030, Space Security and Development Act of 2030) and created new authorities or institutions (Space Czar, U.S. Space Guard, JIATF-SORT, Space Resources Development Center). This pattern of reactive funding and institution-building suggests a systematic underinvestment in space safety infrastructure.

**Institutional Readiness and Response Capabilities.** A consistent theme across scenarios is the lack of clear institutional responsibility and capability for space emergencies. Nearly all scenarios required capabilities the USSF neither possesses, nor have requirements or CONOPS for—large debris deorbit, Cislunar space domain awareness, search and rescue, real-time space traffic control, asteroid deflection. The USSF might respond that they have not been specifically authorized in law or tasked 5100.01[336] with debris clean-up, space rescue, or planetary defense. Congress might respond that 10 U.S. Code § 9081—The United States Space Force tasks the USSF to "protect the interests of the United States in space"[337] and that these are implied tasks they needn't spell out. The White House might point to a decade of national strategy tasks. The lack of preparedness on the part of DoD forced considerations of giving these space control missions to a separate agency and reducing the scope for the USSF.

**Public Communication and Perception Management.** The scenarios consistently highlight the critical importance of managing public perception and communication during space-related crises. Maintaining both public confidence as well as that of our allies was a key factor in crisis response. To be implemented properly it required a well-coordinated narrative across the government and with international partners, which outlined a clear action plan for the future.

If such actions are likely to be forced on the U.S. in the future, wouldn't it be better to begin preparations now to better prepare for foreseeable situations?

## CHAPTER 5 SUMMARY AND RECOMMENDATIONS

- **Introduction.** As Lunar industrialization accelerates, so too do the risks associated with expanding human activity in space. Beyond competition for resources, policymakers must now grapple with the realities of space safety, emergency response, and crisis management. From commercial spaceflight disasters to planetary defense, the ability to respond effectively will define U.S. leadership in the space domain.

- **Scenario 15: Tragedy in Orbit: Call for Tighter Regulations After Fatal Commercial Spaceflight Incident.** A catastrophic accident during a GalaxyZ orbital tourism mission results in 30 casualties and creates hazardous debris. The U.S. must balance safety reforms with commercial space competitiveness, address orbital debris risks, and manage diplomatic fallout. Recommendations include limited commercial flight stand-down, safety board review, and international space safety summit.

- **Scenario 16: Lunar Odyssey Stranded: Is Rescue Possible?** A private Lunar tourism mission suffers a critical failure, stranding its crew in Lunar orbit and exposing gaps in deep space rescue capabilities. Recommendations focus on developing a private-sector rescue framework with government support, establishing a Space Guard for emergency response, and creating international protocols for space rescue operations through the Artemis Accords.

- **Scenario 17: Global Anxiety Swells as Apophis Prepares for Close Earth Approach in 2029.** As a massive asteroid nears Earth, public fear and misinformation threaten market stability, while adversaries exploit the crisis. Key actions include forming a Joint Crisis Communications Center, establishing a U.S. Space Guard for planetary defense, and leading international efforts to develop non-nuclear deflection methods.

- **Scenario 18: China's Asteroid Return: A Scientific Triumph or Public Safety Nightmare?** China's attempt to return an asteroid to Earth raises concerns about safety and space resource competition. Recommendations include enhanced space surveillance, international safety protocols for asteroid reentry, and accelerated U.S. asteroid mining initiatives.

# CHAPTER 6

## *Conclusion—Securing America's Space Future*

### THE NEW SPACE RACE: HIGHER STAKES, GREATER URGENCY

"As an American, I don't want another Sputnik moment. From my standpoint, getting boots on the Moon and setting the groundwork for permanence on the Moon is of national importance and urgency."[338]

—David Limp, CEO of Blue Origin, May 29, 2025

The United States has been challenged to a new Cold War space race but with stakes far grander and consequential than just national prestige. After Apollo, the Strategic Defense Initiative (SDI), and the fall of the Soviet Union, the pace of progress in space was glacial until about 2015. But today, the dwindling cost of space access (due to commercial, reusable rockets), falling cost of space hardware, and access to the means to pursue in-space resources and

239

in-space manufacturing, means that America and its allies stand at the threshold of a transformative era where space will rapidly evolve from the great unknown to a domain dominated by innovation and economic development. Accessing space is no longer optional or merely about "flags and footprints"—it is fundamental to national and economic security, critical infrastructure, and strategic interests. The new imperative is for the United States to remain the leader in space for the remaining decades of the twenty-first century, it must dominate in-space industrialization.

The People's Republic of China clearly understands the strategic value of space industrial development, and has developed a coherent, long-term strategy to 2045 that unifies civil, military, and commercial objectives with the explicit goal of becoming the world's premier space and terrestrial power. In contrast, the United States lacks a comprehensive vision and offers only fragmented responses to this challenge. Though America enjoys certain market and technological advantages, these gains are not coherently deployed to dominate today's strategic challenge. The eighteen scenarios examined in this project demonstrate a sobering reality: if the U.S. continues to pursue reactive space policies, the country is already "late to need"—any remedial actions taken after these events occur will prove both insufficient and prohibitively costly to American interests and its leadership of the international order.

## CRITICAL FINDINGS FROM SCENARIO ANALYSES

While some of the forecasted space events contained in this work may appear to be years—if not decades—away, many can occur as soon as tomorrow. Time is of the essence to prepare for these challenges. After debriefing the wargaming participants and analyzing their responses and plans, several critical insights emerged.

First, there is a profound institutional readiness gap. Despite numerous organizations handling different aspects of U.S. space policy, there is a troubling lack of clear authorities, capabilities, and contingency plans for emerging threats and challenges. Even the National Space Council that was simulated for the exercises in this book lacks permanence (and has routinely been dissolved under disinterested administrations) nor does it have a crisis management structure. In every scenario, the U.S. response was entirely reactive, highlighting a broader pattern: U.S. space policy has consistently been reactive rather than anticipatory, leaving the nation perpetually in catch-up mode.

One reason for this shortfall may be the absence of a compelling strategic narrative to mobilize public support. There is a glaring strategic communication deficit. While industrial thought leaders have proposed a national vision to become multi-planetary or settle and industrialize space to preserve Earth, the nation itself lacks a unified and organizing vision for space—at least for now. A scattershot curiosity, glory, or prestige-based space program is inadequate and ill-matched to the need. The U.S. must clearly convey the economic and security stakes of space to galvanize public interest and support. Once a vision is established, a more integrated approach between the U.S. government and the private sector will be essential. China's civil-military fusion strategy blurs the lines between commercial and government efforts; the U.S. will need a similar, though not identical, approach to harness the full potential of its private sector.

Finally, the strategic implications of achieving space solar and nuclear power, Lunar industrialization, and efficient resource extraction are profound and demand faster U.S. innovation to keep pace with China's ambitious timeline.

## WHY CURRENT APPROACHES FALL SHORT

We have meticulously drafted crisis response frameworks—in coordination with our simulated National Space Council experts—to provide policymakers with plausible and actionable initial responses to the scenarios. However, *upon examination, these plans are clearly inadequate to meet the challenge.* The U.S. must take a step back and reflect on why its space future appears dimmer compared to China's. Why is America falling short in space? One significant issue is that, in the absence of an enduring societal long-term strategic vision or guiding mandate for broader space development, U.S. policy falls victim to four-year presidential policy cycles that are less than ideal for long-term strategic planning. Both the lack of an enduring societal vision and long-term planning has been a fundamental obstacle to robust action.  Equally problematic is NASA's limited mandate. NASA's self-conception of its own mission does not include industrialization or economic development—two essential pillars of a prosperous space future. While NASA may be the face of the American space program, it is far from the only agency handling space matters. The scenarios repeatedly highlighted the overlapping jurisdictions and complete lack of jurisdiction between NASA, Space Force, FAA, and Commerce—this murkiness created confusion during crisis response in every scenario. America suffers from fragmented authority in space governance. With no clear mandate or authority for space economic development, no agency owns this portfolio or takes action to pursue it. As a result, all industrial and economic space development simply falls through the cracks, as neither the Department of Commerce nor the Department of Transportation have clear authority to pursue these objectives, and Congress lacks meaningful mechanisms (such as dedicated budget lines for ISRU and ISAM) to track progress on the development of critical capabilities.

Policymakers also seem to be suffering from a kind of *anti-bold conditioning*. During the scenarios, both the wargame designers and participants were constrained by a political mindset that assumed incremental changes were the only viable option. This paralysis of innovative thought was not confined to one party; both Republican and Democratic participants struggled to think outside the box. Independent reviewers questioned why bolder moves were not considered—though it is worth noting that these wargames occurred prior to the second Trump administration taking office. Since then, Trump administration 2.0 has taken significantly bolder actions, as evidenced by the potentially game-changing presidential action calling for a *Golden Dome for America*. This directive requests an implementation plan for the "development and deployment of proliferated space-based interceptors"—a project that has long been viewed as too destabilizing.[339] If this is the new norm, the responses observed in the scenarios seem tepid by comparison.

Along those same lines, that *anti-bold conditioning* extended to international law, where the Outer Space Treaty (OST) was assumed to be a permanent feature. We did not examine a scenario where a major space power withdrew from the OST, but that is likely due to conditioning rather than the inherent advantages of the OST. Certainly, multiple scenarios we explored stressed the intent of the OST or sought to circumvent it. Nations do leave treaties. Saudi Arabia recently withdrew from the Moon Agreement (in line with the U.S. position), and the second Trump Administration has shown a willingness to withdraw from international organizations and treaties such as the World Health Organization (WHO) and

Paris Climate Accords.[340] Even domestically, former senior officials have stated that we should not be afraid to ask whether it might be to the U.S. advantage to withdraw from the Outer Space Treaty to replace it with something better and more forward looking?[341] Certainly—within or superseding—the OST, the scenarios show a clear need for the U.S. to develop a future-oriented framework, possibly modeled after the Bretton Woods system but in space, which could better enable industrial space dominance by America and its allies.

Ultimately, there is an insufficient scale of investment in the right space projects to secure American economic and security dominance in the space domain. *The most consequential space industrial development lines of effort—ISAM, ISRU, and advanced space power—are embarrassingly underfunded and do not even have dedicated budgetary lines, reflecting a fundamental failure to prioritize the critical capabilities for space dominance.*

## SIX CRITICAL INVESTMENT PRIORITIES FOR SPACE DOMINANCE

If America is in a truly new era and able to make unorthodox choices, what might a bold investment agenda look like? How should the U.S. prioritize space investments?

Throughout the various scenarios players outlined significant spending on the order of several billions of dollars. If we are willing to spend that much in a crisis, this fact suggests that money may be better spent for proactive strategic campaigning. While the numbers below are not meant to be a definitive investment budget, they provide a starting point to challenge and overcome anti-bold thinking in the areas where the U.S. is significantly under invested

244

and should provide new avenues for debate about what the actual numbers should be.

When viewed through a historical lens, the proposed space investment represents a proportionate response to both the strategic challenges and economic opportunities of the current era—more modest than the Apollo mobilization but commensurate with other successful national technology initiatives that secured American leadership during periods of intense great power competition.

Let's examine how $335-620 billion spent over 10 years might advance U.S. space dominance. While the figures may seem eye-popping to our anti-bold conditioning, all combined they are only an increase of $33.5-$62B (average) (less than 0.5-1 percent of current federal expenditures) in overall annual space spending. In many ways these figures are not even close to past national efforts. We should remember that at the peak of the last great power competition, in the latter Cold War and the Reagan build-up (circa1987), total space spending was 2.6 percent of the federal budget.[342] We are now in a new great power competition, and 2.6% of 2024 federal expenditures ($6.752 T) would be $175.552 B. In 2024, combined civil (NASA $24.8B) and military (USSF $29B) is only about $55B, leaving $121.752 billion merely to achieve Reagan build-up levels. The suggested range for annual increase still does not exceed past national efforts—the top of our suggested range of $117B (approximately 1.7 percent of federal expenditure) is still lower than Reagan era. To provide even further perspective, the Reagan peak was also tiny in comparison to the peak of Apollo spending when NASA alone was consuming 4.41 percent of the federal budget.

Our funding estimates in the accompanying chart represent a comprehensive analysis of the capabilities required to secure U.S.

space dominance over the next decade. It is nearly impossible to provide exact values for expenditures, but these best guess ranges are derived from scenario-informed cost assessments. Throughout the book in each scenario response framework section there are footnotes benchmarking cost estimates from existing and historical space programs, and expert evaluations of technological development trajectories. The wide ranges reflect varying levels of ambition and acknowledge the inherent uncertainties in developing new technologies. For example, Space Security & Domain Awareness estimates draw from known costs of programs like the Space-Based Infrared System (SBIRS), while Lunar Industrial Base costs are projected from current NASA ISRU research initiatives scaled to industrial capacity. These investments would be distributed across multiple agencies—including DoD, NASA, Commerce, and Energy—and structured to leverage private sector co-investment through public-private partnerships, particularly in areas like space-based power and Lunar resource utilization.

The following chart outlines the categories of expenditure, the amount spent over ten years, the objective accomplishments, and the risks of inaction.

| Spending Category | 10-Year Funding | Key Objectives | Risk of Inaction |
|---|---|---|---|
| Lunar Industrial Base & Resource Utilization | $75-140B | Establish ISRU technologies, Lunar manufacturing capabilities, infrastructure at strategic locations, commercial partnerships, and economic zones at the Peaks of Eternal Light. | Permanent ceding of critical resources and strategic positions to China; loss of trillion-dollar economic opportunities; inability to sustain long-term space operations. (America may not dominate the industries of the future.) |
| Space-Based Power & Advanced Propulsion | $65-120B | Develop scalable space solar power from 1MW to GW levels, nuclear power for space, advanced propulsion, Lunar power grid, and energy transmission technologies. | Dependence on Chinese energy systems; loss of mobility advantage in Cislunar space; inability to power large-scale operations; China leveraging energy dominance for global influence. (America may cease to be the energy superpower and have to buy energy from a rival state.) |
| Space Security & Domain Awareness Space Security & Domain Awareness | $95-170B | Develop GEO surveillance architecture, counter-ASAT capabilities, space traffic management, rapid reconstitution systems, and Cislunar monitoring networks. | Loss of space superiority to China; vulnerable critical infrastructure; inability to detect and respond to threats; compromised military effectiveness. |
| Space Safety & Rescue Capabilities | $40-75B | Create Space Guard functions, deploy debris remediation systems, establish rescue protocols and vehicles, implement space traffic control, and develop planetary defense capabilities. | Catastrophic loss of human life—both American and international—in space incidents; damage to U.S. credibility; hazardous orbital environment; inability to respond to accidents; abandonment of stranded astronauts. (American citizens will be less safe in space.) |

| Spending Category | 10-Year Funding | Key Objectives | Risk of Inaction |
|---|---|---|---|
| **Space Governance & Commercial Enablement** | $35-65B | Streamline licensing and regulatory systems, establish Space Development Bank, foster public-private partnerships, develop international frameworks, and create standards for responsible space activities. | Private capital flows to more supportive jurisdictions; China setting unfavorable space governance norms; regulatory uncertainty hampering investment; loss of U.S. leadership in space rule-setting. |
| **Space Workforce & Innovation Pipeline** | $25-50B | Implement STEM education for space, fund university research, create manufacturing apprenticeships, establish innovation centers, and develop technology transfer programs. | Critical skills shortages; innovation advantage shifting to China; inability to staff growing space sector; reduced technological competitiveness; dependency on foreign talent. (Fewer jobs for American taxpayers.) |

Regarding implementation, the funding should be pursued using a phased approach. During the first three years, it will be important to focus on critical security capabilities and funding the more transformational technologies. During the following four years, funding should be spent scaling the energy systems and expanding Lunar industrialization. Finally, in the remaining three years there should be a focus on completing the integrated architecture.

It will take time and discipline to stay the course and fulfill the investment strategy to ensure U.S. space primacy—which is admittedly difficult because of austerity and ensuring the U.S. public remains onboard. It may be worthwhile to structure investments with prioritization to ensure some "quick wins" to keep the public engaged and add some momentum. Within the first 24 months, the U.S. could deploy the first phase of a Cislunar Domain Awareness Network using existing commercial capabilities and with accelerated government launches establish an Emergency Space Rescue Protocol with a modest but functional rescue capability based on modified Dragon or Starliner vehicles. These visible accomplishments would demonstrate commitment, continue public support, and create early competitive advantages while the larger strategic initiatives mature.

## JUSTIFYING STRATEGIC SPACE INVESTMENTS AMID FISCAL CONSTRAINTS

In this new era of fiscal austerity where the second Trump administration has emphasized eliminating fraud and waste, it will still be imperative to make wise investments that will benefit the country in the future. Though spending several billions of additional dollars on space may seem potentially wasteful, it's important to note that the space economy is poised to grow significantly—and if the U.S. invests properly the nation can reap the rewards.

Space provides a strategic investment opportunity. The Apollo program serves as a prime example regarding the rates of return on space investment—for every dollar spent during that time the return in economic impact was as high as 15:1, because the space venture created new technologies and industries.[343] In addition to the economic benefits, there are additional national security implications. Like the Soviet Union in the Cold War, China's coordinated strategy carries with it potentially significant advantages that will challenge U.S. leadership. The U.S., for better or worse, has become completely reliant on its indigenous space infrastructure for all parts of daily life—including navigation, communication, intelligence collection, and military affairs. The high cost of losing space superiority would be a small fraction of the price to pay the proposed upfront costs that could better protect space assets from nefarious actors or naturally occurring threats. Finally, investing in space resource development could allow reduced resource competition on Earth, and lower or eliminate entirely the nation's dependence on China for strategic minerals—this would support both economic and national security initiatives.

## IMPLEMENTATION STRATEGY: MOVING FROM CONCEPT TO REALITY

America will need to undergo significant institutional reform to guide this bold investment strategy. On the civilian side, a cabinet-level Department of Space with a broad mandate that includes industrial development, market promotion, as well as licensing and exploration could provide long-term and coherent focus. On the military side, Space Force should be elevated outside of the Air Force to become a separate military department with its own service secretary, and a broad mandate that specifically includes defense of commerce and U.S. Coast Guard-like authorities including planetary defense. National level guidance oversight could also be advanced by creating an interagency planning and coordination group within U.S. Space Command to improve long-term multi-agency strategic foresight and daily operational coordination, including for multi-agency integrated strategic campaign planning[344] and execution for peacetime competition to achieve national objectives.[345] These adjustments will help the U.S. develop clear crisis response protocols and contingency plans that span civilian, commercial, and military domains. Appendix B contains a draft crisis communications plan that can be used in the event any of these scenarios come to fruition before this proposed reorganization is enacted.

However, strategic realignment on an organizational chart is not enough to move the needle on space priorities. The U.S. government must build substantial political support to drive meaningful change. To secure public buy-in, policymakers must clearly articulate why space matters—not just in abstract terms, but in ways that directly impact jobs, economic growth, and national security. The push for space industrialization must feel tangible, with clear answers to the question: How does space superiority and development improve life for the U.S. electorate and our international partners? The U.S. must craft a compelling national space narrative that fosters bipartisan support and mobilizes public enthusiasm to compete with China.

That narrative should be to become the dominant space industrial power enabling the economic development and settlement of space with a uniformed service to protect and enable that vast commerce. It should encompass a vision for energy dominance, vigilance dominance, industrial dominance, providing prosperity and security for current and future Americans.

Once public support is secured, the next challenge is to mobilize the necessary resources. Given the substantial funding requirements and technical sophistication involved, the government cannot accomplish this transformation alone. The U.S. will need to leverage robust public-private partnerships to accelerate space advancement. Developing methods to make financing available through innovative mechanisms—including space development bonds, development corporations, and targeted tax incentives—will be essential. Most importantly, there will need to be strict accountability for execution. Progress must be measured against clear, metrics-based milestones—ensuring that key developments outpace China's strategic timelines and maintain American primacy in space.

## LEARNING FROM HISTORY, LOOKING TO THE FUTURE

Living through the potential futures outlined in these scenarios paints a bleak picture—one of crisis, lost opportunity, and strategic disadvantage. The scale of investment required to prevent such an outcome may seem overwhelming, but history (as well as the scenario responses) show that when faced with substantial adversity, America reacts and—with proper intensity—overcomes. The U.S. was forced to respond to major challenges during the last century and it mobilized resources and talent and rose to the occasion— look no further than the Manhattan Project or the Apollo Program.

This new era of space activity is more than a competition; it is an opportunity to shape the future of humanity beyond Earth and to extend the values of freedom, innovation, and prosperity to the stars as well as at home. The choice before us is stark: proactive leadership may enable centuries of American power with untold prosperity and promise, while reactive and muddled crisis management may doom the nation to becoming hostage to the whims of a foreign power and surrendering the largest canvas for human activity and the liberty of future generations to autocracy. However, our window to act is closing. Every moment of delay increases both the difficulty and cost of catching up should one of these scenarios become reality.

What's ultimately at stake is America's legacy as the leading spacefaring nation for generations to come. The investments and institutional changes outlined here, while substantial, are nothing compared to the economic, strategic, and moral costs of ceding leadership in humanity's greatest frontier. The correct path forward is clear—Congress and the Administration must act decisively now to secure America's space future. Congress should lead by establishing specific mandates and funded initiatives for Lunar industrial development, advanced space power and propulsion, space safety and rescue, and workforce development. The administration should lead with a vision and proposed budget of how to implement those initiatives. The U.S. should begin investing now to ensure a commanding position at the 10-year (2035) timeframe, with phased 10-year plan, starting from an initial investment of ~$30B new dollars gradually rising over five years to peak around $62B. With sufficient leadership and resourcing, the U.S. can ensure America not only remains in a secure future, but a bright and prosperous future with America remains the global engine for growth in the most exciting and productive industries of the future.

## CHAPTER 6 SUMMARY AND RECOMMENDATIONS

- **The New Space Race: Higher Stakes, Greater Urgency.** The United States faces a new space race where the imperative is to dominate in-space industrialization, with higher stakes than mere national prestige due to falling costs of access and the potential for transformative development.

- **Critical Findings from Scenario Analyses.** Analyses reveal a profound institutional readiness gap, absence of a compelling strategic narrative, and need for integrated government-private sector approach to match China's civil-military fusion strategy.

- **Why Current Approaches Fall Short.** U.S. space policy suffers from four-year presidential cycles, NASA's limited mandate excluding industrialization, fragmented authority across agencies, and insufficient investment in critical space capabilities.

- **Six Critical Investment Priorities for Space Dominance.** Strategic investments totaling $335-620 billion over 10 years should focus on Lunar industrial base, space-based power, space security, space safety, space governance, and workforce development. Even at the top range of $62B annually, this funding remains below Reagan-era space spending as a percentage of the federal budget (1.7 percent vs 2.6 percent), yet is critical to prevent China from capturing strategic positions, energy systems, and trillion-dollar economic opportunities.

- **Justifying Strategic Space Investments Amid Fiscal Constraints.** Space investments offer potential 15:1 returns (based on Apollo program data), critical national security benefits, and reduced resource dependence on China for strategic minerals.

- **Implementation Strategy: Moving from Concept to Reality.** Success requires institutional reform including a cabinet-level Department of Space, elevation of Space Force, public buy-in through compelling narratives, and robust public-private partnerships.

- **Learning from History, Looking to the Future.** America's window to act is closing; delay increases both difficulty and cost of catching up, with the nation's space leadership legacy at stake for generations to come.

# APPENDIX A

## *National Space Council Simulation Participants*

**WORKSHOP 1 PARTICIPANTS | FEBRUARY 6, 2024**

| NAME | BRIEF BIO |
|---|---|
| Dr. Greg Autry | Chair of the Safety Working Group on the Commercial Space Transportation Advisory Committee (COMSTAC) at the Federal Aviation Administration. Nominated by the President to serve as the Chief Financial Officer at NASA (due to circumstances of 2020, the U.S. Senate never held a final confirmation vote on the CFO nomination) |
| Mr. Bill Bruner | CEO of New Frontier Aerospace, a space technology development and consulting company; former NASA Assistant Administrator for Legislative and Intergovernmental Affairs |
| Dr. Namrata Goswami | Professor at the Thunderbird School of Global Management at Arizona State University and the Joint Special Forces University; a consultant for Space Fund Intelligence; co-author of the book |
| Dr. Bhavya Lal | Former NASA Associate Administrator for Technology, Policy, and Strategy; Former NASA Chief Technologist (Acting); Former NASA Chief of Staff (Acting) |

| Mr. Douglas Loverro | President of Loverro Consulting and former Deputy Assistant Secretary of Defense for Space Policy |
| --- | --- |
| Dr. John C Mankins | President of Artemis Innovation Management Solutions LLC; former NASA Manager of Exploration Systems Research and Technology within the Exploration Systems Mission Directorate |
| Dr. Kevin Pollpeter | Senior Research Scientist, CNA; author of |
| Mr. Michael Sinclair | Captain, U.S. Coast Guard (retired); Adjunct Professor at George Washington University School of Law; Nonresident Senior Fellow for Space Security in the Forward Defense program of the Atlantic Council's Scowcroft Center for National Security |
| Mr. Joseph Rouge | Former Defense Intelligence Senior Executive Service; former Deputy Director of Intelligence, Surveillance and Reconnaissance, Headquarters U.S. Space Force |
| Mr. Christopher Stone | Senior Fellow for Space Deterrence, National Institute for Deterrence Studies and former Special Assistant to the Deputy Assistant Secretary of Defense for Space Policy |
| Ms. Leonor Tomero | Principal at LeoSpace LLC; former Deputy Assistant Secretary of Defense for Nuclear and Missile Defense Policy in the Office of the Secretary of Defense |
| Ms. Laura Winter | Editor and Host of The DownLink Podcast, an award-winning Defense & Aerospace Report production |

# WORKSHOP 2 PARTICIPANTS | MARCH 6, 2024

| NAME | BRIEF BIO |
|---|---|
| Mr. Marc Berkowitz | Independent consultant and advisor to the U.S. government and private-sector clients; former Assistant Deputy to the Under Secretary of Defense for Space Policy; former Vice President for Strategic Planning at Lockheed Martin Corporation |
| Mr. Robert Brose | Participated as an independent consultant with none of his comments reflecting anything other than personal views; currently serves as the Lead for Special Projects in the U.S. Space Force, Intelligence, Surveillance, and Reconnaissance Directorate |
| Mr. Bill Bruner | CEO of New Frontier Aerospace, a space technology development and consulting company; former NASA Assistant Administrator for Legislative and Intergovernmental Affairs |
| Ms. Kara Cunzeman | Founder and Director of Strategic Foresight, Center for Space Policy & Strategy at Aerospace Corporation; co-founder and co-chair of the Federal Foresight Advocacy Alliance; Director of the U.S. Hub for Teach the Future; engineer and guest instructor |
| Ms. Sandra Erwin | National security reporter on military space programs, policy, technology, and other related topics; senior journalist at |
| Dr. Philip Metzger | Planetary physicist and engineer at the University of Central Florida and Florida Space Institute; co-founder of NASA's Kennedy Space Center Swamp Works team |
| Dr. George Pullen | Chief economist at MilkyWayEconomy; senior economist at the U.S. Commodity Futures Trading Commission; adjunct professor at Columbia University, Eisenhower War College, Johns Hopkins University, and UNH Franklin Pierce School of Law |
| Hon. Manisha Singh | Former Assistant Secretary of State for Economic and Business Affairs; former Acting Under Secretary of State for Economic Growth, Energy, and the Environment |

| Mr. Courtney Stadd | Founder and former President of Capitol Alliance Solutions, LLC; former Chief of Staff and White House Liaison for NASA; Senior Director of the White House National Space Council; former Director of the Office of Commercial Space Transportation |
|---|---|
| Mr. Rick Tumlinson | Founder of SpaceFund, the EarthLight Foundation, and the Permission to Dream Project; co-founder of Deep Space Industries, Orbital Outfitters, the New Worlds Institute, the Space Frontier Foundation, the Texas Space Alliance, LunaCorp, and MirCorp |
| Hon. Robert Walker | Founder and CEO of MoonWalker Associates; advisor to the White House, the U.S. Air Force, the National Space Council, NASA, the Department of Energy, and the Department of Commerce; former Presidential Space Policy Advisor; former appointee to the President's Commission on the Implementation of the U.S. Space Exploration Policy; former congressman |
| Dr. Larry Wortzel | Senior Fellow in Asian Security at the American Foreign Policy Council; former director of the Strategic Studies Institute at the U.S. Army War College; former commissioner on and chairman of the U.S.-China Economic and Security Review Commission; retired U.S. Army colonel |

# WORKSHOP 3 PARTICIPANTS | APRIL 23, 2024

| NAME | BRIEF BIO |
|---|---|
| Mr. Bill Bruner | CEO of New Frontier Aerospace, a space technology development and consulting company; former NASA Assistant Administrator for Legislative and Intergovernmental Affairs |
| Ms. Rose Croshier | International Relations Specialist within the Office of Space Commerce specializing in Africa, South America, India, and parts of Europe |
| Dr. Namrata Goswami | Professor at the Thunderbird School of Global Management at Arizona State University and the Joint Special Forces University; a consultant for Space Fund Intelligence; co-author of the book |
| Dr. David Hardy | President of Dhardyconsulting LLC; Former Associate Deputy Under Secretary of the Air Force for Space; and Deputy Director for the Principal Department of Defense Space Advisor Staff |
| Christopher Hearsey | Founder and CEO of OSA Consulting; space industry consultant at Aegis Trade Law |
| Mr. Gary Henry | Consultant at IINNVision; former Commander of the Launch and Space Systems wing at the Space and Missile Systems Center; former Senior Director of Space Defense & Intelligence at Boeing; and former Senior Director of National Security Space Solutions at SpaceX |
| Dr. Phillip Karber | President of the Potomac Foundation and professor at Georgetown University; member, U.S. Army Science Advisory Board; former strategy adviser to former U.S. Secretary of Defense Caspar Weinberger |
| Mr. Nate Kitzke | Officer in the U.S. Air Force, currently serving as Director of Congressional and Interagency Affairs in the United States Transportation Command |
| Dr. Kevin O'Connell | Founder and CEO at Space Economy Rising; former Director of the Office of Space Commerce in the U.S. Department of Commerce |

| Mr. Bruce Pittman | Associate Fellow at the American Institute of Aeronautics and Astronautics; contractor for NASA's Ames Research Center in Silicon Valley, serving as Chief System Engineer in the NASA Space Portal Office |
| Ms. Lee Steinke | Chief Operating Officer at CisLunar Industries, which provides and processes critical materials and hardware needed for space exploration to government agencies and private enterprises |
| Ms. Laura J. Winter | Editor and host of *The DownLink Podcast*, an award-winning Defense & Aerospace Report production |

# APPENDIX B

## *Crisis Communication Plan*

### CRISIS COMMUNICATION PLAN FOR SPACE SCENARIOS[346]

#### *1. Introduction and Scope*

**Objective:**

To provide a framework for rapid and effective crisis communication to both a domestic and international audience in the event of space-related crises, as outlined in the 18 scenarios in this book.

**Scope:**

- Covers incidents in Low Earth Orbit (LEO), Cislunar space, and beyond.
- Addresses crises impacting military, commercial, and scientific missions.
- Guides internal (U.S. government, interagency) and external (media, international partners, the public) communication.

## 2. Crisis Levels and Escalation Criteria

To standardize the response, categorize crises by potential impact, public concern, and likelihood of escalation:

### Level 1: Advisory

» Minor incidents or anomalies.

» **Examples:** Minor satellite malfunction; narrowly avoided orbital collision with no damage.

» **Response:** Leading agency (NASA, DoT, and so on) Public Affairs Office provides minimal public briefing; and shares what materials have been briefed with the National Space Council Public Affairs Office.

### Level 2: Alert

» Moderate to high public visibility. Potential for limited national security implications.

» **Examples:** Inspector satellite maneuver close to a U.S. asset; partial satellite failure with possible service disruption.

» **Response:**

1. Identify the lead agency and make that Public Affairs Office the lead communicator, with relevant agencies at once feeding germane data and coordinating subsequent messages.

2. Coordinate/liaise with White House Communications Office and/or the White House press Secretary to ensure that White House messaging, while less detailed, is aligned with the lead agency.

3. DoD and DoS Public Affairs Offices should coordinate facts and messaging when and

where appropriate and possible with affected
nations, Allies, and Partners; the lead agency
Public Affairs Office should be included in
decision-making meetings to clearly understand
the leadership's intent and provide strategic
communications advice.

## Level 3: Emergency

» High-impact crisis with potential global repercussions.
» **Examples:** Direct ASAT attack, large-scale Lunar
conflict, catastrophic commercial space accident with
multiple fatalities.
» **Response:** National Space Council convened
1. White House Communications Office is
the Lead Public Affairs Office; there will
be a lead agency, the Public Affairs Office
of which should support the White House
Communications Office.
2. The White House Press Secretary should first
coordinate with the National Security Advisor
and lead agency and then proceed to issue
an initial statement to alert the media of the
Administration's awareness and handling of the
situation, and should include an estimated time
and location (if different from the white House
Press Briefing Room) for a press briefing
3. Shortly thereafter and with more facts about the
situation and what the Administration is doing,
the White House Press Secretary should hold
that press briefing; following press briefings will

also be led by the White House Press Secretary but should include the National Security Advisor and Technical Subject Matter Experts from immediately relevant agencies.

4.  DoS and DoD Public Affairs should immediately begin coordinating with directly affected Allies and Partners as they will also be generating their own messaging and may look to the U.S. for leadership and accurate information, attempt harmonization of or mutually supporting messages where possible.

5.  Only if this is a true threat to the nation and once the President has made a decision on how to proceed, only then should he or she address the nation, not before; the White House Press Secretary should be part of any consequential meetings to effectively provide strategic communications advice and clearly understand the President's intent in order to communicate that to the agencies' Public Affairs Offices and in subsequent press briefings.

## 3. Roles and Responsibilities
### President

- Should speak only on Level 3 crises, if the event illustrates a true threat to the nation, and only after having decided about the way forward.

- Approves Level 3 strategic response and core strategic message; coordinates with a limited number of key heads of state of affected nations, allies, and partners.

## National Space Council (NSpC)

- Convenes for Level 2 and Level 3 crises.

- Members: Develop and approve crisis policy guidance and the strategic messaging plan prior to a crisis.

- Secretariat: Collects, organizes, and maintains all messaging from all agencies; disseminates guidance and strategic messaging to the NSpC Crisis Communications Team: White House Communications Office and agency Public Affairs Offices; socializes, possibly through a secure government website, agencies' pre-crises plans and messages.

## Vice President

- Chairs the NSpC.

- Approves and disseminates key messages and response strategies to agency leads, and when appropriate selected international counterparts, during top-tier crises.

- Directs the NSpC secretariat, the White House Communications Office, and agencies to create a Crisis Communications Team that will consist of one Public Affairs Officer per agency, to ensure that when a crisis occurs, there is already a basic and up-to-date communications framework upon which to build a response.

- Directs the NSpC secretariat, prior to a crisis, to maintain a master list of all draft initial crisis communication messaging for possible or anticipated crises from agencies.

- Designates lead agency and therefore Lead Public Affairs Office/Officer for each crisis.

- In Level 3 crises, at the direction of the President, disseminates/coordinates core strategic messages with lead agency heads, and if appropriate, with key heads of state or counterparts of affected nations, allies, and partners that the President does not.

### Lead Public Affairs Officer or Office (PAO)

- Central coordinator for all communication for a particular crisis; leads and coordinates with the NSpC Crisis Communications Team.

- Maintains an up-to-date list of space relevant and space adjacent PAO officers in NASA, DoD (OSD, U.S. Space Command, USSF, Dept. of the Air Force), DoT (FAA), DoC, DoE, DoS, and USGS.

- Maintains master messaging documents and talking points related to crises.

- In the event of a crisis, attends relevant decision-making meetings to understand leadership's intent and to advise on: how developments are shaping public perception; how decisions will be perceived; and the "if," "how," "what about," and "when" leadership and SMEs should speak publicly.

- Ensures that SMEs have the skills to speak publicly, before meeting the press, and conducts training or support as needed.

- Monitors media and influencers.

- Directs media outreach and manages press conferences.

## Technical Subject Matter Experts (SMEs)
- NASA scientists, DoD, DoS and DoT (FAA) experts, commercial industry representatives as needed.

- Provide to the Public Affairs Office factual up-to-date information and detailed explanations succinctly, in common English, with acronyms spelled out on first use.

- Prior to a crisis, identify "back-up" SME, and both primary and "back-up" SMEs should seek and receive media training from the Public Affairs Office.

## Legal/Policy Advisor
- Ensures communication aligns with national security laws, international treaties, and classification constraints.

- Reviews Public Affairs Office crisis communications plan and imagined space-based crisis; anticipates policy challenges that may arise at a time of crisis.

## Digital Media Specialist
- Oversees official social media channels, real-time monitoring, and addresses misinformation online.

- Coordinates closely with and informs Lead Public Affairs Officer or Office.

### International Liaison

- Coordinates messages with allied and partner nations and relevant international bodies (for example, NATO, UN, ESA).

- Maintains up-to-date contact list of counterparts representing allied and partner nations and relevant international bodies (for example, NATO, UN, ESA).

- In the case of a crisis, monitors relevant international media and influencers.

- In the case of a crisis, coordinates with and informs Lead Public Affairs Officer or Office.

- Adapts or translates messages for global audiences.

### Agency Public Affairs Representatives (NASA, DoD, DoT, DoS, DoC)

- Depending on crisis, may possibly be the lead Public Affairs Office for Level 1 and Level 2 crises, but will provide support to the White House Communications Office and the White House Press Secretary for Level 3 crises.

- If not the lead agency Public Affairs Office, feed specialized details from their respective domains to the lead agency's Public Affairs Office/Officer and into the overall messaging.

- Prior to a crisis that could make this agency the lead, the Public Affairs Office should proactively prepare a plan

and messages for imaginable space-based crises that can
be easily tailored to meet the moment before such a crisis
occurs; seek input from SMEs and Legal Policy Advisors
to anticipate policy and communication challenges; shares
pre-crises plans and messages with NSpC secretariat.

- Maintains an updated list of all internal offices and
  external agencies' PAOs which may have equities in the
  case of a space-based crisis, to in future coordinate crisis
  communications and identify appropriate SMEs; maintains
  an up-to-date contact list of international counterparts if
  applicable.

## Congressional Affairs

- Provides timely updates to congressional committees and
  leadership.

- Assists in preparing testimony if legislative hearings occur,
  and coordinates that testimony with the Public Affairs
  Office to harmonize messaging.

- Monitors messaging originating from Senators and
  Representatives and informs the agency's Public
  Affairs Office.

## Industry Liaison

- Coordinates with private sector (launch providers, satellite
  operators, insurers).

- Gathers technical details and conveys policy decisions to
  commercial stakeholders.

- If the incident or response involves an industry partner, and if appropriate, the Industry Liaison should request a SME/representative of that private sector organization be made available and ready for media events.

- Monitors messaging originating from private sector and informs the agency's Public Affairs Office.

## 4. Core Communication Principles

1. **Always tell the truth without semantic contortion.**

2. **Speed vs. Accuracy Balance**
   - **First Hour:** Confirm basic facts, release a holding statement (for Level 2–3).

   - **Ongoing:** Provide partial, verifiable information in phases; correct errors quickly.

   - **Ongoing:** Respond to complaints or criticisms by communicating an openness to investigate errors and to report back on findings but be careful to avoid guarantees.

3. **One-Voice Strategy**
   - Designate a single spokesperson (or limited set of spokespeople).

   - Through the Crisis Communication Group, coordinate talking points across agencies, the NSpC, and the white House Communications Office to ensure consistency. Note that it is not necessary to deliver the exact same message, but rather supporting messages.

- Centralize major announcements under the White House Press Secretary for high-stakes crises.

## 4. Transparency with Limits

- Default to transparency but protect classified details.

- Offer context on what can be shared and why some details remain restricted.

- Maintain public trust by explaining uncertainties and what is being done to resolve them.

- To further maintain trust with media outlets, and in the case of a particularly thorny or complicated issue that does not yet have a resolution, but there is a desire to prevent misinformation, hold an off-the-record background briefing.

## 5. Proactive Misinformation Management

- Monitor social media and news sources for rumors or false narratives.

- Quickly issue clarifications or corrections with factual evidence.

- Leverage credible third-party voices (media, allies, experts) to amplify correct information.

## 5. Crisis Response Timeline

The detailed timeline below ensures clarity for each stage of communication. Adjust as needed for the crisis level.

### 5.1 Initial Response (First 24 Hours)

1.  **First Hour**
    - **Incident Confirmation:** Verify the situation through official channels (NORAD, NASA mission control, etc.).

    - **Holding Statement:** Provide a brief acknowledgment of the incident, confirming awareness and initial actions.

    - **Activation:** Convene the Crisis Communication Team (CCT) under the Lead PAO's direction if the crisis is Level 2 or 3.

2.  **Hours 2–24**
    - **Situation Briefs:**
        1.  Share updated bulletins every 4–6 hours to press and key stakeholders. Emphasize progress in resolving the crisis: de-escalation steps, rescue efforts, debris cleanup, and so on.
        2.  Emphasize progress, could be in understanding the cause or impact, and if appropriate a response.

    - **Technical Briefings:**
        3.  Deeper press briefing led by the Public Affairs Office with limited but consequential input from SMEs, possibly including NASA, DoD, or commercial reps.
        4.  Explain what is known and unknown about cause and impact, and, if appropriate, response actions in simpler terms for the public.

5. If the technical attributes of the incident are particularly challenging to understand for a non-space sector reporter, and the briefing venue is the White House, issue a FAQ to level set terminology.

- **Media Monitoring:** Track press coverage and social media discussions.

- **Stakeholder Outreach:** Notify congressional leaders, allied partners, and impacted commercial entities.

### 5.2 Crisis Management (Days 2–7)
### 1. Technical Briefings
- In-depth sessions led by SMEs, possibly including NASA, DoD, or commercial reps.

- Explain cause, impact, and response actions in simpler terms for the public.

### 2. Steady Information Flow
- Maintain consistency with scheduled press briefings (for example, daily).

- Provide updates even if no major changes—this reinforces transparency.

- Emphasize progress in resolving the crisis: de-escalation steps, rescue efforts, debris cleanup, etc.

### 3. Misinformation Countermeasures

- Identify viral rumors; use official channels and experts to provide corrections.

- Encourage allied voices to share consistent messaging internationally.

- For particularly thorny or complicated issues that do not yet have a resolution, but there is a desire to support accuracy and prevent misinformation, hold an off-the-record background briefing with a SME.

### 4. International Coordination

- Align statements with key allies if the crisis has broad implications (for example, debris fields affecting other nations).

- If appropriate, consult and coordinate with the UN or other international forums for joint announcements or treaties.

### 5.3 Long-Term Management (Beyond 1 Week)
### 1. Shift to Solutions and Recovery

- Emphasize progress in resolving the crisis: de-escalation steps, rescue efforts, debris cleanup, and so on.

- Highlight policy or procedural changes to prevent recurrence.

## 2. Public Hearings and Reviews

- Prepare for potential congressional or public inquiries.

- Provide data, witness testimony, and official statements as requested.

## 3. After-Action Evaluations

- Conduct interagency reviews to assess communication effectiveness.

- Document lessons learned in the official record and revise protocols accordingly.

## CONCLUSION

This Crisis Communication Plan for Space Scenarios provides a detailed, step-by-step approach for managing and communicating about orbital incidents, Lunar conflicts, ASAT threats, commercial space accidents, and other space-related crises. By adhering to core communication principles, coordinating through a centralized structure, and maintaining flexibility for scenario-specific needs, U.S. policymakers can bolster public trust, reassure global audiences, and uphold America's leadership in space governance and innovation.

# AUTHOR BIOS

**Lt. Col. Peter A. Garretson, USAF (Ret.)** is a Senior Fellow in Defense Studies at AFPC and a co-director of the SPI. He is a prolific writer and is co-author of *The Next Space Race: A Blueprint for American Primacy* (Praeger, 2023) and *Scramble for the Skies: The Great Power Competition to Control the Resources of Outer Space* (Lexington Books, 2020). Previously, Garretson spent over a decade as a transformational strategist for the Department of the Air Force, where he served as a strategy and policy advisor for the Chief of Staff of the Air Force, as Division Chief of Irregular Warfare Strategy Plans and Policy, and as the Chief of the Future Technology Branch of Air Force Strategic Planning. Garretson has extensive wargaming expertise, having helped design, been a player in, and led both red and blue teams in Net Assessment Wargames. Garretson has designed, planned, and executed a diversity of simulations and wargames, including three Title X wargames for HQ U.S. Air Force, the first interagency planetary defense simulation, the U.S.-U.K.-France trilateral strategic initiative airpower wargame, the Air Command and Staff College Joint Warfare wargame, and two Space Horizons Task Force wargames (including one with NASIC). Garretson has designed multiple scenarios supporting

U.S. Space Force Space Futures Workshop, Keplerian Chess, the Nonproliferation Policy Education Center (NPEC), and the AFPC National Space Council Simulation.

**Mr. Richard M. Harrison** is the Vice President of Operations and Director of the Defense Technology Program at AFPC, where he co-directs the AFPC Space Policy Initiative (SPI). He currently serves as managing editor of AFPC's *Defense Dossier* e-journal and as editor of the *Defense Technology Monitor* e-bulletin. Harrison also directs a briefing series on Capitol Hill to educate congressional staff on defense technology issues affecting U.S. national security. He has published numerous articles and is co-author of *The Next Space Race: A Blueprint for American Primacy* (Praeger, 2023) and co-editor of *Cyber Insecurity: Navigating the Perils of the Next Information Age* (Rowman & Littlefield, 2016). Prior to his work at AFPC, Harrison spent several years as a systems engineer in the aerospace sector for Lockheed Martin. He completed his master's degree in Security Studies from Georgetown University's School of Foreign Service and earned a bachelor's degree in Aerospace Engineering from Penn State University.

# INDEX TERMS

# ENDNOTES

1    Alan Wasser, "LBJ's Space Race: what we didn't know then (part 1)," The Space Review, June 20, 2005, https://www.thespacereview.com/article/396/1

## CHAPTER 1 ENDNOTES

2    The U.S. was only able to respond quickly because of actions it had taken years earlier. For example, the U.S. was able to respond to Sputnik via Explorer 1 and Vanguard because of long-standing military rocket development efforts. The Army Ballistic Missile Agency (ABMA), established in 1956, built on years of prior work, including Von Braun's V-2 launches since the 1940s. The Juno rocket, which launched Explorer 1, had its roots in development efforts dating back to 1950. Meanwhile, the Navy's Vanguard program, initiated in 1955, was based on earlier research into sounding rockets dating as far back as 1944. Even crash programs need something from which to build.

3    Remarks by Vice President Pence at the Fifth Meeting of the National Space Council, Huntsville, AL, March 26, 2019, https://trumpwhitehouse.archives.gov/briefings-statements/remarks-vice-president-pence-fifth-meeting-national-space-council-huntsville-al/

4    Bryan Bender, 'We better watch out': NASA boss sounds alarm on Chinese moon ambitions," Politico, January, 1, 2023, https://www.politico.com/news/2023/01/01/we-better-watch-out-nasa-boss-sounds-alarm-on-chinese-moon-ambitions-00075803

5    Melissa Quinn, Caitlin Yilek, "Read the full transcript of Trump's inauguration speech," CBS News, January 20, 2025, https://www.cbsnews.com/news/transcript-trump-inauguration-speech-2025/

6    Peter Garretson and Samuel Havard, "The Starship Singularity," Space Policy Review No. 2, American Foreign Policy Council, February 2023, https://www.afpc.org/uploads/documents/Starship_(SPR)_-_2.22.23.pdf

7    "Space Foundation Announces $570B Space Economy in 2023, Driven by Steady Private and Public Sector Growth," The Space Foundation, July 18, 2024, https://www.spacefoundation.org/2024/07/18/the-space-report-2024-q2/.

8    Ryan Brukardt, "How will the space economy change the world?," McKinsey Quarterly, November 28, 2022, https://www. mckinsey.com/industries/aerospace-and-defense/our-insights/ how-will-the-space-economy-change-the-world

9    In-Space Servicing, Assembly, and Manufacturing (ISAM), NASA, https://nexis. gsfc.nasa.gov/isam/index.html

10   Such large structures and their major components can be built to different standards and large sizes and not be beholden to clever packing schemes or need to be designed to survive the few seconds of high Mach speeds through the Earth's atmosphere and the corresponding launch vibration environment.

11   "In-Space Servicing, Assembly, and Manufacturing National Strategy," National Science and Technology Council, April 2022, https://www.whitehouse.gov/ wp-content/uploads/2022/04/04-2022-ISAM-National-Strategy-Final.pdf.

12   "Moon Missions," NASA Goddard's Solar System Exploration Division for the Science Mission Directorate, https://moon.nasa.gov/exploration/moon-missions/

13   Kyle L. Evanoff, "Bad moonshot rising: The moon's dubious strategic value," Bulletin of the Atomic Scientists, April 19, 2019, https://thebulletin.org/2019/04/ bad-moonshot-rising-the-moons-dubious-strategic-value/

14   "National Cislunar Science and Technology Strategy," National Science and Technology Council, November 2022, https://www.whitehouse.gov/wp-content/ uploads/2022/11/11-2022-NSTC-National-Cislunar-ST-Strategy.pdf

15   Paul D. Spudis, The Value of the Moon: How to Explore, Live, and Prosper in Space Using the Moon's Resources, (Smithsonian Books, April 26, 2016).

16   Randy Korotev, "The Chemical Composition of Lunar Soil," Some Meteorite Information, Washington University in St. Louis, https://sites.wustl.edu/ meteoritesite/items/the-chemical-composition-of-lunar-soil/#CaAl

17   David R. Williams, "Ice on the Moon," NASA, January 1, 2022, https://nssdc.gsfc. nasa.gov/planetary/ice/ice_moon.html

18   Prior to the Trump-Biden administration transition, presidents vacillated on how to move forward with U.S. space objectives. Recently, however, there has been continuity in the push for a return to the Moon through the NASA Artemis program.

19   "Artemis," National Aeronautics and Space Administration, https://www.nasa.gov/ specials/artemis/

20   "Artemis," National Aeronautics and Space Administration, https://www.nasa.gov/ specials/artemis/

21   Eric Berger, "We got a leaked look at NASA's future Moon missions—and likely delays," *Ars Technica*, June 20, 2022, https://arstechnica.com/science/2022/06/we-got-a-leaked-look-at-nasas-future-moon-missions-and-likely-delays/; "Artemis: NASA's Program to Return Humans to the Moon," Congressional Research Service Report, Updated December 5, 2024, https://crsreports.congress.gov/product/pdf/IF/IF11643#:~:text=The%20Artemis%20III%20mission%2C%20planned,such%20as%20a%20lunar%20lander; Jeff Foust, "GAO report warns Artemis 3 landing may be delayed to 2027," *Space News*, December 1, 2023, https://spacenews.com/gao-report-warns-artemis-3-landing-may-be-delayed-to-2027/; William Russell, "NASA ARTEMIS PROGRAMS Lunar Landing Plans Are Progressing, but Challenges Remain," Testimony Before the Subcommittee on Space and Aeronautics, Committee on Science, Space, and Technology, House of Representatives, U.S. Government Accountability Office, January 17, 2024, https://www.gao.gov/assets/d24107249.pdf.

22   "National Low Earth Orbit Research and Development Strategy," National Science and Technology Council, March 2023, https://www.whitehouse.gov/wp-content/uploads/2023/03/NATIONAL-LEO-RD-STRATEGY-033123.pdf

23   Namrata Goswami and Bleddyn Bowen, "HIGH GROUND OR HIGH FANTASY: DEFENSE UTILITY OF CISLUNAR SPACE," Center for Space Policy and Strategy Debate Series, May 2024, https://csps.aerospace.org/sites/default/files/2024-05/Wilson_HighGround_20240416.pdf.

24   "Wu Weiren: Chasing dream of deep space," The National Committee of the Chinese People's Political Consultative Conference, February 21, 2023, http://en.cppcc.gov.cn/2023-02/21/c_860189.htm; "China's Plans for the Moon, Mars and Beyond," *BBC News*, April 19, 2016, https://www.bbc.com/news/av/world-asia-36085659.

25   Andrew Jones, "Space official calls for China to seize crucial opportunity to establish lunar infrastructure," *Space News*, March 31, 2023, https://spacenews.com/space-official-calls-for-china-to-seize-crucial-opportunity-to-establish-lunar-infrastructure/

26   The State Council Information Office of the People's Republic of China, "Full Text: China's Space Program: A 2021 Perspective"; see also "International Lunar Research Station ILRS Guide for Partnership," Chinese National Space Administration, June 16, 2021, http://www.cnsa.gov.cn/english/n6465652/n6465653/c6812150/content.html.

27   Other contemporary sources state 14 and 15 participating states respectfully, see: Farah Ghouri, "Picking sides in space: China's ILRS Moon base or the US Artemis Accords?," Seradata, May 23, 2024, https://www.seradata.com/picking-sides-in-space-chinas-moon-base-or-the-us-artemis-accords/; Andrew Jones, https://x.com/AJ_FI/status/1845816913663865298.

28    Andrew Jones, "Senegal among new members of China's ILRS moon base project," *Space News*, September 5, 2024, https://spacenews.com/senegal-among-new-members-of-chinas-ilrs-moon-base-project/#:~:text=This%20somewhat%20mirroring%20the%20country's,target%20the%20lunar%20south%20pole; "Lunar Space Cooperation Initiatives," Secure World Foundation, January 23, 2025, https://swfound.org/lunar-space-cooperation-initiatives/#:~:text=As%20of%20Sept.

29    Andrew Jones, "Chinese scientists outline major cislunar space infrastructure project," *Space News*, July 30, 2024, https://spacenews.com/chinese-scientists-outline-major-cislunar-space-infrastructure-project/.

30    Andrew Jones, "Chinese scientist proposes solar system-wide resource utilization roadmap," *Space News*, September 4, 2023, https://spacenews.com/chinese-scientist-proposes-solar-system-wide-resource-utilization-roadmap/.

31    Cao Siqi Source, "China mulls $10 trillion Earth-moon economic zone," Global Times, November 1, 2019, https://www.globaltimes.cn/content/1168698.shtml.

32    Andrew Jones, "NASA and China are eyeing the same landing sites near the lunar south pole," SpaceNews, August 31, 2022, https://spacenews.com/nasa-and-china-are-eyeing-the-same-landing-sites-near-the-lunar-south-pole/

33    Richard M. Harrison and Peter A Garretson, *The Next Space Race: A Blueprint for American Primacy*, "Competing with the Chinese Space Vision" by Larry Wortzel, (California: Praeger, 2023), 28-29.

34    For more information see: State of Space Industrial Base Report 2020, https://assets.ctfassets.net/3nanhbfkr0pc/3TLlIb4Z2UZG7szZdyVFuf/bafb12c16a37ee673b1ba30e72935c07/State_of_the_Space_Industrial_Base_2020_Workshop_Report_July_2020_FINAL.pdf; State of Space Industrial Base Report 2021, https://assets.ctfassets.net/3nanhbfkr0pc/43TeQTAmdYrym5DT-Drhjd3/1218bd749befdde511ac2c900db3a43b/Space_Industrial_Base_Workshop_2021_Summary_Report_-_Final_15_Nov_2021.pdf; State of Space Industrial Base Report 2022, https://assets.ctfassets.net/3nanhbfkr0pc/6L5409b-pVlnVyu2H5FOFnc/7595c4909616df92372a1d31be609625/State_of_the_Space_Industrial_Base_2022_Report.pdf

35    Kevin Pollpeter, Timothy Ditter, Anthony Miller, and Brian Waidelich, "China's Space Narrative: Examining the portrayal of the US-China space relationship in Chinese sources and its implications for the United States," China Aerospace Studies Institute, Air University, https://www.airuniversity.af.edu/Portals/10/CASI/Conference-2020/CASI%20Conference%20China%20Space%20Narrative.pdf?ver=FGoQ8Wm2DypB4FaZDWuNTQ%3D%3D; Mark Stokes, Gabriel Alvarado, Emily Weinstein, and Ian Easton, "China's Space and Counterspace Capabilities and Activities," Prepared for: The U.S.-China Economic and Security Review Commission, March 30, 2020, https://www.uscc.gov/sites/default/files/2020-05/China_Space_and_Counterspace_Activities.pdf

36    Richard M. Harrison and Peter A Garretson, *The Next Space Race: A Blueprint for American Primacy*, "Competing with the Chinese Space Vision" by Larry Wortzel, (California: Praeger, 2023), 34-35.

37    Cody Retherford, "The Promise of Space-Based Solar Power," *Space Policy Review* No.1, American Foreign Policy Council, September 22, 2022, https://www.afpc. org/uploads/documents/Space_Policy_Review_-_issue_1_-_9.21.2022.pdf

38    Cody Retherford, "The Promise of Space-Based Solar Power," *Space Policy Review* No.1, American Foreign Policy Council, September 22, 2022, https://www.afpc. org/uploads/documents/Space_Policy_Review_-_issue_1_-_9.21.2022.pdf

39    "DARPA, NASA Collaborate on Nuclear Thermal Rocket Engine," Defense Advanced Research Projects Agency, January 24, 2023, https://www.darpa.mil/ news-events/2023-01-24

40    Christian Davenport, "Chinese rocket tumbles into Pacific Ocean after days in space," *The Washington Post*, November 4, 2022, https://www.washingtonpost.com/ technology/2022/11/04/china-rocket-long-march-earth/

41    Namrata Goswami and Peter Garretson, Scramble for the Skies, Lexington, 2020. Also see, Elizabeth Gamillo, "This Metal-Rich, Potato-Shaped Asteroid Could Be Worth $10 Quintillion," *Smithsonian Magazine*, January 4, 2022, https://www. smithsonianmag.com/smart-news/asteroid-16-psyche-may-be-worth-more-than-planet-earth-at-10-quintillion-in-fine-metals-180979303/

42    Space: The Dawn of a New Age," Citi GPS: Global Perspectives & Solutions, May 2022, https://ir.citi.com/gps/829sRzYY4sQ%2BOhctTEs%2B1WWLgPbyZktiZ-poz3QRCC6ToaLgXov4Kxy852czeh38jOi72XKhJGp0%3D

43    Larry M. Wortzel and Kate Selley, "Breaking China's Stranglehold on the U.S. Rare Earth Elements Supply Chain," *Defense Technology Program Brief* No. 22, American Foreign Policy Council, April 2021, https://www.afpc.org/uploads/ documents/Defense_Technology_Briefing_-_Issue_22.pdf.

44    IISL Directorate of Studies, "Does international space law either permit or prohibit the taking of resources in outer space and on celestial bodies, and how is this relevant for national actors? What is the context, and what are the contours and limits of this permission or prohibition?," 2016, https://iislweb.space/wp-content/ uploads/2020/01/IISL_Space_Mining_Study.pdf

45    "Insight - Encouraging the Recovery and Use of Space Resources: Recommendations for Governmental Policies and Engagement," Secure World Foundation, October 8, 2020, https://swfound.org/news/all-news/2020/10/insight-encouraging-the-recovery-and-use-of-space-resources-recommendations-for-governmental-policies-and-engagement

46    "U.S. Commercial Space Launch Competitiveness Act," Public Law No: 114-90, November 10, 2015, https://www.congress.gov/bill/114th-congress/ house-bill/2262

47    The White House, "Executive Order: Encouraging International Support for the Recovery and Use of Space Resources," April 6, 2020, https://trumpwhitehouse. archives.gov/wp-content/uploads/2020/04/Fact-Sheet-on-EO-Encouraging-International-Support-for-the-Recovery-and-Use-of-Space-Resources.pdf.

48    The Artemis Accords," NASA, https://www.nasa.gov/specials/artemis-accords/ index.html

49    Namrata Goswami, India's space policy and national security posture: what can we expect?," *The Space Review*, April 24, 2023, https://www.thespacereview.com/article/4571/1

50    Liangyu, "China Focus: Capture an asteroid, bring it back to Earth?," *Xinhua*, July 23, 2018, http://www.xinhuanet.com/english/2018-07/23/c_137342866.htm

51    Richard M. Harrison and Peter A Garretson, *The Next Space Race: A Blueprint for American Primacy*, "Competing with the Chinese Space Vision" by Larry Wortzel, (California: Praeger, 2023), 28-29.

52    Briefing with Vice Adm. Jon A. Hill and Michelle C. Atkinson, "Missile Defense Agency Officials Hold a Press Briefing on President Biden's Fiscal 2024 Missile Defense Budget Transcript," U.S. Department of Defense, March 14, 2023, https://www.defense.gov/News/Transcripts/Transcript/Article/3328637/missile-defense-agency-officials-hold-a-press-briefing-on-president-bidens-fisc/

53    Brian Weeden and Victoria Samson, "Global Counterspace Capabilities: An Open Source Assessment," Secure World Foundation, April 2022, https://swfound.org/media/207350/swf_global_counterspace_capabilities_2022_rev2.pdf; "Challenges to Security in Space 2022," Defense Intelligence Agency, U.S. Department of Defense, April 12, 2022, https://www.defense.gov/News/News-Stories/Article/Article/2997723/defense-intelligence-agency-report-details-space-based-threats-from-competitors/

54    Christian Davenport, "Russia threatens commercial satellites that Pentagon sees as its future," Washington Post, October 28, 2022, https://www.washingtonpost.com/technology/2022/10/28/space-war-ukraine-pentagon-russia/

55    Doug Adler, "Why did NASA retire the Space Shuttle?," *Astronomy.com*, November 12, 2020, https://astronomy.com/news/2020/11/why-did-nasa-retire-the-space-shuttle

56    David Nagel, Human Error in Aviation Operations, Science Direct, 1988, https://www.sciencedirect.com/science/article/abs/pii/B9780080570907500151

57    James Gattuso, Air Travel: A Hundred Years of Safety, Mackinac Center, October 6, 2003, https://www.mackinac.org/V2003-30

58    NASA Confirms DART Mission Impact Changed Asteroid's Motion in Space, NASA, October 11, 2022, https://www.nasa.gov/press-release/nasa-confirms-dart-mission-impact-changed-asteroid-s-motion-in-space

## CHAPTER 2 ENDNOTES

59    Theresa Hitchens, "China's space moves: Highly mobile satellites stalking GEO spook Space Force," *Breaking Defense*, December 10, 2024;

60    Andrew Jones, "A Chinese Spacecraft Has Been Checking Out US Satellites High Above Earth," Space.com, March 3, 2023, https://www.space.com/chinese-spacecraft-tjs-3-inspecting-us-satellites

61    Jones, "A Chinese Spacecraft Has Been Checking Out US Satellites High
      Above Earth"; for additional reading on space war tactics read, Colin Clark, "US,
      China, Russia Test New Space War Tactics: Sats Buzzing, Spoofing, Spying,"
      *Breaking Defense*, October 28, 2021, https://breakingdefense.com/2021/10/
      us-china-russia-test-new-space-war-tactics-sats-buzzing-spoofing-spying/

62    At present, the U.S. has no publicly advertised anti-satellite weapon capabilities.

63    According to NATO Article 4, "Any member country can formally invoke Article
      4 of the North Atlantic Treaty. As soon as it is invoked, the issue is discussed
      and can potentially lead to some form of joint decision or action on behalf of
      the Alliance." https://www.nato.int/cps/on/natohq/topics_49187.htm; "Article
      5 provides that if a NATO Ally is the victim of an armed attack, each and every
      other member of the Alliance will consider this act of violence as an armed attack
      against all members and will take the actions it deems necessary to assist the Ally
      attacked." https://www.nato.int/cps/uk/natohq/topics_110496.htm?selectedLo-
      cale=en#:~:text=Article%205%20provides%20that%20if,to%20assist%20the%20
      Ally%20attacked.

64    While the participants did not propose estimated costs, ballpark estimates supplied
      from a ChatGPT-4 query suggest a range from $8-$15 billion. The total is based
      on SBIRS ($19B+ over life cycle) and Next-Gen OPIR (~$14B). Autonomy and
      distribution drive cost.

65    While the participants did not propose estimated costs, ballpark estimates supplied
      from a ChatGPT-4 query suggest a range from $10-$20 billion. Scaling from
      ABL ($5B) and Starfire-like concepts. Power, cooling, and platform costs drive
      variability.

66    While the participants did not propose estimated costs, ballpark estimates supplied
      from a ChatGPT-4 query suggest a range from $3-$7 billion. Scaled from SSA
      programs (e.g., SPADOC, GSSAP) and terrestrial air traffic control system
      development (~$10B for FAA NextGen).

67    Donald J. Trump, "The Iron Dome for America," para (iii), The White House,
      January 27, 2025, https://www.whitehouse.gov/presidential-actions/2025/01/
      prioritizing-military-excellence-and-readiness/.

68    Stephanie Schappert, "China Plans to Crush Starlink With Constellation
      of Satellites," *Cybernews*, February 27, 2023, https://cybernews.com/tech/
      china-plans-satellite-constellation-starlink-rivalry/

69    Moving satellites from their predicted orbits complicates the ability of the
      adversary to target them.

70    While the participants did not propose estimated costs, ballpark estimates supplied
      from a ChatGPT-4 query suggest a range from $6-$12 billion. Based on PWSA
      (~$16B planned through 2028). Rapid acceleration increases launch and integra-
      tion costs.

71    While the participants did not propose estimated costs, ballpark estimates supplied
      from a ChatGPT-4 query suggest a range from $2-$5 billion. Derived from
      Blackjack ($175M+) and responsive space launch (~$2B est. per year).

72      While the participants did not propose estimated costs, ballpark estimates supplied
        from a ChatGPT-4 query suggest a range from $10-$18 billion. Modeled after
        SDA's future layers (~$15B) and AI-driven autonomy scaling costs.

73      While the participants did not propose estimated costs, ballpark estimates
        supplied from a ChatGPT-4 query suggest a range from $5-$12 billion. Based
        on ISS FabLab costs, Northrop's plans (~$9B), and debris removal studies ($5B+
        per system).

74      Independent reviewers find it highly unlikely that, in a real-world scenario, the
        United States would refrain from fielding or commissioning the development of at
        least a comparable—if not more sophisticated—space control system in response.
        Furthermore, the independent reviewers are concerned that such a restrained
        approach may reflect a broader hesitation within the established space policy
        community. U.S. policymakers may wish to consider that the perspectives could, at
        times, be shaped by institutional caution and past conditioning rather than a focus
        on strategic imperatives.

75      "Russian Direct-Ascent Anti-satellite Missile Test Creates Significant,
        Long-Lasting Space Debris," U.S. Space Command, November 15, 2018,
        https://www.spacecom.mil/Newsroom/News/Article-Display/Article/2842957/
        russian-direct-ascent-anti-satellite-missile-test-creates-significant-long-last/.

76      Greg Hadley, "Saltzman: China's ASAT Test Was 'Pivot Point' in Space Oper-
        ations," *Air and Space Forces,* January 13, 2023, https://www.airandspaceforces.
        com/saltzman-chinas-asat-test-was-pivot-point-in-space-operations/; Brian
        Weeden, "2007 Chinese Anti-Satellite Test Fact Sheet," Secure World Foundation,
        November 23, 2010, https://swfound.org/media/9550/chinese_asat_fact_sheet_
        updated_2012.pdf.

77      Doris Elin Urrutia, "India's Anti-Satellite Missile Test Is a Big Deal. Here's Why,"
        Space.com, August 10, 2022, https://www.space.com/india-anti-satellite-test-sig-
        nificance.html.

78      Vann H. Van Diepen, "Modest Beginnings: North Korea
        Launches Its First Reconnaissance Satellite," 38 North,
        November 28, 2023, https://www.38north.org/2023/11/
        modest-beginnings-north-korea-launches-its-first-reconnaissance-satellite/.

79      "Iran Launches New Research Satellite Chamran-1 Into Orbit," *Al
        Jazeera,* September 14, 2024, https://www.aljazeera.com/news/2024/9/14/
        iran-launches-new-research-satellite-chamran-1-into-orbit.

80      "Sounding Rockets," NASA, https://sites.wff.nasa.gov/code810/files/Sounding%20
        Rockets_NASA_fact_sheet.pdf.

81      "Vice President Harris Advances National Security Norms in
        Space," The White House, April 18, 2022, https://www.white-
        house.gov/briefing-room/statements-releases/2022/04/18/
        fact-sheet-vice-president-harris-advances-national-security-norms-in-space/.

82    While the participants did not propose estimated costs, ballpark estimates supplied
      from a ChatGPT-4 query suggest a range from $4-$9 billion. Based on responsive
      launch programs (~$2B per year), R&D for non-kinetic capabilities, and 72-hour
      rapid deployment challenges.

83    While the participants did not propose estimated costs, ballpark estimates supplied
      from a ChatGPT-4 query suggest a range from $5-$10 billion. Scaling from
      commercial satellite maneuverability upgrades and DoD multi-domain integration
      efforts (~$8B est.).

84    While the participants did not propose estimated costs, ballpark estimates supplied
      from a ChatGPT-4 query suggest a range from $2-$5 billion. Modeled after
      DARPA & DIU funding for rapid tech innovation and certification (~$3B).

85    While the participants did not propose estimated costs, ballpark estimates supplied
      from a ChatGPT-4 query suggest a range from $10-$20 billion. Derived from
      Next-Gen OPIR ($14B), SDA satellite networks, and ISAM infrastructure
      development.

86    While the participants did not propose estimated costs, ballpark estimates supplied
      from a ChatGPT-4 query suggest a range from $8-$16 billion. Based on GPS
      modernization ($12B) and resilient PNT alternatives like LEO-based navigation
      ($10B est.).

87    While the participants did not propose estimated costs, ballpark estimates supplied
      from a ChatGPT-4 query suggest a range from $1-$3 billion. Comparable to
      NASA and DoD space workforce development initiatives ($1.5B per year).

88    Such actions were taken at the UN and it had very little impact upon China,
      Russia, Iran and North Korea, who all voted no on the test ban. While this might
      have been thought effective during the simulation, it may be less effective than
      envisioned.

89    Michael Kan, "Researchers Suggest China 'Suppress' Starlink Using Own Satellite
      Constellation," *PC Magazine*, February 24, 2024, https://www.pcmag.com/news/
      researchers-suggest-china-suppress-starlink-using-own-satellite-constellation

90    While the participants did not propose estimated costs, ballpark estimates supplied
      from a ChatGPT-4 query suggest a range from $2-$6 billion. Based on prior
      cybersecurity partnership models (e.g., CISA & industry), DIU cyber investments,
      and R&D for secure comms.

91    While the participants did not propose estimated costs, ballpark estimates supplied
      from a ChatGPT-4 query suggest a range from $8-$15 billion. Scaled from GPS
      anti-jamming upgrades (~$10B) and past counter-EW investments.

92    While the participants did not propose estimated costs, ballpark estimates supplied
      from a ChatGPT-4 query suggest an annual increase of $200 million per year
      to subsidize another satellite broadband provider. Based on existing Starlink,
      Starshield, and SES O3B contracts.

93    Andrew Jones, "China's Spaceplane Conducted Proximity and Capture Maneuvers
      With Subsatellite, Data Suggests," Space News, May 11, 2023, https://spacenews.
      com/chinas-spaceplane-conducted-proximity-and-capture-maneuvers-with-subsa-
      tellite-data-suggests/.

94    Namrata Goswami and Peter Garretson, "The Strategic Implications of China's 'Divine Dragon' Spaceplane," *The Diplomat*, January 12, 2024, https://thediplomat.com/2024/01/the-strategic-implications-of-chinas-divine-dragon-spaceplane/.

95    At the time this scenario was written China organized its space forces under the Strategic Support Force with its cyber forces. Recently China split its space and cyber forces with its space specific forces typically translated as the Aerospace Defense Force (even though it does not appear to have any aero component).

96    One independent reviewer found this response wholly inadequate because none of these recommendations addresses the current problem of the Chinese squadron now.

97    NorthStar is an example of a company that conducts orbit monitoring services. See https://northstar-data.com

98    "AEGIS Weapon System," U.S. Navy, September 20, 2021, https://www.navy.mil/Resources/Fact-Files/Display-FactFiles/Article/2166739/aegis-weapon-system/

99    An independent reviewer suggested that a better plan would be to field a militarized version of the Starship, which "would make quick work of any of these things and would be infinitely more capable and cost-efficient."

100    Mike Wall, "SpaceX catches giant Starship booster with 'Chopsticks' on historic Flight 5 rocket launch and landing (video)," Space.com, October 13, 2024, https://www.space.com/spacex-starship-flight-5-launch-super-heavy-booster-catch-success-video.

101    Peter Garretson and Samuel Havard, "The Starship Singularity," *Space Policy Review*, American Foreign Policy Council, February 2023, no. 2, https://www.afpc.org/uploads/documents/Starship_(SPR)_-_2.22.23.pdf.

102    Namrata Goswami, "Long March 9 Rocket Will Be a Game-changer for China's Space Program," *The Diplomat*, October 3, 2023, https://thediplomat.com/2023/10/long-march-9-rocket-will-be-a-game-changer-for-chinas-space-program/.

103    Andrew Jones, "China Plans Full Reusability for Its Super Heavy Long March 9 Rocket," *SpaceNews*, April 27, 2023, https://spacenews.com/china-plans-full-reusability-for-its-super-heavy-long-march-9-rocket/.

104    Andrew Jones, "Chinese launch startup Cosmoleap secures funding for rocket featuring chopstick recovery system," SpaceNews, November 1, 2024, https://spacenews.com/chinese- launch-startup-cosmoleap-secures-funding-for-rocket-featuring-chopstick- recovery-system/.

## CHAPTER 3 ENDNOTES

105    Multiple independent reviewers expressed concern that no one thought to provide subsidies for domestically produced reusable launch vehicles until the U.S. is once again in the lead.

106    While the participants did not propose estimated costs, ballpark estimates supplied from a ChatGPT-4 query suggest a range from $3-$6 billion. Modeled after Apollo-era education initiatives (~$1B in 1970s, ~$6B today) and modern workforce training programs (NASA's Artemis-focused initiatives).

107    While the participants did not propose estimated costs, ballpark estimates supplied from a ChatGPT-4 query suggest a range from $2-$5 billion. Based on STEM workforce development efforts like NSF's STEM Innovation Programs (~$3B annually).

108    While the participants did not propose estimated costs, ballpark estimates supplied from a ChatGPT-4 query suggest a range from $4-$8 billion. Comparable to national STEM programs (e.g., DoD STEM scholarships & NASA's workforce initiatives).

109    Ji Gao, Xinbin Hou, and Li Wang, "Solar Power Satellites Research in China," Online Journal of Space Communication Volume 9 Issue 16 Solar Power Satellites (Winter 2010), https://ohioopen.library.ohio.edu/cgi/viewcontent.cgi?params=/context/spacejournal/article/1398/&path_info=SolarPowerSatellitesResearchInChina_GoaJi_HouXinbin_WangLi.pdf

110    Cody Retherford, "The Promise of Space-Based Solar Power," *Space Policy Review,* American Foreign Policy Council, September 2022, no. 1, https://www.afpc.org/uploads/documents/Space_Policy_Review_-_issue_1_-_9.21.2022.pdf.

111    Chinese Edition  by Wang Li, Zhang Xing, Hua Hou and Xin Bin (Author), *Space Solar Power Station Introduction* (Chinese Edition), May 1, 2020; Lu Hongyan, "Launching Ceremony of 'Space Solar Power Station Project' Held in Xi'an," *China Daily*, December 24, 2018, https://www.chinadaily.com.cn/a/201812/24/WS5c20a2a7a3107d4c3a0028ce.html.

112    Stephen Chen, "China Plans to Start Building First-Ever Solar Power Plant in Space by 2028," *South China Morning Post*, July 7, 2022, https://www.scmp.com/news/china/science/article/3180627/china-brings-forward-plans-space-solar-power-plant; Andrew Jones, "China Aims for Space-Based Solar Power Test in LEO in 2028, GEO in 2030," *Space News*, June 8, 2022, https://spacenews.com/china-aims-for-space-based-solar-power-test-in-leo-in-2028-geo-in-2030/

113    Readers should be aware that at least for microwave systems, the U.S. Department of Defense should be able to determine if the satellite is being used as a directed energy weapon.

114    Andrew Jones, "China Aims for Space-Based Solar Power Test in LEO in 2028, GEO in 2030," *SpaceNews*, June 8, 2022, https://spacenews.com/china-aims-for-space-based-solar-power-test-in-leo-in-2028-geo-in-2030/.

115    "Solar Arrays on the International Space Station," NASA, April 14, 2015, https://www.nasa.gov/image-article/solar-arrays-international-space-station-2/.

116    Kelsey A. W. Horowitz, Timothy Remo, Brittany Smith, and Aaron Ptak, "A Techno-Economic Analysis and Cost Reduction Roadmap for III-V Solar Cells," NREL, November 2018, https://www.nrel.gov/docs/fy19osti/72103.pdf

117    "U.S. Army Selects Lockheed Martin to Deliver 300 kW-class, Solid State Laser Weapon System," Lockheed Martin, October 10, 2023, https://news.lockheedmartin.com/2023-10-10-US-Army-Selects-Lockheed-Martin-to-Deliver-300-kW-class-Solid-State-Laser-Weapon-System.

118     "February 3, 2010: Testing of YAL-1 Airborne Laser Test Bed," Air Force Test Center, February 3, 2021, https://www.aftc.af.mil/News/On-This-Day-in-Test-History/Article-Display-Test-History/Article/2462050/february-3-2010-testing-of-yal-1-airborne-laser-test-bed/.

119     A solar power satellite in a geosynchronous orbit spends about 99% of the time in sunlight and about 1% in Earth's shadow during the spring and autumn equinoxes.

120     Despite a National Level Strategy to prioritize in-space servicing assembly and manufacture, NASA cancelled OSAM-2 in September of 2023, and OSAM-1 in September of 2024, see: https://web.archive.org/web/20220404131954/https://www.whitehouse.gov/wp-content/uploads/2022/04/04-2022-ISAM-National-Strategy-Final.pdf; White House, "In-Space Servicing, Assembly, and Manufacturing National Strategy," April 2022; Frank Millard, "Made in Space," Aerospace Testing International, January 30, 2024, https://www.aerospacetestinginternational.com/features/made-in-space.html; Jeff Foust, "NASA reaffirms decision to cancel OSAM-1," SpaceNews, September 5, 2024, https://spacenews.com/nasa-reaffirms-decision-to-cancel-osam-1/

121     Fan Anqi, "China to study assembly mechanics of kilometer-level extra-large spacecraft," Global Times, August 25, 2021, https://www.globaltimes.cn/page/202108/1232426.shtml;  Andrew Jones, "China researching challenges of kilometer-scale ultra-large spacecraft," SpaceNews, August 27, 2021, https://spacenews.com/china-researching-challenges-of-kilometer-scale-ultra-large-spacecraft/

122     EXIM Bank and DFC provide attractive financing in emerging markets so they can purchase U.S. products and services.

123     The Defense Production Act (DPA) authorizes the President to ensure the availability of domestic industry for defense, essential civilian, and homeland security requirements and The DPA Title III program targets investments that create, maintain, protect, expand, or restore domestic industrial base capabilities; see OSD, "Defense Production Act Title III Overview," 2022, https://www.bis.doc.gov/index.php/documents/2022-update-conference/3064-dpat3-overview-mz/file; Matthew Seaford, "Title III of theDefense Production Act," DOE, https://www.energy.gov/eere/bioenergy/articles/title-iii-defense-production-act

124     One independent reviewer suggested considering use of the U.S. energy production sector because SBSP is not a competitor with Big Oil and the U.S. would need to think beyond the space community here.

125     One independent reviewer expressed disappointment in repeatedly seeing similar solutions, such as, STEM funding, studies, norms, rather than expeditiously getting equipment in space.

126     For example, participants specifically mentioned DPALs (Diode Pumped Alkali Lasers).

127     DOE, "System for Nuclear Auxiliary Power (SNAP) Overview," n.d., https://www.energy.gov/etec/system-nuclear-auxiliary-power-snap-overview

128    Stephen Chen, "China's Nuclear Spaceships Will Be 'Mining Asteroids and
       Flying Tourists' as It Aims to Overtake US in Space Race," South China Morning
       Post, November 17, 2017, https://www.scmp.com/news/china/policies-politics/
       article/2120425/chinas-nuclear-spaceships-will-be-mining-asteroids.

129    Andrew Jones, "Chinese scientist proposes solar system-wide resource utili-
       zation roadmap," Space News, September 4, 2023, https://spacenews.com/
       chinese-scientist-proposes-solar-system-wide-resource-utilization-roadmap/.

130    YiCan Wu, "Design and R&D of megawatt lithium-cooled space nuclear reactor,"
       SciEngine, October 12, 2023, https://www.sciengine.com/SST/doi/10.1360/
       SST-2023-0202

131    White House, "Memorandum on the National Strategy for Space Nuclear
       Power and Propulsion (Space Policy Directive-6) Infrastructure & Technology,"
       December 16, 2020, https://trumpwhitehouse.archives.gov/presidential-actions/
       memorandum-national-strategy-space-nuclear-power-propulsion-space-policy-di-
       rective-6/

132    NASA, "Fission Surface Power," n.d., https://www.nasa.gov/
       space-technology-mission-directorate/tdm/fission-surface-power/.

133    Such a program would likely be more than $1B. Based on adjusted numbers of past
       nuclear development projects (Jetson, $35M; Timberwind, $322M; Pele, $538M;
       DRACO, $550M; Prometheus, $760M; NERVA, $5,055M) none of which have
       made it to flight test.

134    While the participants did not propose estimated costs, ballpark estimates supplied
       from a ChatGPT-4 query suggest a range from $10-$25 billion. Modeled after
       terrestrial microreactor costs ($1B per unit), NASA Fission Surface Power (~$4B+),
       and Lunar infrastructure setup (~$10B est.).

135    Peter Garretson, "Why the next Space Policy Directive needs to be to the Secretary
       of Energy," The Space Review, July 1, 2019, https://www.thespacereview.com/
       article/3744/1

## CHAPTER 4 ENDNOTES

136    Fan Anqi, "Putin signs into law joint building of lunar base with China as Beijing
       expands circle of friends in Moon exploration," Global Times, Jun 13, 2024,
       https://www.globaltimes.cn/page/202406/1314079.shtml; Andrew Jones, "China
       wants 50 countries involved in its ILRS moon base," SpaceNews, July 23, 2024

137    NASA, "Artemis Accords," n.d., https://www.nasa.gov/artemis-accords/; NASA,
       "NASA's Lunar Exploration Program Overview," September 2020, https://www.
       nasa.gov/wp-content/uploads/2020/12/artemis_plan-20200921.pdf

138    Tom Kalil, "Bootstrapping a Solar System Civilization," White House Blog,
       October 14, 2014, https://obamawhitehouse.archives.gov/blog/2014/10/14/
       bootstrapping-solar-system-civilization; Philip T. Metzger et al., "Affordable, rapid
       bootstrapping of space industry and solar system civilization," Arvix, https://arxiv.
       org/pdf/1612.03238

139    "Replicating Systems Concepts: Self-Replicating Lunar Factory and Demon-
       stration," in *Advanced Automation for Space Missions*, ed. Robert A. Freitas, Jr.,
       and William P. Gilbreath. NASA Conference Publication 2255 (NASA and
       American Society for Engineering Education, 1980), https://ntrs.nasa.gov/api/
       citations/19830007081/downloads/19830007081.pdf.

140    Gregory S. Chirikjian, "An Architecture for Self-Replicating Lunar Facto-
       ries," Final Report, April 26, 2004, https://www.niac.usra.edu/files/studies/
       final_report/880Chirikjian.pdf.

141    Justin Lewis-Weber, "Lunar-Based Self-Replicating Solar Factory," *New
       Space* 4, no. 1 (2016): 53–62, https://space.nss.org/wp-content/uploads/
       Lunar-Based-Self-Replicating-Solar-Factory.pdf.

142    Philip T. Metzger, Anthony Muscatello, Robert P. Mueller, and James Mantovani,
       "Affordable, Rapid Bootstrapping of Space Industry and Solar System Civiliza-
       tion," *Journal of Aerospace Engineering* 26, no. 1 (2013): 18–29, https://arxiv.org/
       pdf/1612.03238.

143    Andrew Jones, "Chinese scientist proposes solar system-wide resource utilization
       roadmap," SpaceNews,  September 4, 2023, https://spacenews.com/

144    Cao Siqi, "China mulls $10 trillion Earth-moon economic zone," Global Times,
       November 1, 2019, https://www.globaltimes.cn/content/1168698.shtml

145    Xinhua, "Exploiting earth-moon space: China's ambition after space station,"
       China Daily, March 8, 2016, https://www.chinadaily.com.cn/china/2016-03/08/
       content_23775949.htm

146    Andrew Jones, "China researching challenges of kilometer-scale ultra-
       large spacecraft," SpaceNews, August 27, 2021, https://spacenews.com/
       china-researching-challenges-of-kilometer-scale-ultra-large-spacecraft/

147    Aedan Yohannan, "China's Space Strategy Dwarfs U.S. Ambitions," National
       Interest, March 11, 2024, https://nationalinterest.org/blog/techland/
       chinas-space-strategy-dwarfs-us-ambitions-209959

148    Avery S., "Building on the Moon: China's 3D Printing Mission,"
       *3D Printing News*, April 25, 2023, https://www.3dnatives.com/en/
       building-on-the-moon-chinas-3d-printing-mission-250420236/.

149    Andrew Jones, "A Prototype Robotic 'Mason' Could Fly on the Chang'e 8
       Lunar South Pole Mission," Space.com, April 18, 2023, https://www.space.com/
       china-moon-3d-printing-bricks-change-8-2028; Andrew Jones, "Building blocks:
       How China plans to make bricks on the moon for lunar habitats," Space.com,
       December 3, 2024, https://www.space.com/space-exploration/human-spaceflight/
       building-blocks-how-china-plans-to-make-bricks-on-the-moon-for-lunar-habitats.

150    "China to Test Out 3D Printing Technology on Moon to Build Habitats,"
       Reuters, April 24, 2023, https://www.reuters.com/technology/space/
       china-test-out-3d-printing-technology-moon-build-habitats-2023-04-24/.

151    American Foreign Policy Council translation of presentation at 3rd Annual Space Science Conference, hosted by the Chinese Society of Space Research and the Zhe Jiang Province Science and Technology Association, "Proposal to Develop China's Lunar Orbital Space Station and Moon," October 15, 2023, https://www.youtube.com/watch?v=7fKlNCi879o.

152    Avery S., "Building on the Moon."

153    Independent reviewers considered that none of the proposals were reactive enough to constitute a sufficient response given the long-term implications.

154    While China states it has "commercial" or "private sector" space area it is all tied to their government, which is at contrast with Western/U.S. commercial sector that has external interests.

155    An independent reviewer noted that given much of the China decoupling has already been mandated by U.S. Law (like Wolf Amendment, etc…) it is not clear how U.S. corporations are even active in China in other ways beyond just selling equipment, which according to ITAR and EAR rules are not the top end U.S. products.

156    Scott Pace, "Space Development, Law, and Values," Executive Secretary of the National Space Council Lunch Keynote at IISL Galloway Space Law Symposium, December 13, 2017, https://spacepolicyonline.com/wp-content/uploads/2017/12/Scott-Pace-to-Galloway-Symp-Dec-13-2017.pdf.

157    An independent reviewer noted that declassification of China's debris generation will not accomplish much because China is one of the biggest offenders in not passivating upper stages and draining satellite batteries and propellant, so creating debris in a much more open Lunar environment will not likely sway public opinion.

158    Matt Williams, "New Idea: Use the Starship HLS to Create a Lunar Base!," Universe Today, October 30, 2021, https://www.universetoday.com/153061/new-idea-use-the-starship-hls-to-create-a-lunar-base/; Casey Handmer, "Starship Moon Base Design Principles," Casey Handmer's Blog, June 28, 2021, https://caseyhandmer.wordpress.com/2021/06/28/starship-moon-base-design-principles/; Adam Abdin et al., "Solutions for Construction of a Lunar Base: A Proposal to Use the SpaceX Starship as a Permanent Habitat," ResearchGate, https://www.researchgate.net/figure/Conceptual-overview-of-the-lunar-base-showing-the-Starship-lander-in-its-horizontal_fig1_356285358.

159    Independent reviewers note that the proposals for reaction stress the appearance of action rather than a coherent strategy to regain the initiative. Further these actions need to be synchronized with a specific end state in mind and it is likely already too late to gain the advantage without having a more proactive policy.

160    While the participants did not propose estimated costs, ballpark estimates supplied from a ChatGPT-4 query suggest a range from $2-$5 billion. Based on NASA's EPSCoR (~$0.2B annually) and state-university aerospace R&D programs (~$3B for Artemis-related projects).

161    David Whitehouse, "China Denies Manned Moon Mission Plans," BBC, May 21, 2002, http://news.bbc.co.uk/2/hi/sci/tech/2000506.stm.

162 Aedan Yohannan, "China's Space Strategy Dwarfs U.S. Ambitions," American Foreign Policy Council, March 11, 2024, https://www.afpc.org/publications/articles/chinas-space-strategy-dwarfs-u.s-ambitions.

163 Xinhua, "Exploiting Earth-Moon Space: China's Ambition After Space Station," *China Daily*, March 8, 2016, https://www.chinadaily.com.cn/china/2016-03/08/content_23775949.htm.

164 Cao Siqi, "China Mulls $10 Trillion Earth-Moon Economic Zone," *Global Times*, November 1, 2019, https://www.globaltimes.cn/content/1168698.shtml#:~:-text=China%20is%20mulling%20of%20establishing,generate%20%2410%20trillion%20a%20year.

165 Andrew Jones, "Egypt Joins China's ILRS Moon Base Initiative," *SpaceNews*, December 7, 2023, https://spacenews.com/egypt-joins-chinas-ilrs-moon-base-initiative/.

166 White House, "Remarks by Vice President Pence at the Fifth Meeting of the National Space Council | Huntsville, AL," March 26, 2019, https://trumpwhitehouse.archives.gov/briefings-statements/remarks-vice-president-pence-fifth-meeting-national-space-council-huntsville-al/.

167 White House, "National Space Policy of the United States of America," December 9, 2020, https://trumpwhitehouse.archives.gov/wp-content/uploads/2020/12/National-Space-Policy.pdf.

168 Jeff Foust, "GAO Report Warns Artemis 3 Landing May Be Delayed to 2027," *SpaceNews*, December 1, 2023, https://spacenews.com/gao-report-warns-artemis-3-landing-may-be-delayed-to-2027/.

169 Paul Kessler, Tracie Prater, Tiffany Nickens and Danny Harris, "Artemis Deep Space Habitation: Enabling a Sustained Human Presence on the Moon and Beyond," NASA, 2022, https://ntrs.nasa.gov/api/citations/20220000245/downloads/Artemis%20Deep%20Space%20Habitation%20Enabling%20a%20Sustained%20Human%20Presence%20on%20the%20Moon%20and%20Beyond%20(3).pdf.

170 White House, "National Space Strategy," December 9, 2020, https://trumpwhitehouse.archives.gov/wp-content/uploads/2020/12/National-Space-Policy.pdf.

171 White House, "National Cislunar Science & Technology Strategy," November 2022, https://web.archive.org/web/20221117163444/https://www.whitehouse.gov/wp-content/uploads/2022/11/11-2022-NSTC-National-Cislunar-ST-Strategy.pdf.

172 Casey Handmer, "SLS is still a national disgrace," *Casey Handmer's Blog*, October 2, 2024, https://caseyhandmer.wordpress.com/2024/10/02/sls-is-still-a-national-disgrace/.

173   Eric Berger, "We got a leaked look at NASA's future Moon missions—and likely delays," *Ars Technica*, June 20, 2022, https://arstechnica.com/science/2022/06/we-got-a-leaked-look-at-nasas-future-moon-missions-and-likely-delays/; "Artemis: NASA's Program to Return Humans to the Moon," Congressional Research Service Report, Updated December 5, 2024, https://crsreports.congress.gov/product/pdf/IF/IF11643#:~:text=The%20Artemis%20III%20mission%2C%20planned,such%20as%20a%20lunar%20lander; Jeff Foust, "GAO report warns Artemis 3 landing may be delayed to 2027," *Space News*, December 1, 2023, https://spacenews.com/gao-report-warns-artemis-3-landing-may-be-delayed-to-2027/; William Russell, "NASA ARTEMIS PROGRAMS Lunar Landing Plans Are Progressing, but Challenges Remain," Testimony Before the Subcommittee on Space and Aeronautics, Committee on Science, Space, and Technology, House of Representatives, U.S. Government Accountability Office, January 17, 2024, https://www.gao.gov/assets/d24107249.pdf.

174   Jeff Foust, "Blue Origin protests NASA Human Landing System award," *Space News*, April 26, 2021, https://spacenews.com/blue-origin-protests-nasa-human-landing-system-award/; Jeff Foust, "Federal agencies caught in environmental crossfire over Starship launches," *Space News*, December 15, 2023, https://spacenews.com/federal-agencies-caught-in-environmental-crossfire-over-starship-launches/#:~:text=That%20new%20licensing%20process%20included,pad%20after%20the%20second%20launch; Jack Daleo, "SpaceX takes aim at FAA after latest Starship launch delay," *Astronomy.com*, September 11, 2024, https://www.astronomy.com/space-exploration/spacex-takes-aim-at-faa-after-latest-starship-launch-delay/.

175   "NASA's Development of Next-Generation Spacesuits," NASA Office of the Inspector General, Report No. IG-21-025, August 10, 2021, https://oig.nasa.gov/wp-content/uploads/2024/02/IG-21-025.pdf; Joey Roulette, "NASA's new space suits are delayed, making a 2024 Moon landing 'not feasible'," The Verge, August 10, 2021, https://www.theverge.com/2021/8/10/22618275/nasa-spacesuits-delay-inspector-general-report-2024-artemis; Kenneth Chang, "New Moon Suit for NASA's Artemis Astronauts Unveiled," *New York Times*, March 15, 2023, https://www.nytimes.com/2023/03/15/science/nasa-moon-suit-astronauts.html.

176   Andrew Jones, "China Sets Sights on Crewed Lunar Landing Before 2030," *SpaceNews*, May 29, 2023, https://spacenews.com/china-sets-sights-on-crewed-Lunar-landing-before-2030/; Mike Wall, "How China Will Land Astronauts on the Moon by 2030," Space.com, July 13, 2023, https://www.space.com/china-astronauts-moon-landing-2030-plan.

177   Andrew Jones, "China to Launch Moon Astronauts' New Spacecraft for 1st Time in 2027 or 2028," Space.com, July 20, 2023, https://www.space.com/china-launch-new-astronaut-moon-spacecraft-2027.

178   Xinhua, "China Achieves Progress in Equipment Development for Manned Moon Landing," July 22, 2023, https://english.news.cn/20230722/1ec49c6d1b9e4307898293bf88368381/c.html.

179   Note, the PRC space program is a single military civilian fusion initiative
coordinated by the State Administration of Technology and Industry for National
Defense (SASTIND) with significant presence and influence by the PLA and
its subordinate units, such as the Aerospace Force (formerly part of the Strategic
Support Force). CNSA, a subordinate agency of SASTIND, is a public facing
organization that puts a civilian face on the broader military-civil fusion program.

180   See "Governance Case Studies" pages 64-85 in Charles Miller et al., "Economic
Assessment and Systems Analysis of an Evolvable Lunar Architecture that
Leverages Commercial Space Capabilities and Public-Private-Partnerships,"
NexGen Space LLC, July 13, 2015, https://nss.org/wp-content/uploads/Evolv-
able-Lunar-Architecture.pdf; Michael Castle-Miller, Alfred Anzaldúa, and Hoyt
Davidson, "The Lunar Development Cooperative: A new idea for enabling lunar
settlement," The Space Review, April 27, 2020, https://www.thespacereview.com/
article/3928/1.

181   Independent reviewers noted that if China has a presence on the Moon they
will be setting rules by practice, so having discussion on norms will not matter if
the U.S. or its allies do not also have hardware on the surface—this will cede the
advantage to China.

182   An independent reviewer remarked that new alliances, treaties, funding entities,
and trade zones could be individually powerful and necessary, if properly
constructed and coordinated, but without a clear overall purpose, however, these
proposals run the risk of being easily defeated by concentrated adversary action and
potentially even counterproductive by themselves.

183   One independent reviewer questioned the reactive approach and what the
establishment of Lunar Economic and Trade Zones within Artemis Accords would
hope to accomplish.

184   This was a player-imagined capability in this timeframe, an expected derivative of
the X-37B spaceplane.

185   Allison Zuniga, Dan Rasky and Bruce Pittman, "Lunar COTS: Using the
Moon's Resources to Enable an Economical and Sustainable Pathway to
Mars and Beyond," NASA, https://ntrs.nasa.gov/api/citations/20200001552/
downloads/20200001552.pdf; Allison F. Zuniga, nDaniel Rasky, Robert B.
Pittman, Edgar Zapata, and Roger Lepsch, "Lunar COTS: An Economical and
Sustainable Approach to Reaching Mars," NASA, https://smad.com/wp-content/
uploads/2023/01/Lunar_COTS_An_Economical_and_Sustainable.pdf; . A. F.
Zuniga, D. J. Rasky , R. B. Pittman, "Lunar COTS: Using The Moon's Resources
To Enable An Economical And Sustainable Pathway To Mars And Beyond,"
https://www.hou.usra.edu/meetings/leag2016/pdf/5003.pdf.

186   While the participants did not propose estimated costs, ballpark estimates
supplied from a ChatGPT-4 query suggest a range from $8-$15 billion. Based on
Artemis Base Camp estimates (~$10B+), Lunar Gateway (~$3B), and supporting
infrastructure.

187    While the participants did not propose estimated costs, ballpark estimates supplied from a ChatGPT-4 query suggest a range from $6-$12 billion. Comparable to SDA missile-tracking layers (~$8B) and past DoD ISR space investments.

188    While the participants did not propose estimated costs, ballpark estimates supplied from a ChatGPT-4 query suggest a range from $4-$10 billion. Modeled after historical aerospace tax credits (~$2B/yr) and government-backed space funding programs.

189    While the participants did not propose estimated costs, ballpark estimates supplied from a ChatGPT-4 query suggest a range from $2-$5 billion. Based on NASA's ISS partner contributions and Artemis international agreements.

190    One reviewer questioned which nations would have access to participate in this initiative.

191    For example, see work (report and videos) sponsored by the European Space Agency: GEⵟ Lunar Power Station, 2023, https://nebula.esa.int/content/ge%E2%8A%95-lunar-power-station; Arthur Woods, Andreas Vogler, Patrick Collins, and Dmitrijis Gasperovics, "Greater Earth Lunar Power Station (GEⵟ-LPS) Final Report," AstroStrom, June 2023, https://nebula.esa.int/sites/default/files/neb_study/2753/GEO-LPS-Final-Report_June_2023.pdf; see also: Space Research Associates, "Solar Power Satellite Built of Lunar Materials," SSI, September 21, 1985, https://nss.org/wp-content/uploads/2017/07/1985-SPS-Lunar-Materials-Study.pdf; Justin Lewis-Weber, "Lunar-Based Self-Replicating Solar Factory," New Space, 2016, https://nss.org/wp-content/uploads/2017/07/Lunar-Based-Self-Replicating-Solar-Factory.pdf; General Dynamics Convair Division, "Lunar Resources Utilization For Space Construction Final Report Volume I," April 30, 1979, https://nss.org/wp-content/uploads/2017/07/1979-Lunar-Resources-Utilization-1-Summary.pdf; Space Systems Laboratory (MIT), "Extraterrestrial Processing and Manufacturing of Large Space Systems, Volume 1, Final Report," NASA, September 1979, https://ntrs.nasa.gov/api/citations/19790025056/downloads/19790025056.pdf.

192    NASA, "The Artemis Accords," https://www.nasa.gov/artemis-accords/.

193    Matt Hrodey and Tree Meinch, "No One Owns Outer Space, but Could Space Mining Change That?" *Discover*, September 11, 2023, https://www.discovermagazine.com/technology/no-one-owns-outer-space-but-could-space-mining-change-that.

194    NASA, "Beresheet," https://science.nasa.gov/mission/beresheet/.

195    NASA, "Peregrine Mission 1 (Astrobotic)," https://nssdc.gsfc.nasa.gov/nmc/spacecraft/display.action?id=PEREGRN-1.

196    Ellyn Lapointe and Morgan McFall-Johnsen, "NASA Is Back on the Moon—With the First Commercial Lunar Landing Ever," *Business Insider*, February 22, 2024, https://www.businessinsider.com/intuitive-machines-im-1-odysseus-moon-Lunar-landing-mission-nasa-2024-2.

197    Iram Ghafoor, "Top 15 Offshore Tax Havens in the World," Yahoo Finance, May 31, 2023, https://finance.yahoo.com/news/top-15-offshore-tax-havens-102342802. html; and "Top Ten Caribbean Tax Havens for Offshore Banking," Global Citizen Solutions, July 29, 2024, https://www.globalcitizensolutions.com/ top-ten-offshore-tax-havens-in-the-caribbean/

198    Anna Fleck, "Flags of Convenience Dominate Maritime Freight," Statista, January 11, 2023, https://www.statista.com/chart/29086/flags-of-convenience/#:~:tex-t=The%20figures%20from%20the%20United,of%20the%20world's%20cargo%20 capacity.

199    "Outer Space Treaty Parties Map," Wikipedia, March 1, 2022, https://en.wikipedia. org/wiki/Outer_Space_Treaty#/media/File:Outer_Space_Treaty_parties_map_ colors_updated_03012022.svg.

200    An independent reviewer cautioned there would be no risk of co-option if compa- nies are licensed according to regulation and law to include ITAR/EAR rules.

201    An independent reviewer observed that the authors noted that scenario partici- pants neglected to deal directly with Starlight claims and warned approaches like "revise licensing requirements" may not be very effective unless these proposals are driven into a particular direction that attempts to mitigate the immediate problem as well as future issues that may arise from the general problem. Policy makers will need to consider the successful "victorious" end state desired from all scenarios and real-world events to generate effective responses.

202    While the participants did not propose estimated costs, ballpark estimates supplied from a ChatGPT-4 query suggest a range from $12-$25 billion. Based on Artemis Base Camp (~$10B+), Lunar communications & surveillance (~$5B), and security infrastructure for Cislunar ops and comparable to SDA tracking layers (~$8B) and global ISR networks (e.g., space-based radar).

203    See prior work on space economic development: Bruce Cahan, Mandy Vaughn, Mir Sadat, Casey DeRaad, and Scott Maethner, "Space Budgeting for Modern Times Industrial Space Capabilities with less waste, delay, and obsolescence," NewSpace Nexus, https://newspacenm-cf.rtscustomer.com/wp-content/ uploads/2022/09/Space-Budgeting-for-Modern-Times-092421.pdf; Bruce Cahan and Mir Sadat, "US Space Policies for the New Space Age: Competing on the Final Economic Frontier," NewSpace Nexus, https://newspacenm-cf.rtscustomer. com/wp-content/uploads/2022/09/US-Space-Policies-for-the-New-Space-Age- Competing-on-the-Final-Economic-Frontier-010621-final.pdf

204  Note the White House tasking: "3.1.1 Identify and prioritize research and development needed to support extension of U.S. SSA capabilities into Cislunar space, to include aiding planetary defense, improved debris population modeling, and detection, tracking, and characterization of satellites in the Cislunar volume. This process will be based upon capability needs identified by interagency stakeholders and consider commercial and international development to the maximum extent practicable. (Lead: DOD and NASA, Support: DOC)" White House, National Cislunar Science & Technology Action Plan, December 2024, https://bidenwhitehouse.archives.gov/wp-content/uploads/2024/12/Cislunar-Implementation-Plan-Final.pdf

205  Martin Elvis, Tony Milligan, and Alanna Krolikowski, "The Peaks of Eternal Light: A Near-Term Property Issue on the Moon," *Space Policy* 38 (November 2016): 30–26, https://www.sciencedirect.com/science/article/abs/pii/S0265964616300194.

206  Recently the PRC has also indicated an interest in equatorial landing sites. See: Andrew Jones, "China invites bids for lunar satellite to support crewed moon landing missions," Space News, February 14, 2025, https://spacenews.com/china-invites-bids-for-lunar-satellite-to-support-crewed-moon-landing-missions/#:~:text=The%20description's%20mention%20of%20low,interest%20and%20potential%20landing%20sites.

207  Noor Al-Sibai, "Awkward! The US and China Are Looking at the Same Moon Landing Sites," Futurism, September 24, 2022, https://futurism.com/the-byte/us-china-moon-landing-sites.

208  Malcolm Davis, "Space: The Next South China Sea," Australian Strategic Policy Institute, July 12, 2018, https://www.aspistrategist.org.au/china-the-us-and-the-race-for-space/.

209  Bryan Bender, "'We Better Watch Out': NASA Boss Sounds Alarm on Chinese Moon Ambitions," *Politico*, January 1, 2023, https://www.politico.com/news/2023/01/01/we-better-watch-out-nasa-boss-sounds-alarm-on-chinese-moon-ambitions-00075803.

210  Huong Le Thu, "Fishing While the Water Is Muddy: China's Newly Announced Administrative Districts in the South China Sea," Asia Maritime Transparency Initiative, May 6, 2020, https://amti.csis.org/fishing-while-the-water-is-muddy-chinas-newly-announced-administrative-districts-in-the-south-china-sea/.

211  Jaemin Lee, "China's Declaration of an Air Defense Identification Zone in the East China Sea: Implications for Public International Law," *ASIL Insights*, August 19, 2014, https://www.asil.org/insights/volume/18/issue/17/china%E2%80%99s-declaration-air-defense-identification-zone-east-china-sea.

212  Note, a similar series of crisis games explored similar concerns at a more operational level with a near-term developed infrastructure, and multiple international players at NSS Space Settlement Summit, and the Spacecon conference, see Peter Garretson, Donald Comstock, Andre Sonntag, "Will it be a Lunar War," January 2025.

213  An independent reviewer commented that this scenario is one of the most likely that the U.S. will lose its superpower dominance.

214    One independent reviewer stated that given China often disregards international rulings like ICJ on SCS claims of the Philippines vs. China, would it be better to acknowledge it and increase presence in this area of the moon as well as in international forum?

215    See David Buehler, Eric Felt, Charles Finley, Peter Garretson, Jaime Stearns, and Andy Williams, "Posturing Space Forces for Operations Beyond GEO," Space Force Journal, January 31, 2021, https://spaceforcejournal.org/posturing-space-forces-for-operations-beyond-geo/.

216    For example, see this ESA-sponsored video: Astrostrom, "Greater Earth Synergies," 2023, https://www.youtube.com/watch?v=UfoWgs3dL-U.

217    According to an independent reviewer, the scenario participants did not address what many space experts consider to be the most important attributes of the Peaks of Eternal Light—the likelihood that they are the most important strategic positions in the solar system for their military, economic and development potential. The participants' focus on exceedingly short-term stock market shocks for example, may not be particularly fruitful for long-term national economic and strategic health.

218    See also, Bryan Bender, "As Trump pushes Space Force, support quietly builds for 'Space Guard': A constabulary force modeled on the Coast Guard is viewed as 'more Swiss Army knife than Ka-Bar.'," Politico, July 8, 2018, https://web.archive.org/web/20200406084058/https://www.politico.com/story/2018/07/08/trump-space-force-coast-guard-666917.

219    Whether and what roles the USSF should assume is a topic of controversy. Those who believe the U.S. will have substantial commercial interests in space and that there will be enduring great power competition for control of resources in the space domain advocate for mission expansion and see those missions as enabling while those skeptical of in-space industrial development see such missions as not core to warfighting and a distraction.  See discussion: Peter Garretson, "What War in Space Might Look Like Circa 2030-2040?," NPEC, August 13, 2020, https://npolicy.org/article_file/What_War_In_Space_Might_Look_Like_In_The_Next_One_To_Two_Decades.pdf or https://npolicy.org/wp-content/uploads/2021/05/Space_and_Missile_Wars-chapter_2.pdf; Peter Garretson, "Bluewater and Brownwater Space Strategies and Their Budgetary Profiles," NPEC, 2023, https://npolicy.org/wp-content/uploads/2023/08/Bluewater-and-Brownwater-Space-Strategies-and-Their-Budgetary-Profiles.pdf; See DIU, "State of the Space Industrial Base 2021, page 40, "Space Futures Workshop explored how the expanding area of responsibility and increased activity are likely to drive expanded roles, missions and technology investments, concluding that "USSF is committed to its broader strategic purpose to support freedom of civil, commercial, military operations; environmental monitoring, stewardship and debris clean-up; protection of critical space national infrastructure; enforcing space law and norms of behavior; Search and Rescue / Personnel Recovery (PR) / Non-Combatant Evacuation (NEO); and planetary defense.";

220   While the participants did not propose estimated costs, ballpark estimates supplied from a ChatGPT-4 query suggest a range from $15-$30 billion. Based on NASA's Fission Surface Power (~$4B per unit), solar-based power grids ($10B+ est.), and logistics for Lunar energy distribution.

221   While the participants did not propose estimated costs, ballpark estimates supplied from a ChatGPT-4 query suggest a range from $10-$20 billion. Modeled after ISS development (~$150B total, adjusted for smaller Lunar scope) and Artemis Base Camp projections (~$10B+).

222   Cao Siqi, "China Mulls $10 Trillion Earth-Moon Economic Zone."

223   American Foreign Policy Council translation of presentation at 3rd Annual Space Science Conference. See: Aedan Yohannan, "China's Space Strategy Dwarfs U.S. Ambitions," *National Interest*, March 11, 2024, https://nationalinterest.org/blog/techland/chinas-space-strategy-dwarfs-us-ambitions-209959

224   Xinhua, "Exploiting Earth-Moon Space."

225   White House, "A New Era for Deep Space Exploration and Development," National Space Council, July 23, 2020, https://csps.aerospace.org/sites/default/files/2021-08/NSpC New Era for Space 23Jul20.pdf; and White House, "National Cislunar Science & Technology Strategy," Cislunar Technology Strategy Interagency Working Group of the National Science & Technology Council, November 2022, https://www.whitehouse.gov/wp-content/uploads/2022/11/11-2022-NSTC-National-Cislunar-ST-Strategy.pdf.

226   Mark Whittington, "Republican Party Platform Goes All in on Space Exploration," *Washington Examiner*, July 19, 2024, https://www.washingtonexaminer.com/restoring-america/courage-strength-optimism/3090928/republican-party-platform-goes-all-in-space-exploration/.

227   White House, NATIONAL CISLUNAR SCIENCE & TECHNOLOGY STRATEGY, November 2022, https://bidenwhitehouse.archives.gov/wp-content/uploads/2022/11/11-2022-NSTC-National-Cislunar-ST-Strategy.pdf.

228   White House, National Cislunar Science and Technology Action Plan, December 2024, https://bidenwhitehouse.archives.gov/wp-content/uploads/2024/12/Cislunar-Implementation-Plan-Final.pdf.

229   NASA, "Moon to Mars Objectives," September 2022, https://www.nasa.gov/wp-content/uploads/2022/09/m2m-objectives-exec-summary.pdf?emrc=119caf.

230   Fibertek, "DARPA 10-Year Lunar Architecture Capabilities Study (LunA-10), Lunar Infrastructure Optical Node (LION)," https://www.darpa.mil/attachments/DISTRO%20A%20-%20LunA-10%20LSIC%20Presentation_Fibertek.pdf.

231   Steven J. Butow, Thomas Cooley, Eric Felt, and Joel B. Mozer, "State of the Space Industrial Base 2020: A Time for Action to Sustain US Economic & Military Leadership in Space," https://assets.ctfassets.net/3nanhbfkr0pc/3TLlIb-4Z2UZG7szZdyVFuf/bafb12c16a37ee673b1ba30e72935c07/State_of_the_Space_Industrial_Base_2020_Workshop_Report_July_2020_FINAL.pdf.

232   NASA, "Lunar Resources Utilization for Space Construction," April 30, 1979, https://nss.org/wp-content/uploads/2017/07/1979-Lunar-Resources-Utilization-1-Summary.pdf; NASA, "Solar Power Satellite Built of Lunar Materials," September 21, 1985, https://nss.org/wp-content/uploads/2017/07/1985-SPS-Lunar-Materials-Study.pdf.

233   Lewis-Weber, "Lunar-Based Self-Replicating Solar Factory."

234   "Replicating Systems Concepts: Self-Replicating Lunar Factory and Demonstration."

235   Chirikjian, "An Architecture for Self-Replicating Lunar Factories."

236   Metzger et al., "Affordable, Rapid Bootstrapping of Space Industry and Solar System Civilization."

237   Astrostrom, "Greater Earth Lunar Power Station: Final Report," June 2023, https://nebula.esa.int/sites/default/files/neb_study/2753/GEO-LPS-Final-Report_June_2023.pdf.

238   Astrostrom, "Greater Earth Energy Synergies," https://www.youtube.com/watch?v=UfoWgs3dL-U.

239   Henry Kolm, "L5: Mass Driver Update," L5 News, September 1980, https://nss.org/l5-news-mass-driver-update/; Leonard David, "Could we launch resources from the moon with electromagnetic railguns?," Space.com, June 24, 2024, https://www.space.com/electromagnetic-launch-moon-mass-drive; "Lunar Electromagnetic Launch for Resource Exploitation to Enhance National Security and Economic Growth," AFOSR, September 30, 2023.

240   Robert A. Heinlein, *The Moon Is a Harsh Mistress* (New York: Penguin, 2018).

241   Matt Williams, "China proposes magnetic launch system for sending resources back to Earth," Phys.org, August 26, 2024, https://phys.org/news/2024-08-china-magnetic-resources-earth.html; Linn Xin, "Chinese scientists planning rotating launch system on the moon," SCMP. https://www.scmp.com/news/china/science/article/3274828/chinese-scientists-planning-rotating-launch-system-moon; Bojan Stojkovski,"China could develop rotating launcher on moon to send lunar resources to Earth: The system will use solar and nuclear energy, with over 70 percent of energy recovered after each launch," Interesting Engineering, August 18, 2024; Zhang Wei, Hideshi Chu, Xia Guojin, Han Fei, Zhai Maochun, "New technology of lunar-based magnetic levitation rotary ejection return system," Shanghai Aerospace, https://cstj.cqvip.com/Qikan/Article/Detail?id=7111898473.

242   House Committee on Natural Resources, "The Mineral Supply Chain and the New Space Race," December 12, 2023, https://www.youtube.com/watch?v=QbD2ka_1tZI&t=1721s; Greg Autry, "The Mineral Supply Chain and the New Space Race," *Forbes*, December 16, 2023, https://www.forbes.com/sites/gregautry/2023/12/16/the-mineral-supply-chain-and-the-new-space-race/.

243   Blue Origin, "Blue Alchemist Technology Powers Our Lunar Future," Febuary 10, 2023, https://www.blueorigin.com/news/blue-alchemist-powers-our-lunar-future.

244     Justine Calma, "These companies are making solar cells out of fake Moon dirt," The Verge, February 14, 2023, https://www.theverge.com/2023/2/14/23599260/ blue-origin-lunar-resources-solar-cells-moon-regolith; Lunar Resources, "MW Program," n.d., https://www.lunarresources.space/#projects.

245     One independent reviewer believes this is a late to need idea, which should be advocated years prior to this situation emerging. Now that it happened in the scenario, the time to leverage COTS now as R&D is not effective today.

246     An independent reviewer believes that while sanctions are one option, one could argue for a military strike on the military factory to enforce OST/international law—they believe in other areas the U.S. has had a more aggressive response for less significant event. If the U.S. can prove these are military factories, we can, target them and use UN Security Council and Congress to make this known. Additionally, if the U.S. has an inadequate Space Force still, then that could take time or a rapid alteration of a program of record that can be transported to Lunar orbit (using tech from Clementine type efforts).

247     While the participants did not propose estimated costs, ballpark estimates supplied from a ChatGPT-4 query suggest a range from $5-$12 billion. Based on NASA's Lunar ISRU research (~$3B), historical R&D grants, and SBSP feasibility studies ($10B+ est.).

248     While the participants did not propose estimated costs, ballpark estimates supplied from a ChatGPT-4 query suggest a range from $4-$8 billion. Modeled after Lunar regolith processing studies, ISRU prototype programs, and scaled commercial partnerships.

249     While the participants did not propose estimated costs, ballpark estimates supplied from a ChatGPT-4 query suggest a range from $10-$25 billion. Based on historical SBSP concepts, projected launch/infrastructure costs, and energy beaming experiments (~$15B+).

250     PWC, "The CHIPS Act: What it means for the semiconductor ecosystem," n.d., https://www.pwc.com/us/en/library/chips-act.html; Congress, "Public Law 117–167: CHIPS ACT OF 2022," August 9, 2022, https://www.congress.gov/117/ plaws/publ167/PLAW-117publ167.pdf.

251     NASA, "National Aeronautics and Space Act of 1958 (Unamended)," April 19, 2024, https://www.nasa.gov/history/ national-aeronautics-and-space-act-of-1958-unamended/.

## CHAPTER 5 ENDNOTES

252     Jared Isaacman, X, December 4, 2024, https://x.com/rookisaacman/ status/1864346915183157636?lang=en

253     Scott Detrow and Geoff Brumfiel, President-elect Trump selects Jared Isaacman to lead NASA, NPR: All Things Considered, December 7, 2024, https://www.npr.org/2024/12/07/nx-s1-5217693/ president-elect-trump-selects-jared-isaacman-to-lead-nasa.

254　Federal Aviation Administration, "Report to Congress: U.S. Department of Transportation Evaluation of Commercial Human Space Flight Activities Most Appropriate for New Safety Framework," September 29, 2023, https://www.faa.gov/sites/faa.gov/files/2023_10_06%20PL_114-90_Sec_111_7_Commercial_Human_Spaceflight_Activities.pdf.

255　dearMoon Project, https://dearmoon.earth/.

256　Micheal Sheetz, "Elon Musk Says SpaceX's Starship Rocket Will Launch 'Hundreds of Missions' Before Flying People," CNBC, September 1, 2020, https://www.cnbc.com/2020/09/01/elon-musk-spacex-starship-to-fly-hundreds-of-missions-before-people.html.

257　Marcia Smith, "FAA Reauthorization Clears Congress, Extends Learning Period," SpacePolicyOnline.com, May 16, 2024, https://spacepolicyonline.com/news/faa-reauthorization-clears-congress-extends-learning-period/.

258　Consider the spectacle of SpaceX Starship Test 7: The Launch Pad, "WOW! SpaceX Starship Breaks Up Over Caribbean," Youtube, https://www.youtube.com/watch?v=oCtz76L_d34.

259　" U.S. Department of Transportation Evaluation of Commercial Human Space Flight Activities Most Appropriate for New Safety Framework," Federal Aviation Administration, Report to Congress, September 29, 2023, https://www.faa.gov/sites/faa.gov/files/2023_10_06%20PL_114-90_Sec_111_7_Commercial_Human_Spaceflight_Activities.pdf.

260　Stephen Clark, "Industry united in push to extend ban on human spaceflight regulations," *Ars Technica*, October 18, 2023, https://arstechnica.com/space/2023/10/industry-united-in-push-to-extend-ban-on-human-spaceflight-regulations/.

261　Note: NASA is not a regulator, but essentially fills this role when it certifies the safety of commercial providers (such as Crewed Dragon flights to ISS) where NASA astronauts are involved.

262　Elizabeth Howell, "Meet the dearMoon crew of artists, athletes and a billionaire riding SpaceX's Starship to the moon," *Space.com*, December 26, 2022, https://www.space.com/meet-dearmoon-crew-spacex-moon-mission.

263　Brian Wang, "NASA Says Up to 20 SpaceX Starship Refueling Launches Per Moon Mission," *Next Big Future*, December 3, 2023, https://www.nextbigfuture.com/2023/12/nasa-says-up-to-20-spacex-starship-refueling-launches-per-moon-mission.html.

264　Brian Wang, "SpaceX Lunar Starship and Refueling in Orbit Might Slip from 2025 to 2027," *Next Big Future*, December 4, 2023, https://www.nextbigfuture.com/2023/12/spacex-lunar-starship-and-refueling-in-orbit-might-slip-from-2025-to-2027.html.

265　Andrew Jones, "China puts models of its future crewed moon landing spacecraft on display (video)," *Space.com*, February 1, 2024, https://www.space.com/china-puts-models-crewed-moon-landing-spacecraft-on-display#:~:text=%22China%20has%20announced%20the%20goal,moon%20for%20more%20scientific%20experiments.%22.

266　Independent reviewers thought this would send the wrong message.

267  Note: at present the USSF has no such capability.

268  Independent reviewers suggested it would be important to remind the public that 100 percent safety is not realistic and pushing the boundaries and frontiers always has risk, but we must not shirk from the rewards that come from bravely pushing them into the future.

269  While the participants did not propose estimated costs, ballpark estimates supplied from a ChatGPT-4 query suggest a range from $8-$18 billion. Based on Northrop Grumman's MEV servicing costs (~$1B per unit), DARPA's Robotic Servicing of Geosynchronous Satellites (RSGS), and proposed debris mitigation programs (~$10B+ for operational scaling).

270  While the participants did not propose estimated costs, ballpark estimates supplied from a ChatGPT-4 query suggest a range from $6-$15 billion. Comparable to SDA's tracking layers (~$8B), DARPA's Hallmark program, and Cislunar tracking proposals requiring high-precision deep-space sensors.

271  John E. Shaw, Jan Purgaon, Amy Soilau, "Sailing the New Wine-Dark Sea: Space as a Military Area of Responsibility," Aether, Vol. 1, No. 1, Spring 2022, https://www.airuniversity.af.edu/Portals/10/AEtherJournal/Journals/Volume-1_Issue-1/06-Shaw.pdf.

272  "2. COMMON MILITARY SERVICE FUNCTIONS. The Army, the Navy, the Air Force, the Marine Corps, and the Space Force...h. Organize, train, and equip forces to contribute unique service capabilities to the joint force commander to conduct the following functions across all domains, including land, maritime, air, space, and cyberspace: (4) Personnel recovery operations in coordination with USSOCOM and other Combatant Commands, the Military Services, and other DoD Components." From: DoD, "DoD Directive (DoDD) 5100.1 Functions of the Department of Defense and Its Major Components," September 17, 2020, page 39, para b.(7), https://www.esd.whs.mil/portals/54/documents/dd/issuances/dodd/510001p.pdf.

273  "USSPACECOM continues to support NASA's Commercial Crew Program for contingency rescue operations for crewed flights to and from the International Space Station as part of our Human Space Flight Support role. USSPACECOM is committed to assuring the safe exploration of space and is supporting NASA's planned lunar missions by providing crew and spacecraft recovery for the upcoming Artemis program and associated training events.", "USSPACECOM is entrusted to protect and defend our nation's most critical space assets. The UCP assigns me the responsibility to "protect and defend U.S. and, as directed, allied, partner, and critical commercial space operational capabilities.", "USSPACECOM... continues to pursue increased resources and capabilities to...to protect and defend U.S., allied, partnered, and commercial space capabilities." From: James H. Dickinson, Fiscal Year 2023 Priorities and Posture of United States Space Command, SASC, March 1, 2022, https://www.armed-services.senate.gov/imo/media/doc/USSPACE-COM%20FY23%20Posture%20Statement%20SASC%20FINAL.pdf.

274    Space Force, "Space Force announces new mission statement," September 6, 2023, https://www.spaceforce.mil/News/Article-Display/Article/3517324/space-force-announces-new-mission-statement/

275    Elizabeth Howell, "Meet the dearMoon Crew of Artists, Athletes and a Billionaire Riding SpaceX's Starship to the Moon," Space.com, December 26, 2022, https://www.space.com/meet-dearmoon-crew-spacex-moon-mission.

276    Jeff Foust, "House Speaker Introduces Bill to Extend Commercial Spaceflight Regulatory Learning Period," *SpaceNews*, September 22, 2023, https://spacenews.com/house-speaker-introduces-bill-to-extend-commercial-spaceflight-regulatory-learning-period/.

277    Leonard David, "How Will Space Tourism Be Impacted by the Titan Submersible Tragedy?" Space.com, July 28, 2023, https://www.space.com/spaceflight-titan-submersible-tragedy-impacts.

278    Ian Whittaker, "Astronauts Are Stuck on the International Space Station After Yet More Problems With Boeing's Beleaguered Starliner," *The Conversation*, July 15, 2024, https://theconversation.com/astronauts-are-stuck-on-the-international-space-station-after-yet-more-problems-with-boeings-beleaguered-starliner-234409.

279    Grant Cates, "The In-Space Rescue Capability Gap," Center for Space Policy and Strategy, July 29, 2021, https://csps.aerospace.org/papers/space-rescue-capability-gap.

280    Bruce McClintock, Dan McCormick, Katie Feistel, et al., "Select Space Concepts for the New Space Era," RAND Corporation, November 2023, https://www.rand.org/content/dam/rand/pubs/perspectives/PEA2600/PEA2644-1/RAND_PEA2644-1.pdf.

281    Bryan Bender, "A Space Rescue Service? Calls Grow to Create a Quick Response Force for Astronauts in Distress," *Politico*, November 2, 2022, https://www.politico.com/news/2022/11/02/space-rescue-service-astronauts-00064633.

282    J. Olson, S. Butow, E. Felt, T. Cooley, and J. Mozer, "State of the Space Industrial Base 2021," https://assets.ctfassets.net/3nanhbfkr0pc/43TeQTAmdYrym5DT-Drhjd3/1218bd749befdde511ac2c900db3a43b/Space_Industrial_Base_Workshop_2021_Summary_Report_-_Final_15_Nov_2021.pdf.

283    John E. Shaw, Jean Purgason, and Amy Soileau, "Sailing the New Wine-Dark Sea: Space as a Military Area of Responsibility," *Æther* 1, no. 1 (2022): 35–44, https://www.airuniversity.af.edu/Portals/10/AEtherJournal/Journals/Volume-1_Issue-1/06-Shaw.pdf.

284    Brian Desautels, "Personnel Recovery in Space: A New Venture for Human Space Flight Support", ACSC, AY2016; Alexander B. Layendecker, "That Others May Live Among The Stars: Implementing A Space Rescue Arm Within The United States Space Force," ACSC, February 2024; Mari Manifold, "Personnel Recovery in Space," Air University, April 10, 2017, https://www.airuniversity.af.edu/Portals/10/ASPJ_Spanish/Journals/Volume-29_Issue-4/2017_4_10_manifold_s_eng.pdf.

285  DoD, "DoD Directive (DoDD) 5100.1 Functions of the Department of Defense and Its Major Components," September 17, 2020, page 39, para b.(7), https://www. esd.whs.mil/portals/54/documents/dd/issuances/dodd/510001p.pdfhttps://www. esd.whs.mil/portals/54/documents/dd/issuances/dodd/510001p.pdf.

286  Grant R. Cates, "The In-Space Rescure Capability Gap," The Aerospace Corporation, August 2021, https://csps.aerospace.org/sites/default/files/2021-08/ Cates_SpaceRescue_20210728.pdf.

287  Jan Osburg, Grant Cates, Robin Dickey, "2024 RAND and Aerospace Space Rescue Workshop," RAND, February 1, 2024, https://www.rand.org/ events/2024/02/space-rescue.html.

288  JARUS, "First International Lunar SAR Conference," October 13, 2022, ; ISSF, "IAASS Conference: International Lunar Search and Rescue: Managing Risk in Space, Hainan, People Republic of China 13-15 Oct 2022," n.d., https://spacesafe-tyfoundation.org/space-safety-events/conferences/.

289  Benjamin J. Johnis, "Lunar Search and Rescue: The Next Step for Human Spaceflight Recovery," Air Force Institute of Technology (AFIT) Scholar Theses and Dissertations, 6996, March 2023, https://scholar.afit.edu/cgi/viewcontent. cgi?article=7999&context=etd.

290  Benjamin J. Johnis and Peter Garretson, "Strategic implications of China winning the space rescue race (part 1)," The Space Review, April 1, 2024, https://www. thespacereview.com/article/4767/1; Benjamin J. Johnis and Peter Garretson, "Strategic implications of China winning the space rescue race (part 2)," The Space Review, April 8, 2024, https://www.thespacereview.com/article/4771/1.

291  Independent reviewers felt the government should have a more forward leaning posture and place a higher value on rescuing U.S. citizens and that this would be demanded by the public.

292  According to an independent reviewer, the authors note that in all likelihood, such a real-time issue would immediately spark an "all hands on deck" approach that would quickly inventory all available space capabilities with any ability to assist in immediate recovery. Contracting with a private company will probably be the most likely approach since it is probable only private companies would have any human-rated Lunar capabilities at all. But this is the point, reactive scenarios can only be reactive. Should actions be taken now that would allow for more capabilities—civil, military, and commercial—to be deployed before such an event as lunar tourism takes place?

293  Near-Earth Objects Coordination Centre, "Close Approaches," European Space Agency, https://neo.ssa.esa.int/close-approaches.

294  Peter Garretson, "Clarifying the Planetary Defense Mission," *Defense Technology Program Brief* No. 24, American Foreign Policy Council, June 2021, https://www. afpc.org/uploads/documents/Defense_Technology_Briefing_-_Issue_24.pdf.

295  Tricia Talbert, "Five Years After the Chelyabinsk Meteor: NASA Leads Efforts in Planetary Defense," NASA, February 15, 2018, https://www.nasa.gov/solar-system/ five-years-after-the-chelyabinsk-meteor-nasa-leads-efforts-in-planetary-defense/.

296  "Apophis," NASA, https://science.nasa.gov/solar-system/asteroids/apophis/.

297 "Earth's gravity will alter Apophis' orbit during 2029 flyby," The European Space Agency, March 26, 2021, https://www.esa.int/ESA_Multimedia/Images/2021/03/Earth_s_gravity_will_alter_Apophis_orbit_during_2029_flyby.

298 Elizabeth Howell, "Chelyabinsk Meteor: A Wake-Up Call for Earth," *Space.com*, January 9, 2019, https://www.space.com/33623-chelyabinsk-meteor-wake-up-call-for-earth.html.

299 Andrew Jones, "China is getting serious about planetary defense," *The Planetary Society*, June 2, 2022, https://www.planetary.org/articles/china-planetary-defense-plans.

300 "'CITADEL' INTERNATIONAL PLANETARY DEFENCE SYSTEM AS PROPOSED FOR ESTABLISHMENT," Fifty-second session of the Scientific and Technical Subcommittee of the Committee on the Peaceful Uses of Outer Space, United Nations, February 2-13, 2015, https://www.unoosa.org/pdf/pres/stsc2015/tech-07E.pdf.

301 Space Mission Planning Advisory Group (SMPAG), United Nations, Office for Outer Space Affairs, December 2016, https://www.unoosa.org/oosa/en/ourwork/topics/neos/smpag.html.

302 Both China and Russia have articulated the need for nuclear explosives for planetary defense. China: On April 27 1996, the Chinese participants to CTBT negotiations argued that "peaceful nuclear explosions" might be necessary in the future to combat the "asteroid threat," NTI, page 54, https://media.nti.org/pdfs/china_nuclear.pdf; "'The door to peaceful nuclear explosions should not be closed, at least not now,' the Foreign Ministry said…China is arguing that mankind needs to keep developing "peaceful" nuclear weapons in case a giant asteroid is discovered careering through space on a collision course with the earth." from Patrick E. Tyler, "Chinese Seek Atom Option to Fend Off Asteroids," New York Times, April 27, 1996, in LexisNexis, https://www.nytimes.com/1996/04/27/world/chinese-seek-atom-option-to-fend-off-asteroids.html; Russia: "Mainly devices of short-term (impulse) action will be used – kinetic hypervelocity impactors and nuclear explosive devices, if needed…The development of kinetic and nuclear means for action will be based on the experience of similar devices created for military purposes" from: Planetary Defence Centre, "International Planetary Defence System "Citadel" Concept For Creation", 2002, https://pdc.su/images/Citadel-e.pdf; COPUOUS, "Information on research in the field of near-Earth objects carried out by Member States, international organizations and other entities,(Russian Federation)" March 28, 2006, https://www.unoosa.org/pdf/reports/ac105/AC105_863Add1E.pdf; UNOOSA, "'Citadel' International Planetary Defence System As Proposed For Establishment," 2015, https://www.unoosa.org/pdf/pres/stsc2015/tech-07E.pdf;

303 An independent reviewer noted that the potential for devastating side effects of a nuclear detonation depends on where the intercept is and how big the yield. This concern could be a non-issue or at least less of a concern if detonation occurs further away from Earth.

304     The 2007 NASA report to congress key finding (page 2, see also Figure 4, p23) was that, "Nuclear standoff explosions are assessed to be 10-100 times more effective than the non-nuclear alternatives analyzed in this study"; NASA, "Near-Earth Object Survey and Deflection Analysis of Alternatives Report to Congress," March 2007, https://nss.org/2007-Near-Earth-Object-Survey-And-Deflection-Analysis-Of-Alternatives-NASA/; The White House strategy states, "Continue the study of circumstances when only use of a nuclear explosive device would provide the necessary capability to mitigate an impending NEO impact threat," White House, "National Preparedness Strategy and Action Plan for Near-Earth Object Hazards and Planetary Defense," April 2023, https://assets.science.nasa.gov/content/dam/science/psd/planetary-science-division/2025/2023-NSTC-National-Pre-paredness-Strategy-and-Action-Plan-for-Near-Earth-Object-Hazards-and-Plan-etary-Defense.pdf.

305     An independent reviewer noted that the same intent could be met without a new agency, but by giving coast guard like authorities to the Space National Guard.

306     See for example, NASA, "Pi – Terminal Defense for Humanity," February 19, 2022 https://www.nasa.gov/general/pi-terminal-defense-for-humanity/; UCSB, "PI-Multimodal Planetary Defense," n.d., https://www.deepspace.ucsb.edu/projects/pi-terminal-planetary-defense

307     Brian Bender, "As Trump pushes Space Force, support quietly builds for 'Space Guard', July 8, 2018, " Military.com, https://www.politico.com/story/2018/07/08/trump-space-force-coast-guard-666917; James C. Bennett, "Proposing a 'Coast Guard' for Space," The New Atlantis, Winter 2011, https://www.thenewatlantis.com/publications/proposing-a-coast-guard-for-space; Cynthia A. S. Mckinley, "The Guardians of Space Organizing America's Space Assets for the Twenty-First Century," Spring 2000, https://mly.bof.mybluehost.me/spacefaringamerica.com/wp-content/uploads/2018/06/McKinley-Guardians-of-Space-ADA519071.pdf; Michael Sinclair, "The US Needs A 'Coast Guard' For Space: Semper Paratus Exteriores Spatium," Breaking Defense, May 21, 2018, https://breakingdefense.com/2018/05/the-us-needs-a-coast-guard-for-space-semper-paratus-exteriores-spatium/; Michael R. Sinclair, "To Fight To Save…In Space: A Legal Argument That A Space 'Coast Guard' Is Increasingly Necessary For Effective 21st Century Space Governance," May 17, 2018, https://papers.ssrn.com/sol3/papers.cfm?abstract_id=3172287; Michael R. Sinclair, "Model a Space Force on the Coast Guard," USNI, September 2018, https://www.usni.org/magazines/proceed-ings/2018/september/model-space-force-coast-guard; Michael R. Sinclair, "Why the US needs a 'Coast Guard' in space, ORF, May 25, 2018, https://www.orfonline.org/expert-speak/why-us-needs-coast-guard-space.

308     While the participants did not propose estimated costs, ballpark estimates supplied from a ChatGPT-4 query suggest a range from $10-$25 billion. Modeled after U.S. Coast Guard (~$13B annual budget), NASA's planetary defense programs (~$1B), and large-scale debris mitigation and rapid response operations.

309    Ashley Strickland, "An asteroid has a 2% chance of hitting Earth in 2032. Here's
       how astronomers are tracking it," CNN, February 15, 2025, https://www.cnn.
       com/2025/02/15/science/asteroid-2024-yr4-earth-tracking/index.html.

310    By Helen Davidson, "China opens recruitment for 'planetary defense force' amid
       fears of asteroid hitting Earth," Taipei Times, February 15, 2025, https://www.
       taipeitimes.com/News/feat/archives/2025/02/15/2003831906; Business Today,
       "China to save Earth? Country launches planetary defense force as asteroid impact
       risk in 2032 spikes," February 14, 2025.

311    NASA, "Double Asteroid Redirection Test (DART)," n.d., https://science.nasa.
       gov/mission/dart/

312    Business Today, "China to save Earth? Country launches planetary defense force as
       asteroid impact risk in 2032 spikes," https://www.businesstoday.in/science/story/
       china-to-save-earth-country-launches-planetary-defense-force-as-asteroid-impact-
       risk-in-2032-spikes-464746-2025-02-14

313    White House, "United States Space Priorities Framework," December 2021,
       https://apps.dtic.mil/sti/pdfs/AD1155604.pdf

314    State Dept, "A Strategic Framework for Space Diplomacy," May 2, 2023, https://
       www.state.gov/wp-content/uploads/2023/05/Space-Framework-Clean-2-May-
       2023-Final-Updated-Accessible-5.25.2023.pdf

315    White House, "National Space Policy of the United States of America, December
       9, 2020, https://trumpwhitehouse.archives.gov/wp-content/uploads/2020/12/
       National-Space-Policy.pdf.

316    An independent reviewer notes that while some policy may be in place there is
       no real funding and resources allocated to procuring or developing equipment to
       complete this mission.

317    White House, "National Near-Earth Object Preparedness Strategy," December
       2016, https://csps.aerospace.org/sites/default/files/2021-08/NEO%20Prepared-
       ness%20Strategy%20Dec16.pdf.

318    White House, "National Near-Earth Object Preparedness Strategy And Action
       Plan, " June 2018, https://www.nasa.gov/wp-content/uploads/2022/03/ostp-neo-
       strategy-action-plan-jun18.pdf

319    White House, "National Preparedness Strategy & Action Plan for Near-Earth
       Object Hazards and Planetary Defense," April 2023, https://assets.science.nasa.
       gov/content/dam/science/psd/planetary-science-division/2025/2023-NSTC-Na-
       tional-Preparedness-Strategy-and-Action-Plan-for-Near-Earth-Object-Hazar-
       ds-and-Planetary-Defense.pdf.

320    NASA, "NASA Planetary Defense Strategy And Action Plan: In support of
       the National Preparedness Strategy and Action Plan for Near-Earth Object
       Hazards and Planetary Defense," April 2023, https://www.nasa.gov/wp-content/
       uploads/2023/06/nasa_-_planetary_defense_strategy_-_final-508.pdf.

321　White House, "National Preparedness Strategy and Action Plan for Near-Earth Object Hazards and Planetary Defense," April 2023, https://assets.science.nasa.gov/content/dam/science/psd/planetary-science-division/2025/2023-NSTC-National-Preparedness-Strategy-and-Action-Plan-for-Near-Earth-Object-Hazards-and-Planetary-Defense.pdf.

322　DoD 3100.10 Space Policy also failed to incorporate other White House strategies: The National Space Weather Strategy, the National LEO R&D Strategy, the National ISAM Strategy, and the National ISAM Strategy and Action Plan.

323　White House, "National Cislunar Science & Technology Action Plan," December 2024, https://bidenwhitehouse.archives.gov/wp-content/uploads/2024/12/Cislunar-Implementation-Plan-Final.pdf.

324　Michael J. Shannon, "The Clementine Satellite," Satellite Technology, June 1994, https://www.llnl.gov/sites/www/files/2020-05/clementine-etr-jun-94.pdf;

325　EOportal, "Clementine Lunar Mission," May 29, 2012, https://www.eoportal.org/satellite-missions/clementine#mission-status.

326　Gunter's Space Page, "Clementine 2 (DSPSE 2),"

327　Clementine 2 was line item vetoed by President Clinton along with the Military Spaceplane. Science News Staff, "Clinton Kills Asteroid Mission," Science.org, October 21, 1997

328　Stephen Chen, "China's Nuclear Spaceships Will Be 'Mining Asteroids and Flying Tourists' as It Aims to Overtake US in Space Race," *South China Morning Post*, November 17, 2017, https://www.scmp.com/news/china/policies-politics/article/2120425/chinas-nuclear-spaceships-will-be-mining-asteroids.

329　Andrew Jones, "China to Launch Near-Earth Asteroid Sample Return Mission in 2025," *SpaceNews*, September 25, 2024, https://spacenews.com/china-to-launch-near-earth-asteroid-sample-return-mission-in-2025/.

330　Robert Lea, "China Plans to Deflect an Asteroid by 2030 to Showcase Earth Protection Skills," Space.com, July 11, 2024, https://www.space.com/china-planning-planetary-defense-asteroid-mission; Andrew Jone, "China Targets Its First Planetary Defense Test Mission," Planetary Society, July 2, 2024, https://www.planetary.org/articles/china-targets-its-first-planetary-defense-test-mission.

331　"China Focus: Capture an Asteroid, Bring It Back to Earth?" Xinhua, July 23, 2018, http://www.xinhuanet.com/english/2018-07/23/c_137342866.htm ; Phillip Keane, "China's Asteroid Capture Plan," SpaceTech Asia, October 22, 2018, https://www.spacetechasia.com/chinas-asteroid-capture-plan/.

332　Nicole Arce, "China Plans To Capture An Asteroid And Bring It Down To Earth," *Tech Times*, July 26, 2018, https://www.techtimes.com/articles/232692/20180726/china-plans-to-capture-an-asteroid-and-bring-it-down-to-earth.htm.

333　Independent reviewers noted the focus on governance, but few concrete actions or alterations of program of record while China continues to move resources and people around to advance asteroid mining.

334 An independent reviewer noted that most recommendations focus on reclaiming U.S. leadership from China but overlook preparations for the asteroid return event. The proposal for a Joint Task Force (JTF) seems insufficient—should it instead focus on early warnings, evacuations, or missile defense options? The scenario highlights the need for proactive planning by policymakers.

335 An independent reviewer noted that this authority can be assigned to the Executive Secretary and Special Assistant to the President for the Council as this role, no need to duplicate effort reporting.

336 DoD, "DoD Directive (DoDD) 5100.1 Functions of the Department of Defense and Its Major Components," September 17, 2020, page 39, para b.(7), https://www.esd.whs.mil/portals/54/documents/dd/issuances/dodd/510001p.pdfhttps://www.esd.whs.mil/portals/54/documents/dd/issuances/dodd/510001p.pdf.

337 "Functions.—The Space Force shall be organized, trained, and equipped to—(1) provide freedom of operation for the United States in, from, and to space; (2) conduct space operations; and (3)protect the interests of the United States in space." From: U.S. Congress, "10 U.S. Code § 9081 - The United States Space Force," Cornell, n.d., https://www.law.cornell.edu/uscode/text/10/9081.

## CHAPTER 6 ENDNOTES

338 Stephen Clark, "Blue Origin boss: Government should forget launch and focus on "exotic" missions," *Ars Technica*, May 30, 2025, https://arstechnica.com/space/2025/05/blue-origin-boss-government-should-forget-launch-and-focus-on-exotic-missions/#:~:text=still%20need%20you-,Blue%20Origin%20boss%3A%20Government%20should%20forget%20launch%20and%20focus%20on,to%20the%20Moon%20with%20humans.%22.

339 The Iron Dome for America, Presidential Action from The White House, January 27, 2025, https://www.whitehouse.gov/presidential-actions/2025/01/the-iron-dome-for-america/.

340 Withdrawing the United States from the World Health Organization, Presidential Action from The White House, January 20, 2025, https://www.whitehouse.gov/presidential-actions/2025/01/withdrawing-the-united-states-from-the-worldhealth-organization/; Putting America First in International Environmental Agreements, Presidential Action from The White House, January 20, 2025, https://www.whitehouse.gov/presidential-actions/2025/01/putting-america-first-in-international-environmental-agreements/.

341 "Space as a Warfighting Area of Responsibility (AOR) with John Shaw (LTG, US Space Force RET) is almost here," Real Space Strategy Podcast, February 19, 2025.

342 Anthony Imperato, Peter Garretson, Richard M. Harrison, "U.S. Space Budget Report," AFPC, May 2021, https://www.afpc.org/uploads/documents/Defense_Technology_Briefing_-_Issue_23.pdf

343 James Donovan, "America spent billions to put a man on the moon. Was it worth it?," *Los Angeles Times*, July 4, 2019, https://www.latimes.com/opinion/op-ed/la-oe-donovan-moon-cold-war-apollo-program-20190704-story.html.

344    Joint Concept for Integrated Campaigning, Joint Chiefs of Staff, March 16, 2018,
       https://www.jcs.mil/Portals/36/Documents/Doctrine/concepts/joint_concept_inte-
       grated_campaign.pdf?ver=2018-03-28-102833-257

345    U.S. Naval Institute Staff, "Pentagon's Joint Concept for Compet-
       ing," *USNI News*, March 9, 2023, https://news.usni.org/2023/03/09/
       pentagons-joint-concept-for-competing; Joint Concept for Competing,
       Joint Chiefs of Staff, February 10, 2023, https://drive.google.com/
       file/d/13WAYsbN5fyF-guDZH94UwDwoR1XWwQQx/view

346    We thank Laura Winter, host of the award winning The Downlink Podcast, for
       her suggestion to create such an appendix and her substantial authorship of the
       language included in this Crisis Communication Plan.

www.ingramcontent.com/pod-product-compliance
Lightning Source LLC
Chambersburg PA
CBHW020525270326
41927CB00006B/448